Kunst
Haus
Graz

Barbara Steiner
Sophia Walk
Anna Lena von Helldorff
Katia Huemer

jovis

Kunst
Haus
Graz

2007

(friendly alien

Photo by Marie Neugebauer

2003

(**friendly alien**

Drawing by a pupil from BG/BRG Carneri, created during the construction phase of the Kunsthaus

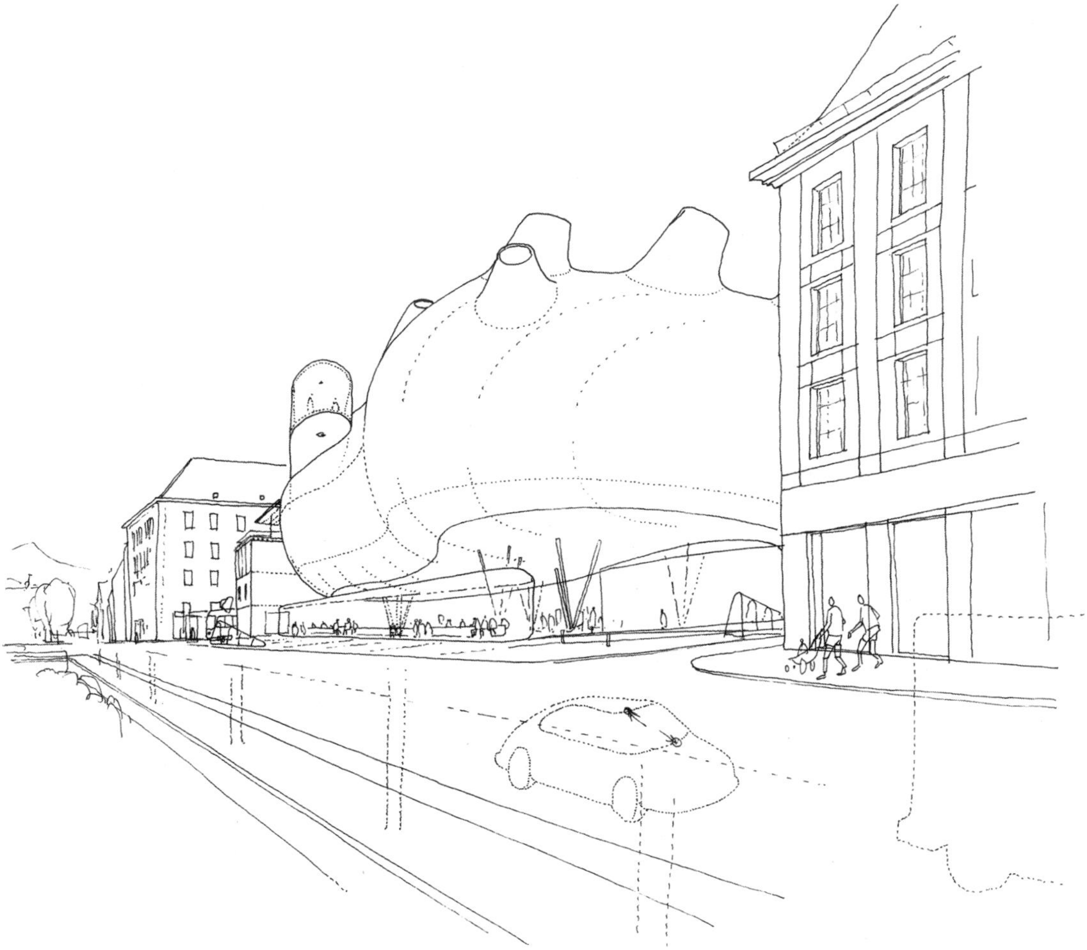

View along Lendkai. Sketch from the preliminary design, Niels Jonkhans

↗ p. 51
↗ p. 159

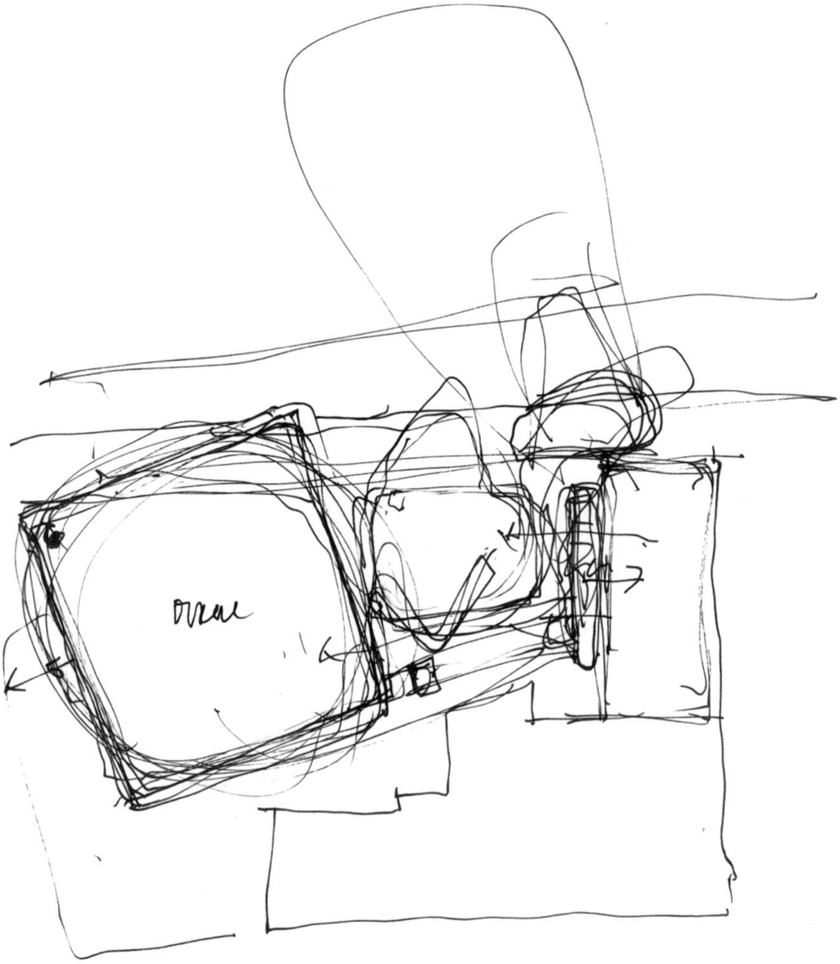

Design sketch from the competition, consisting of spatially separated functions, Colin Fournier

2017

(**friendly alien**

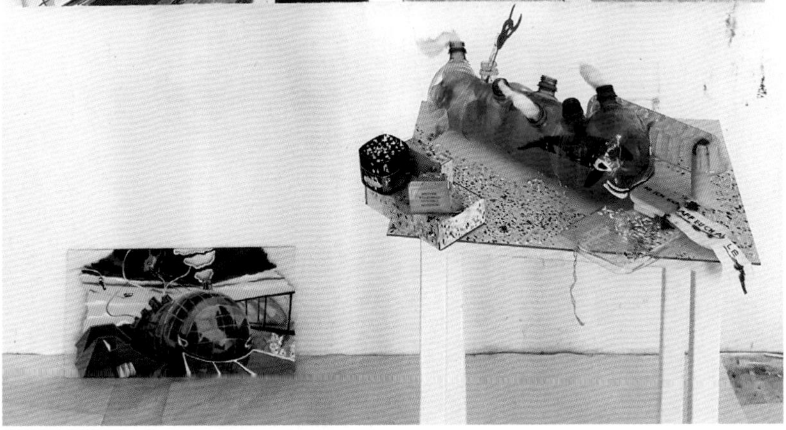

Anna Meyer explores transition zones between house, animal and human. In her paintings and models, wall becomes skin and building becomes human-like. Created for the exhibition **Up into the Unknown**.

→ 037)
→ 107)

Haus Tier, Anna Meyer

2004

Kunst
Haus
Graz

2000

Kunst
Haus
design

Skin
→171)
→176)
↗ p. 39
↗ p. 41
↗ p. 43
↗ p. 45
↗ p. 47
↗ p. 77
↗ p. 299

Black: Organic, moving **Skin**, supported by slabs. Red: Floor plan with a stair or ramp construction between functional areas that are still spatially separated, Peter Cook, design sketch from the competition

2001

Kunst
Haus
Graz
design

View of Mariahilfer Straße.
Sketch from the preliminary design, Niels Jonkhans

2020

Kunst
Haus
Graz

Photo by Eva Mohringer

Photo by Renesmee van Fraatenblad

(About the book:) a kaleidoscope

'We are making a radical gesture. But we're making it in a city that has already seen a series of radical experiments.'
Colin Fournier

When you look through it, a kaleidoscope reassembles what you see and, when turned, creates ever-new images.
The friendly alien has become a familiar image, and yet over time perspectives on the building have changed, and will continue to change in the future. In this book, we take a kaleidoscopic look at the Kunsthaus Graz, mainly focusing on the use and application of the building. The interval of time that has passed offers us the chance to take another look at this once brave experiment, to examine how spacelab's extraordinary achievement is put to use, and to recognise its worth.

The architects **Sir Peter Cook** and **Colin Fournier**, together with **Niels Jonkhans**, who as a **spacelab** partner was significantly involved in the concept development and became the competition team's representative on site, talk about the period of its creation, their ideas at the time, and how their view of the Kunsthaus has changed since then (↗ p. 291). **Pablo von Frankenberg** and **Anselm Wagner** contextualise the Kunsthaus both at an international and local level, so placing it in relation to global developments in museum architecture (↗ p. 99) and to Graz architecture (↗ p. 259). **Barbara Steiner** looks at the genesis and use of the building from an institutional and curatorial perspective and explores the potential of the non-perfect for exhibiting (↗ p. 37).
Sophia Walk focuses on linguistic and other forms of use of the Kunsthaus (↗ p. 219). A conversation between **Barbara Steiner**, **Sophia Walk** and **Pablo von Frankenberg** explores various architectural concepts and notions of space since the 1960s (↗ p. 135).
Katia Huemer lists all of the exhibitions that have taken place at the Kunsthaus so far and includes a commentary on those that reveal a special relationship to its architecture. (↗ p. 350)
Elisabeth Schlögl examines the **BIX façade** projects and describes how the Kunsthaus constantly relates to the city in new and different ways (↗ p. 323).

Texts and images run parallel throughout the book and each follow their own numbering – and yet both levels enter into symbiosis at certain points, images refer to text passages, and vice versa.
The narrative of the images featured in the publication tells – more or less – the history of the Kunsthaus Graz and the utilisation of its spaces.
It is essentially a 'tour' through space and time, interrupted at certain points to take new twists and turns. It begins with the imagination: spacelab's first ideas take shape as drawings, thoughts are sketched out, developed, modified or sometimes discarded. These visions flow into a spatial-sculptural approach. Models and construction drawings explore and test various ways of implementing the plans. Depictions of the building or significant architectural elements are interspersed in between.
From outside, the reader enters the building via the **foyer** and the **'Travelator'**, up into the exhibition rooms (**Space01**, **Space02**) into the **Needle**, onto the roof and back again via the **staircase** to the **forecourt** of the Kunsthaus.
The selection of illustrations also encompasses different types of representation: Classical professional architectural photography tends to focus on the visual impact of the architecture, while largely hiding its usage. **Martin Grabner** and **Arthur Zalewski** come from the realm of art photography. **Martin Grabner's** series echoes the question Sophia Walk put to users of the building, asking them to name an architectural element that embodied their use of the Kunsthaus. It shows people who use the Kunsthaus in a range of different ways, revealing the broad scope of its use. **Arthur Zalewski** adopts an essayistic understanding of photography: he approaches the objects featured from different perspectives and highlights the traces of use left in and around the Kunsthaus. Held especially for the book, a photo competition on social media highlights a sample of the media appropriation performed millions of times by visitors. These photos circulate on the internet, spreading the image of the Kunsthaus across the world and contributing significantly to the development of its profile.

Our **sincere thanks** go to all those who contributed to this book, to the authors mentioned above and to the translators Louise Bromby, Kate Howlett-Jones and Teresa Faudon. We would like to thank Doris Kleilein and Theresa Hartherz for their faith in the project, and Jochen Visscher for his mediating and supportive role in getting the publication off the ground.
We hope that this book will play a role in continuing active engagement with the Kunsthaus over the coming decades.

The editors

↗ p. 39

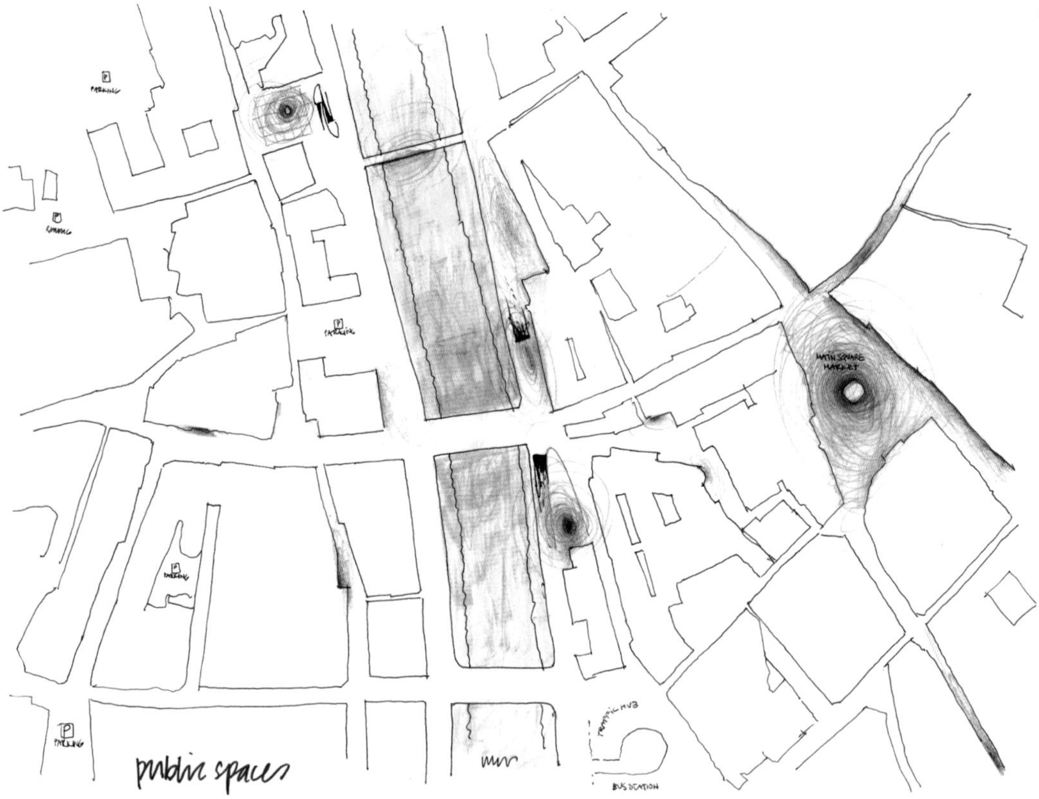

One of the first sketches from the competition.
No building is shown, just the location of public spaces nearby,
Niels Jonkhans

(Text contributions)

2000

(**Kunst**
(**Haus**
(**Graz**
(**Iron House**
(design

Iron House
→ 020)
↗ p. 41
↗ p. 303

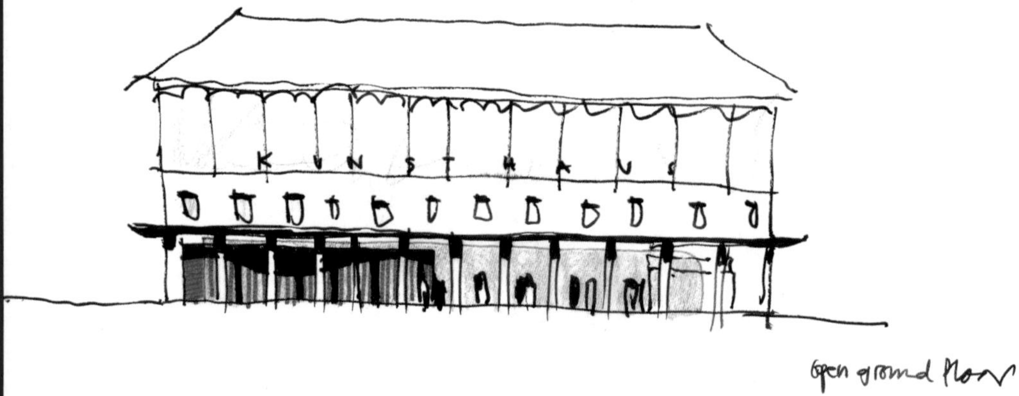

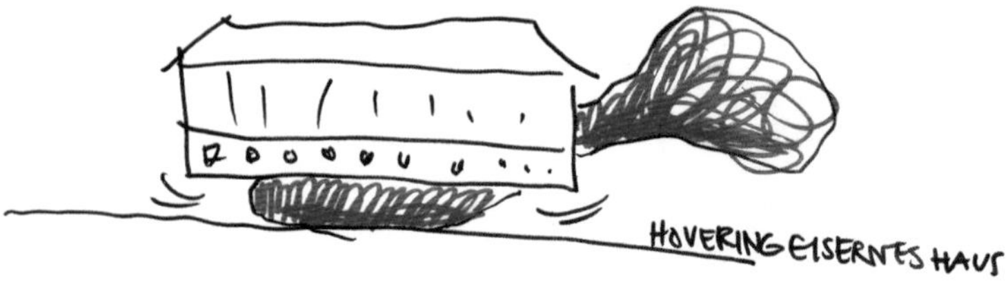

The Iron House with the open, public and vibrant **ground floor**.
Early sketch from the competition, Niels Jonkhans

(Kunst
(Haus
(Graz
(Iron House

café
→ 024)

Photo taken by Laura Treiblmayr

2003

Iron House
former Medienkunstlabor
former shop

shop
→ 059

Images)

(Architectural photography

→ 015) **former shop**
→ 046) **foyer**
→ 048) **foyer**
→ 061) **former café Les Viperes**
→ 086) **Space02**

(Favoriten

Arthur Zalewski took photographs inside and outside the Kunsthaus Graz. At first glance, many of his photos seem like snapshots; they appear unspectacular and arbitrary, almost as though the artist had pressed the shutter release button at random. However, the images are based on a series of decisions – Zalewski consistently photographs with a focal length of 60 mm, slightly zooming in on the motif. The subject and framing are chosen precisely, and a similar precision is shown in the selection and presentation of the pictures. Whilst photographing, Zalewski proceeds in an associative manner, combining coincidence with an interest in precise image construction. Although the single objects and the single image retain their autonomy, they are conceived and treated in relation to one another. Essentially, Zalewski adopts an essayistic understanding of photography – he approaches the objects he wishes to photograph from various perspectives, subjectively, unsystematically, discovering surprising cross connections and views of the architecture of Graz, whereby architecturally demanding and purely pragmatic projects, architectural works of art and functional buildings without design ambitions are given equal consideration. The photos in the book are a selection from a series created in the context of the exhibitions **Graz Architecture** and **Up into the Unknown**, Kunsthaus Graz 2017, and were shown as a slide projection.
→ 39)
→ 155)

(Construction and reconstruction phase

→ 042) 2018 **Kunst Haus façade**
→ 047) 2001 **Kunst Haus Space01 Foyer**
→ 050) 2017 **Kunst Haus foyer**
→ 051) 2017 **Kunst Haus foyer**
→ 057) 2019 **Haus Foyer façade**
→ 060) 2017 **Kunst Haus foyer info**
→ 063) 2017 **Kunst Haus foyer Travelator**
→ 196) 2017 **Haus façade foyer**
→ 197) 2018 **Haus façade foyer**

(**Iron House**
(usage

'The room is located directly behind the façade of the **Iron House**, which is of such great historic importance. Although a statue of Polyhymnia, the muse of sacred poetry, is mounted on its outside wall, the materiality of this façade made it just as modern when it was built as the blue acrylic glass **Skin** of the Kunsthaus appears to us today.'

Tanja Gasser, paper restorer

(Which architectural element at the Kunsthaus corresponds to your use?

Sophia Walk addressed this question to the people who work indirectly or directly with the Kunsthaus Graz. During the resulting conversation, the users showed her various places in the Kunsthaus and pointed out the positions of the chosen elements that reveal their use of the building. **Martin Grabner** documented the users' interaction with the architecture in photographs. His series paints a picture that is more than the sum of its parts. In the book Martin Grabner's photos fit naturally into the tour of the building and the associated image narrative. They tell of the people who use the Kunsthaus.

2001

Haus
ground floor
design

floor plan
↗ p. 345
↗ p. 83

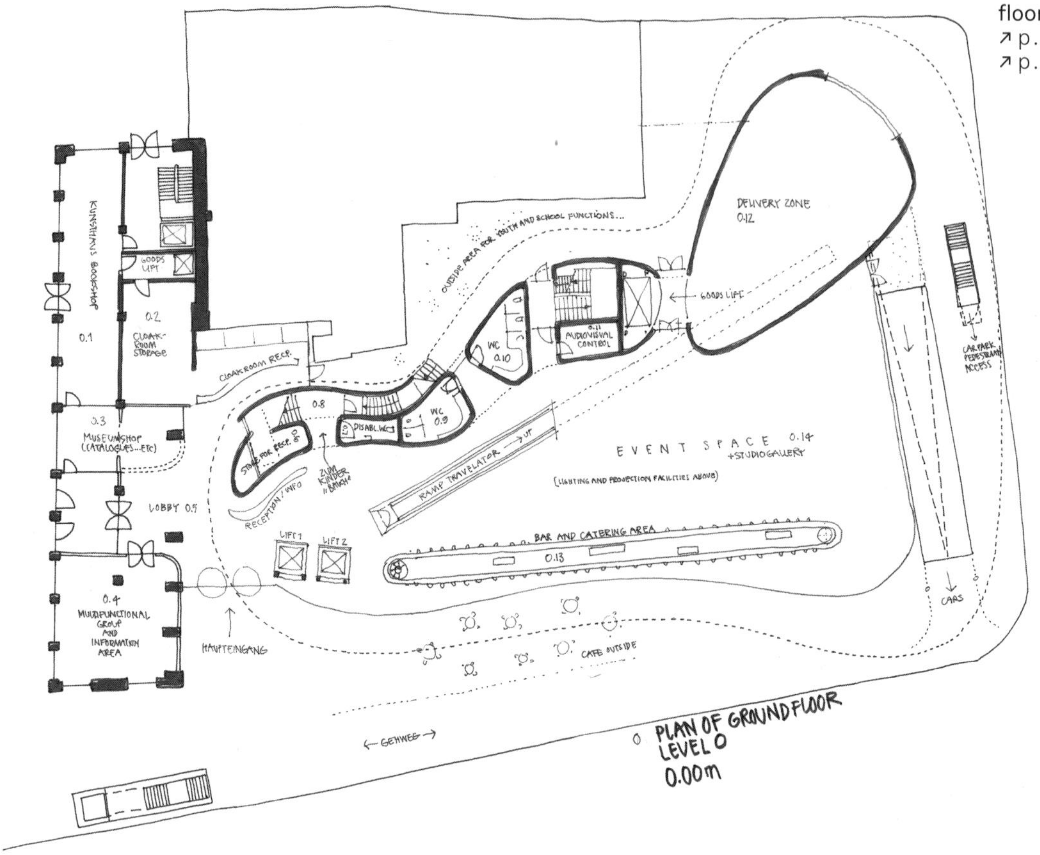

Floor plan variant of the open **ground floor**.
Study from the preliminary design, Niels Jonkhans

(Designs and sketches

→ 003) 2001 View along Lendkai
→ 004) 2000 Design sketch from the competition
→ 007) 2000 Organic, moving Skin
→ 008) 2001 View of Mariahilfer Straße
→ 011) 2000 Location of public spaces nearby
→ 012) 2000 The Iron House with the open, public and vibrant ground floor
→ 017) 2001 Floor plan variant of the open ground floor
→ 020) 2001 View from across the Hauptbrücke
→ 025) 2000 Amorphous building
→ 026) 2001 Isometric sectional drawings
→ 033) 2000 The floating Bubble
→ 034) 2000 Organic shapes
→ 040) 2000 Distribution of functions
→ 041) 2000 Floor plan variant of the open ground floor
→ 076) 2001 Cross section of the Bubble
→ 077) 1997 Reference: The Tongue
→ 081) 2000 The Travelator
→ 082) 2001 Exhibition level
→ 083) 2001 Exhibition floor
→ 084) 2001 Exhibition floor
→ 085) 2004 Videodreams
→ 106) 1997 Reference: The Tongue
→ 151) 2000 Pathways / open ground floor
→ 153) 2001 Escape routes
→ 154) 2001 Ground floor
→ 171) 2000 Organic shell with embedded functions
→ 173) 2000 Outer Skin with Nozzles
→ 174) 2002 3D drawing of the supporting structure
→ 176) 2000 Studies for the organic shell and supporting structures
→ 208) 2003 Animation on the simulation software of the BIX façade

(friendly alien

→ 001) 2007
→ 002) 2003
→ 005) 2017
→ 010) 2020
→ 027) 2004
→ 029) 2004
→ 038) 2003
→ 078) 2004
→ 141) 2003
→ 152) 2004
→ 218) 2004
→ 221) 2019
→ 222) 2003

2019

Kunst
Haus
Needle

Needle
→ 021)

Photo by Suza Lesjak

('The special Kunsthaus photo'

Photos from the competition
'SEND US YOUR SPECIAL KUNSTHAUS PHOTO', 2020

→ 001) **Bubble** Photo by Marie Neugebauer
→ 009) **Bubble** Photo by Eva Mohringer
→ 018) **Needle** Photo by Suza Lesjak
→ 071) **façade** Photo by Georg Weinseiss
→ 194) **façade** Photo by Christoph Edlinger
→ 195) **façade** Photo by Martina Margarete Berger
→ 198) **façade** Photo by Gerhard Moderitz
→ 199) **façade** Photo by Gerlinde Becker
→ 200) **façade** Photo by Meinrad Hopfgartner

(References

→ 029) Instant City Airships, Visit to a Small Town, 1970
→ 030) Instant City, 1969
→ 031) Bâtiment Public Monte Carlo, 1969/70
→ 032) Plan for the Living City Exhibition, Archigram, 1963
→ 055) The Museum of Modern Art, New York City, 1950
→ 056) Some lines in the net that stretches between the museum and iconic architecture, 2020
→ 062) Cuestión de Pasta, Fausto Grossi, 2000
→ 077) The Tongue, Peter Cook, Colin Fournier, 1997
→ 103) Raumstadt, Frederick Kiesler, Paris, 1925
→ 106) The Tongue, Peter Cook, Colin Fournier, 1997
→ 156) A Walking City, Ron Herron, 1964
→ 157) Bau. Schrift für Architektur und Städtebau 20, 1965
→ 158) Bau. Schrift für Architektur und Städtebau 21, 1966
→ 159) Agglomeration of devices for satisfying requirements, Konrad Frey, 1966
→ 160) Cushicle, Michael Webb, 1966–67
→ 161) Cowicle/Kuhwickel, Konrad Frey, 1966–67
→ 162) Archegram 1 + 2, Bernhard Hafner, 1962
→ 163) Building, Planning & Resources und Anthony Hunt Associates, Sundome – Shell structure for halls, 1971
→ 164) AEC-Pavilion, Victor Lundy, 1965
→ 165) Refurbishment of church block, Kaiser-Josef-Platz, Graz, Konrad Frey, 1967
→ 166) Interments Palace, Leicester Square (The Sin Centre), Michael Webb, 1962
→ 167) Refurbishment of church block, Kaiser-Josef-Platz, Graz, Konrad Frey, 1967
→ 168) Multipurpose hall at the Schulschwestern in Graz-Eggenberg, Günther Domenig / Eilfried Huth 1973–77
→ 169) Vegetated / Smooth Lump, Peter Cook, 1973
→ 170) Greenhouses, University of Graz Botanical Gardens, Volker Giencke, 1982–95

2019

(Kunst (Haus (Graz

Space01
→ 138)

(Exhibitions, projects

Since the opening of the Kunsthaus Graz in 2003, its exhibition programme and artistic practice have been – and still are today – shaped by an engagement with the architecture of the Kunsthaus itself. Artists have frequently been commissioned to produce new works that reflect on the space directly, or investigate spatial perception at media boundaries. It would exceed the format of this book to present all of these projects in full, which is why the following list includes all exhibitions and selected events with just a fraction of these described in greater detail. These particular projects were selected due to their focus on architectural aspects.

(Kunst (Haus (foyer (

(Kunst (Haus (Needle (foyer (

(Kunst (Haus (inner courtyard (project space (

(Kunst (Haus (Space04 (

2001

Kunst
Haus
Graz
Iron House
design

Iron House
→ 012)
→ 022)
→ 023)
↗ p. 83
↗ p. 303

View from across the Hauptbrücke.
Sketch from the preliminary design, Niels Jonkhans

(Kunst
(Haus
(Space02
(

→ 085) **Videodreams. Between the Cinematic and the Theatrical,** 2004
→ 087) **Werner Reiterer. Eye Sucks World,** 2007
→ 093) **Graz Architecture. Rationalists, Aesthetes, Gut Instinct Architects, Democrats, Mediacrats,** 2017/18
→ 095) **Where Art Might Happen. The Early Years of CalArts,** 2020
→ 097) **Hollerer/Marte. 'Do we need to have an accident?',** 2011
→ 098) **Sofie Thorsen. Cut A-A',** 2012
→ 099) **The Paradise the Downfall. Hartmut Skerbisch – Media Works,** 2015/16
→ 100) **Karl Neubacher. Media Artist, 1926–1978,** 2014
→ 101) **James Benning. Decoding Fear,** 2014
→ 102) **Tatiana Trouvé. Il Grande Ritratto,** 2010
→ 121) **BLESS N°41. Retrospectives Home,** 2010

(Kunst
(Haus
(Space01)
(

→ 028) **Bill Fontana. Primal Energies,** 2020
→ 037) **Up into the Unknown. Peter Cook, Colin Fournier and the Kunsthaus,** 2017/18
→ 107) **Up into the Unknown. Peter Cook, Colin Fournier and the Kunsthaus,** 2017/18
→ 108) **Sol LeWitt. Wall,** 2004
→ 111) **Michael Kienzer. Logic and Self-Will,** 2012
→ 112) **Antje Majewski. The World of Gimel. How to Make Objects Talk,** 2011/12
→ 116) **Erwin Wurm. Football-sized lump of clay on light blue car roof,** 2017
→ 124) **Maria Lassnig, Liz Larner. Two or Three or Something,** 2006
→ 125) **Berlinde De Bruyckere. In the Flesh,** 2013
→ 126) **Constantin Luser. Music Tames the Beast,** 2016
→ 127) **Diana Thater. Gorillagorillagorilla,** 2009
→ 128) **Bill Fontana. Primal Energies,** 2020
→ 130) **Katharina Grosse. 'Who, I? Whom, You?',** 2014
→ 131) **Pedro Cabrita Reis. True Gardens #6,** 2008
→ 135) **Corporate. Xu Zhen (Produced by MadeIn Company),** 2015/16
→ 136) **Romuald Hazoumè. Beninese Solidarity with Endangered Westerners,** 2013/14
→ 139) **Cittadellarte. Sharing Transformation,** 2012/2013

(Kunst
(Haus
(Space01
(Space02
(

→ 080) Travelator **Narratives. -35/65+ Two Generations,** 2006/2007
→ 088) Space02 **Inventory. Works from the Herbert Collection,** 2006
→ 089) Space02 **Protections. This is not an exhibition,** 2006
→ 091) Space02 **Connected. Peter Kogler with ...,** 2019
→ 094) Space02 **Arts ↔ Crafts. Between Tradition, Discourse and Technologies,** 2019/2020
→ 104) Space02 **Herbert Brandl. TOMORROW,** 2020
→ 113) Space01 **Rock – Paper – Scissors. Pop Music as Subject of Visual Art,** 2009
→ 114) Space01 **Chikaku. Time and Memory in Japan,** 2005
→ 115) Space01 **Einbildung. The Perception in Art,** 2003/04
→ 117) Space01 **The Artist, the Work and the Exhibition,** 2019
→ 119) Space01 **M City. European Cityscapes,** 2005/06
→ 122) Space01 **Herbert Brandl. TOMORROW,** 2020
→ 129) Space01 **Connected. Peter Kogler with ...,** 2019
→ 133) Space01 **Herbert Brandl. TOMORROW,** 2020
→ 134) Space01 **Congo Stars,** 2018/2019
→ 137) Space01 **ARTS ↔ CRAFTS. Between Tradition, Discourse and Technologies,** 2019/2020
→ 138) Space01 **Jun Yang. The Artist, the Work, and the Exhibition,** 2019

2019

(**Kunst**
(**Haus**
(Needle

Needle
→ 018)
Kunsthaus
→ 221)

In the run-up to the national elections, the Kunsthaus Graz showed the multi-channel video installation **What Is Democracy?** by Oliver Ressler. The exhibition location for this sombre work was the visitor platform of the building, the **Needle**, which created a visible connection to the city from the inside as well as from the outside, ensuring that the large lettering with which Ressler broadcast his question to the public was visible from afar.

Oliver Ressler, What Is Democracy?

(**Kunst**
(**Haus**
(**Needle**
(**Space01**
(**Space02**
(

→ 118) Space01 **China welcomes you ... Desires, Struggles, New Identities,** 2007
→ 146) Needle **China welcomes you ... Desires, Struggles, New Identities,** 2007

(**Kunst**
(**Haus**
(**Needle**)
(

→ 143) **Dizziness. Navigating the Unknown,** 2017
→ 147) **keep drawing! Part of the UNIQA Family Day,** 2017
→ 021) **Oliver Ressler. What Is Democracy?,** 2019

(**Kunst**
(**Haus**
(**Space03**)
(

→ 179) **Mieke Bal. nothing is missing,** 2010

(**Kunst**
(**Haus**
(**staircase**
(

→ 182) **Site/Cite. Speaking in Tongues While Splitting One's Own. Birke Gorm,** 2016/17

(**Kunst**
(**Haus**
(**Space01**
(**Space02**
(**Space04**
(**foyer**
(**Needle**
(**freight elevator**
(**delivery space**
(**staircase**
(**basement**
(**forecourt**
(

→ 073) freight elevator **'I don't think I am trying to commit suicide'. Performance Now,** 2019
→ 145) Needle **The Museum as a Gym. Aldo Giannotti,** 2016
→ 183) basement **The Big Draw Graz – ARTopie – Drawing Makes Sense!,** 2016
→ 184) staircase **The Museum as a Gym. Aldo Giannotti,** 2016
→ 188) forecourt **The Big Draw Graz,** 2015

2000
~1900

Iron House
Graz

Iron House
↗ p. 41
→ 012)
→ 020)

The Iron House before the state of construction 2000 and around 1900

café
→ 061)

'When the tender was issued for catering at the Kunsthaus, it soon became clear to me that a café would only really work well if you expanded it out onto Südtiroler Platz with an al fresco terrace. I wanted to open up this space with the folding doors.'

Michael Schunko, café manager

↗ p. 83

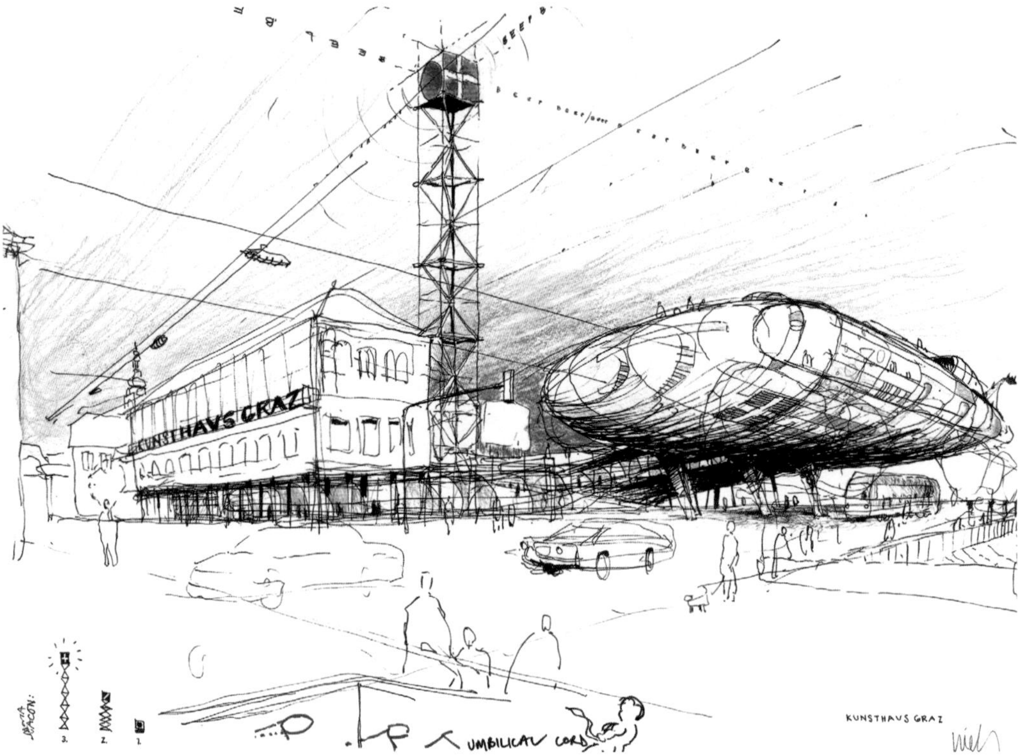

Amorphous building projecting over Lendkai.
Sketch of a design variant from the competition,
Niels Jonkhans

The potential of the non-perfect

Barbara Steiner

intersection
↗ p. 346

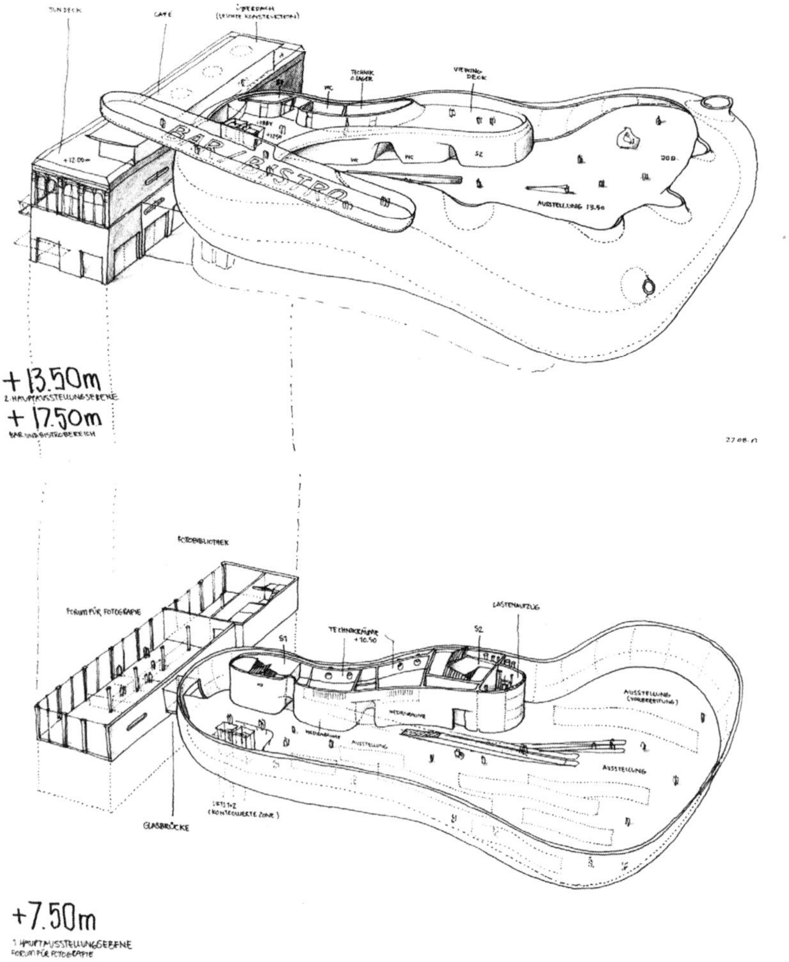

Isometric sectional drawings of the exhibition floors.
Extract from sketchbooks, Niels Jonkhans

The potential of the non-perfect

Shortly after the opening of the Kunsthaus, the journalist Ute Woltron remarked in the Austrian daily newspaper *Der Standard* that the building seemed 'as though Space Barbie were being carried to her grave on a sarcophagus of cold German bank architecture'. She went on to draw the conclusion: 'The Kunsthaus experiment has been carried out, albeit without success. There is too wide a gap between the concept and its actual realisation, the visionary aspect of the architecture remained extraterrestrial, it shattered on the limits of earthly feasibility.'[1] In fact, the concept changed considerably over the course of time – not only between the birth of the design and its realisation, but also during the implementation phase. Central parts of the competition design were never implemented, for example a building that was to float freely above the square and a transparent, permeable external skin with a constantly changing appearance. This was a disappointment for many people who had been following the construction of the Kunsthaus from the beginning. But to say that the visionary element of the design shattered on the limits of earthly feasibility? Not in my opinion, and I will explain why below.

History, site and competition

In 1963, the tri-national biennial *trigon* was founded by Hanns Koren, the State Councillor for Culture at the time. Its goal was to present the current art scene in Austria, Italy and the former Yugoslavia, and to promote cultural exchange across the borders. Later, the 'trigon territory' was extended to include Hungary, Germany, France, Great Britain, Spain and the Czech Republic. As the biennials became firmly established, the idea of a 'trigon museum' soon arose. In 1988, following discussions lasting many years, the Styrian State Building Authority held an architectural competition in which representatives from the 'trigon region' were invited to participate. The Viennese office Schöffauer Schrom Tschapeller won the competition, and immediately began the planning process. Although a site was available in the city centre (at Pfauengarten), along with financing and preliminary planning, the project was shelved when the government changed in 1991. A short time later, the architect Klaus Gartler was commissioned to perform a site study, whose results he presented in 1996. A second competition was announced, with international participation, this time for the Schloßberg – Palais Herberstein location. This was won by the Swiss firm Weber Hofer Partner Architekten. Their proposals were rejected in a public referendum held in 1998. In the third attempt, an area opposite the old town was under consideration, in the so-called 'red light district'. Because Graz had applied to become the European Capital of Culture in 2003, there was now a real chance for the museum of modern and contemporary art to finally be realised. For many people, this would be a dream come true.

From the beginning, the decision to erect the building on the right bank of the Mur was motivated by urban development concerns. Attention was drawn to the districts of

Luchezar Boyadjiev, idea sketch, produced in the context
of the Dispositiv Trigon conference

Lend and Gries, which had previously been in the shadow of the areas on the left bank of the Mur. An empty site between Lendkai and Mariahilfer Straße was designated as the future location. The 'Iron House', marking the end corner of Annenstraße, was to connect directly with the new building; the listed façade with its cast-iron structure on the upper floor would remain unchanged. The first cast-iron building in continental Europe was built as early as 1848 – before the famous Crystal Palace in London – by Josef Benedict Withalm (1771–1864). Withalm, who was the architect, owner and first operator, had not only imported the new cast iron technology from England, but also developed a modern concept for the utilisation of the building: it was to be a department store with large, inviting shop windows on the ground floor, a fine café – the *Café Meran* – on the first floor, and a bar in the basement. In his first design, the building was a two-storey glazed cast-iron structure, above which a recessed third storey with a flat roof was situated. Having undergone numerous structural changes in the 150 years since it had been in use, the 'Iron House' was cleared and gutted in 2001/02; its iron façade was exposed and the original proportions of the storeys were restored.

→ design 011)
→ design 012)
→ Iron House 023)

The object of the international architectural competition at the end of 1999 was 'the construction of an art museum incorporating the listed building, the Iron House.' The new complex was to house 'an exhibition space, a media centre, a photography forum, a catering area, commercial facilities and all necessary adjoining rooms.' The 'Iron House' was to be given 'a flat roof (= roof terrace) with a penthouse.'[2] A spatial and functional programme for the Kunsthaus Graz, developed by the museum planner Dieter Bogner on behalf of the city of Graz, was linked with the call for tender. A total of 102 projects were submitted to the competition; nine were considered worthy of a prize, and one prize was awarded. On 7 April 2000, the jury, chaired by the Graz architect Volker Giencke, unanimously selected the project by Peter Cook and Colin Fournier as the winner. Their competition design envisaged a 'building floating freely over the square' with an outer membrane that was to be 'coated with Teflon, inflammable, tear-resistant and translucent.' All additional rooms were to be housed 'in the double-walled outer **Skin**.'[3] In the statement made by the jury, which consisted of Odile Decq, Dietmar Feichtinger, Kasper König, Harald Szeemann, Kjetil Thorsen, Dieter Bogner, Wolfgang Lorenz, Klaus Gartler, Gerfried Sperl and Rudolf Schilcher, special mention was given to the fact that 'the building volume fits into its environment perfectly' and yet 'instantly recognisable.'[4]

↗ jury statement p. 349

In February 2001, the financing for the Kunsthaus was agreed by the Styrian parliament and the city council of Graz. The Austrian partner of the British architects was Architektur Consult (Günther Domenig, Hermann Eisenköck and Herfried Peyker). They joined forces with spacelab (Peter Cook and Colin Fournier) and Bollinger + Grohmann Engineers to form ARGE Kunsthaus, which was responsible for the realisation of the building. The architect Niels Jonkhans, a partner of spacelab, had already played an important role in the concept development phase in London. He became the competition team's representative on site.

2020

Kunst
Haus
Needle
BIX

↗ p. 55
↗ p. 299
↗ p. 325

The **BIX façade**
Project: Bill Fontana, Graphic Waves

The unpredictable nature of the space

The spatial programme of the competition design was based on the idea of flexible, adaptable 'platforms'. The exterior also followed this principle – transitions between transparency and opacity, along with reflections, were to ensure that the external **Skin** of the building constantly changed its appearance. Initially conceived as a seamless laminated membrane, it was intended to house photovoltaic elements (solar and wind energy) and light-emitting diodes; the skin was also to be used as a digital screen. Suggestions concerning the possible composition of such a skin were taken from the field of professional yacht sailing.[5] This concept was consistent with the idea that the future Kunsthaus did not have to house a permanent collection. It was intended – and this was one of Colin Fournier's favourite ideas – 'potentially to allow' the Kunsthaus to be more like a chameleon, always changing its appearance both externally, by means of its programmable electronic façade, and internally, to fit the fresh needs and style of each ephemeral show.'[6] In this context, it was conceptually important to integrate 'element of novelty and shock'[7] – visitors would enter the interior of the Kunsthaus on the so-called **Travelator**, a kind of conveyor belt that also led to the various floors, thus gliding 'into the unknown,' to use Peter Cook's catchy description.[8] Each exhibition was to produce a 'new spatial feeling' and 'constantly create the illusion of an unknown building.'[9] Film and city were used as an analogy: just as 'an unforgettable film is one in which something unexpected happens, an unexpected city is one that changes its mood or character.' The Kunsthaus had to promise a series of surprises in its '"nooks and crannies", on the small platforms, under things'.[10] Along with the focus being on temporary exhibitions, the decision to create several entrances and points of access inside – the **Travelator, staircase, lift** and open platforms – in short, the multidirectional spatial conception, formed the basic framework that allowed visitors to make surprising discoveries.

→ design 034) 176)

→ Travelator 079) 080)

→ access 151) 153) 189)

Colin Fournier, in particular, had long pursued the vision of a fluid architecture, 'which, with the help of robotics and artificial intelligence, will one day be able to really come alive and respond to environmental influences and human needs and desires.'[11] The idea of permanent change became the key to the architectural conception. It referred not only to the building itself, but also to the things it was capable of unleashing, as a motor so to speak. It was to have 'an important influence on the regeneration of the western half of the city' and, following the examples of the Centre Pompidou in Paris, the Guggenheim in Bilbao or the Tate Modern in London, 'be an effective catalyst for change.'[12]

→ reference 062)

First ideas on lively, communicative and changing buildings and cities emerged long before the Kunsthaus competition, in the midst of an environment shaped by pop culture – London in the 1960s, in the circles surrounding Cedric Price und Archigram. The *Fun Palace* (1960/61), which Price developed in collaboration with the theatre director Joan Littlewood, was designed as a light, modular structure. Movable walls, floors, ceilings and corridors, ramps, air barriers, warm air curtains and fog machines were to support various activities in its interior, adapting to individual needs.[13] With the help of

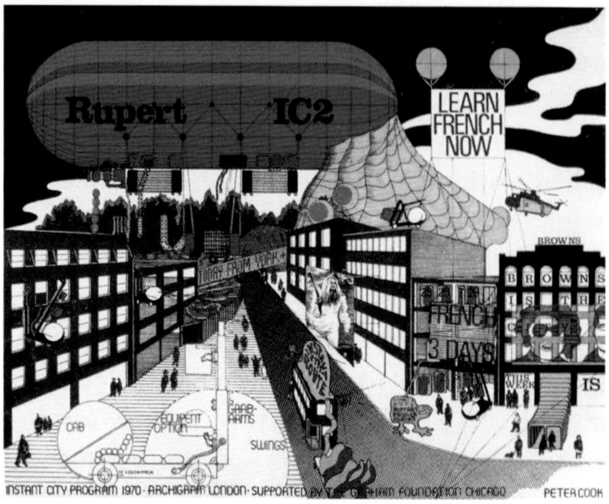

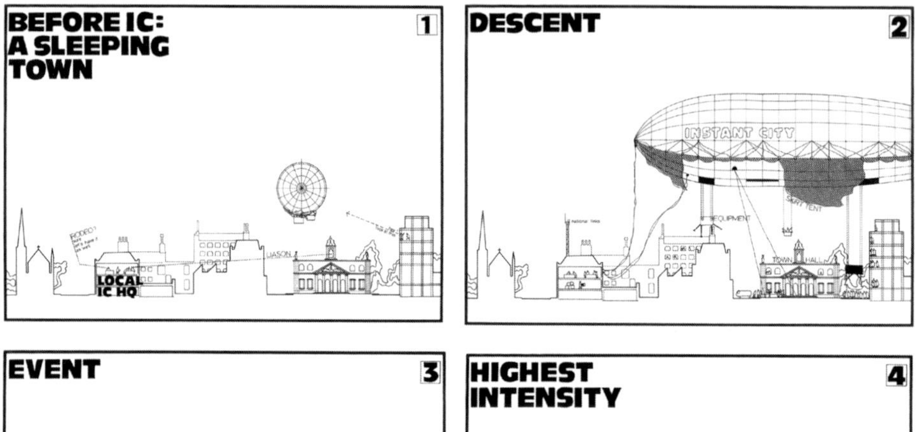

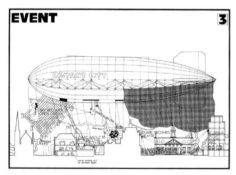

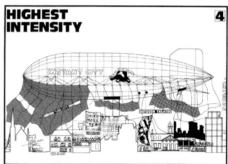

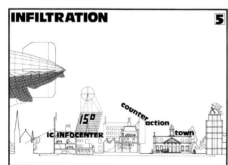

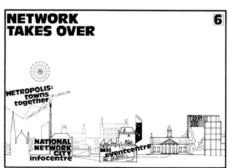

(top) Instant City Airships, Visit to a Small Town
(bottom) Instant City, Collection Frac Centre-Val de Loire;
Peter Cook, Archigram

a crane, the spatial constellation could be changed as required. Archigram, founded in 1961 by Peter Cook, Michael Webb and David Greene, placed great emphasis on its visionary ideas, which were published in a journal founded especially for the purpose. The group distanced itself from the pragmatism that was widespread in the architecture of the time. Its members envisioned periscopes rising up from buildings, spaceships settling in sleepy cities, spongy, landscape-like zones and variable skins for their buildings. Their bold urban and architectural designs made a particularly strong impact on the younger generation.

Several of Archigram's projects share specific characteristics with the Kunsthaus Graz. For example, the layout of the exhibition ***Living City*** (ICA London, 1963), designed and curated by Archigram, has a clear affiliation with the floor plan of the exhibition levels and geometrical inner skin of the Kunsthaus. The London exhibition featured a periscope pointing in the direction of Piccadilly, and this element also appears in a modified form in Graz, with its opening facing towards the Schloßberg, the so-called 'naughty **Nozzle**'. In both cases, the periscope directs the visitor's gaze towards a popular tourist spot. *Instant City* (1969) by Archigram has clear characteristics that can be transferred to the situation in Graz: an airship comes from the outside, settles in a less developed part of a city and provides information, education and entertainment via (provisional) structures. The Lend district, in which the Kunsthaus is situated, was also an urban area neglected by politics until the arrival of the Kunsthaus. Even though the building in Graz was certainly never intended to be provisional, it is based on the programmatic ambition of permanent transformation. If you exchange the term 'airship' for '**friendly alien**,' a similar gesture can be recognised – something comes from the outside, intervenes in existing structures and continues to merge with its environment.

→ reference 032)
→ Nozzle 122) 123)
→ reference 029) 030) 037)

The first joint project undertaken by Cook and Fournier was *Bâtiment Public* in Monte Carlo.[14] It was intended to provide a platform for all kinds of activities, assimilating various functions such as go-cart track, circus, venue for chamber music concerts and ice hockey field. The architecture, conceived in terms of fluidity, would become apparent through the events; it would be a 'feature space,' or a space with special attributes. The plans showed 'service nodes' recessed in the floor and the dome ceiling, along with machines like robots that generated spatial solutions for the various functional requirements, following a 'plug-in' principle. In this way, it was intended to create a kind of stage area with constantly changing spatial, colour or acoustic features, which would even allow the architectural shell to be forgotten. In this project, the architects emphasised the special meaning of the unknown, of having no idea what to expect. Even then, the architects were considering a '**Travelator**' that would lead visitors into the building. In 1997, Cook and Fournier took part in an international competition for a museum of modern and contemporary art on the Schloßberg in Graz, the project preceding today's Kunsthaus. The roof with its organic appearance and changing '**Nozzles**,' the polymorphic lining of the interior, the plans for a double-shell skin and the bold, striking colour scheme clearly link *The Tongue* with the design of the Kunsthaus in its current location. Like a coloured tongue stretching from the hill between the buildings to the street below, it is integrated into the urban environment, yet retains

→ reference 031)
→ reference 106)
→ reference 077)

1972
1969–70
(**reference**

↗ p. 45
↗ p. 55
↗ p. 57
↗ p. 157
↗ p. 295

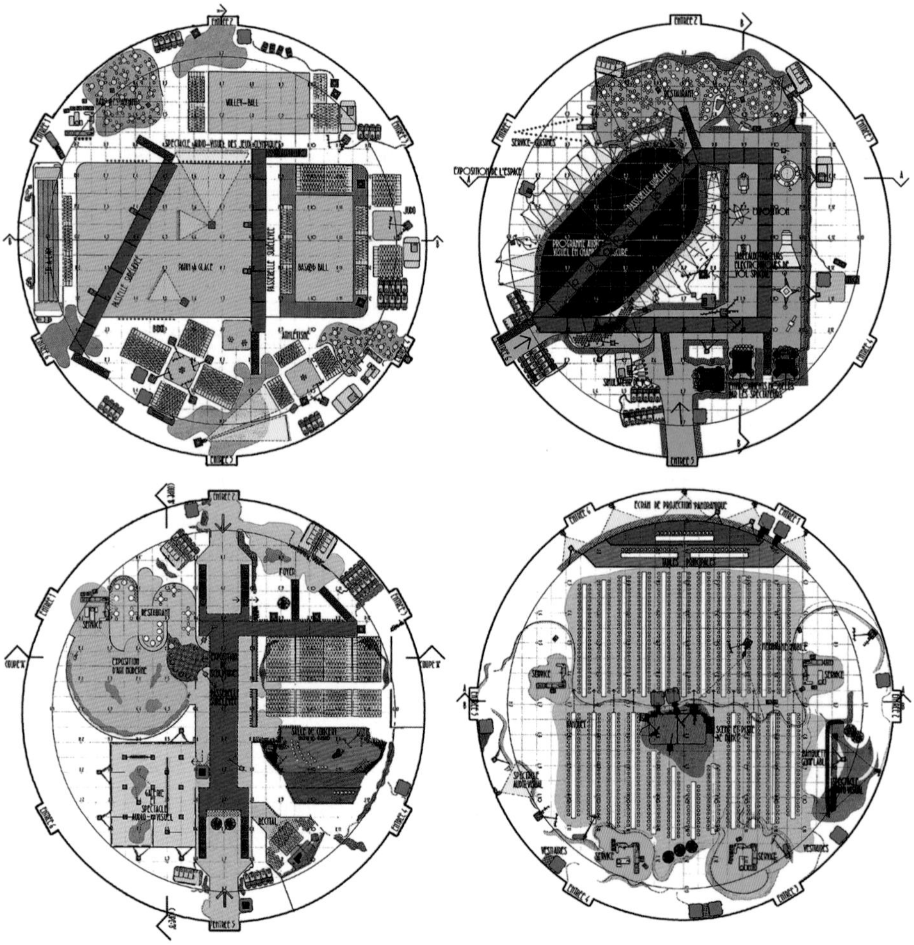

Bâtiment Public, Monte Carlo, Archigram Architects
(top) Features Monte Carlo, Foyer Principal;
(bottom) Plan arrangement for four uses: sports activities; exhibition of space exploration; cultural event; banquet

its self-confident architectural presence – in a similar way to the blue roof structure of the Kunsthaus, which inscribes itself into the surrounding Baroque roof landscape. → Kunsthaus 221)

Unknown territory

In the publication on his exhibition of the same name – *digital real Blobmeister* – Peter Cachola Schmal turns his attention to the architecture of the 1990s, which increasingly used digital tools to generate free forms. He coined the term 'Fegefeuer des Bauens' (purgatory of building) to describe the agonising process these designs had to pass through on the way to realisation.[15] Deviations from the original concept are an integral part of the building process, simply because legal, technological, economic and political conditions – and sometimes even constraints – force compromises to be made. However, this applies all the more to the ambitious architectural projects of the 1990s, which broke new ground. The Kunsthaus was no exception. It may sound incredible from today's perspective, but when the building permit was applied for, no viable technical solutions existed for some of the central design ideas formulated in the competition design, such as the free-standing form and the double-walled outer skin.
When the application for the building permit was made, the reference project was the BMW Pavilion at the IAA in Frankfurt/Main in 1999, a 'bubble' designed by Bernhard Franken/ABB Architects. The structural engineers of the Kunsthaus, Bollinger + Grohmann, were involved in its implementation. Due to the size of the Kunsthaus Graz, this reference example could not be directly transferred: '... we were working in all areas with systems that had never been tested. Virtually everything was new, and we had to take constant risks. It was basically procedural approach,'[16] explained Herfried Peyker, partner architect, ARGE Kunsthaus. Gernot Stangl, who was responsible for the 3D planning, remembers: 'When we were concreting the lower part of the building, we still didn't know how we were going to tackle the top half.'[17] The construction of the shell presented a particular structural challenge, whereby a square meshed net was transformed into a triangular structure for the planar sandwich layers of the building. Sigrid Brell-Cokran, who had digitalised the competition model before ARGE Kunsthaus was founded, mentions that 'at that time, commercially available CAD programmes did not provide a solution for the planarisation of square structures for the entire layered construction.'[18] These statements reveal that the architectural visions were far more advanced than the available knowhow. Even though research on free-standing forms was being carried out all over the world, there was simply a lack of experience in how to implement them.[19] There were huge expectations on the part of politicians and local citizens. 'After people had seen the design, we were expected to implement it immediately in a feasible way,' says Niels Jonkhans, although in his opinion a longer planning phase would have been required. Basically, different planning cultures collided at a very early stage. Visionary thinking, which was striving to develop in unforeseen directions, both conceptually and also as a result of the real technological challenges, encountered a pragmatic approach that was heading straight towards a concrete goal (the opening of the Kunsthaus in the year of the European Capital of Culture in 2003).

→ Nozzle 120)

→ Space02 087) 174)

↗ p. 45
↗ p. 55

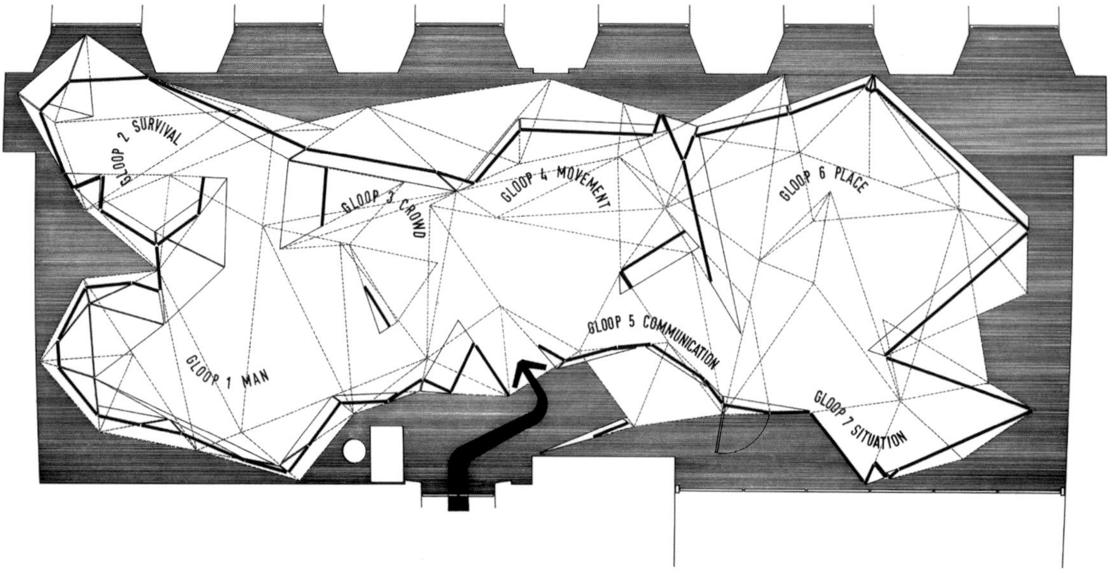

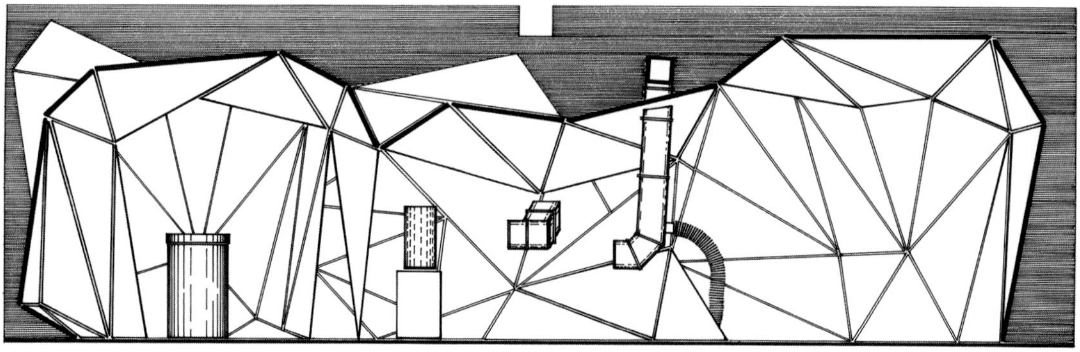

Living City, Archigram
(top) Plan for the Living City exhibition
(bottom) Intersection of the exhibition structure

In practical terms, a decision was made to build a steel primary construction, a kind of double concrete table. The 'belly' of the building was hung underneath it, and the free-form construction was built over it.[20] The light cocoon membrane of the Kunsthaus, as originally envisioned, gave way to a very solid, non-transparent construction. The **'Nozzles'** that characterise the roof landscape of the Kunsthaus are set in a fixed position; they cannot change direction, and they let very little natural light into the interior through the slats. For budget reasons, the spiral neon tubes in the **'Nozzle'** funnels were not concealed under light covers, but retained their expressive appearance.[21] The original lighting system, consisting of rows of small LED light sources placed close together and integrated into the surface of the inner skin, was dropped at an early stage. The concept of the two open platforms and the **'Travelator'** allowing visitors to glide into the exhibition zone remained in place. Another central idea – that of allowing the building to float above a freely accessible ground floor – had to be abandoned, mainly for reasons related to climate and conservation.[22] Nevertheless, it was possible to create a visual, open connection with the urban surroundings of the Kunsthaus by introducing a glass façade for the ground floor and its three entrances. Conceived as a low-threshold communication and event space, the ground floor initially housed the **Medienkunstlabor** (media art laboratory) and the 'media lounge',[23] along with the **events room**, **café**, **restaurant** and **shop**. Today, this zone features the **events room**, the **restaurant** and the **shop**, along with permanently installed works of art and the **Katzenbaum für die Kunst** (**Cat-Tree for the Arts**), a display sculpture for smaller temporary exhibitions. It was also possible to create a vaulted mediation room for children in the **belly** of the Kunsthaus, completely lined with carpet, which offers a view of the **ground floor** and the **forecourt** through portholes. However, the 'Pin-and-Skin Bar' at the Mur-riverside front was not realised. It was replaced by a viewing platform, known as the **'Needle,'** which is often used as an extended part of the exhibition, but also rented out for special occasions.

→ design 076) 174)
→ design 171)
→ Nozzle 172)
→ Nozzle 111) 135)
→ design 076) 082)
→ foyer 057) 065) 196)
→ Medienkunstlabor 014)
shop 015)
→ foyer 186)
→ Cat-Tree 049) 053)
→ Space03 177) 178) 179)
→ Needle 143) 146) 148)

'Crap-tech'

While the Kunsthaus was being built, budget restrictions and the pressures of time often made it necessary to rely on 'crap-tech' (crap technology).[24] This is characterised by the use of standard elements and materials combined with improvised, ingenious detailed solutions. An important example of this kind of improvisation is the internal skin of the Kunsthaus – the fine-meshed net, usually used in sewage treatment plants, is inexpensive, light and very elegant in appearance. In the construction of the Kunsthaus, it was not only necessary to improvise and find ad hoc solutions to save money, but also to compensate for discrepancies – between the manually drawn design and its digital translation, and also between digital production and manual implementation. The positioning of the Kunsthaus in relation to its urban setting and its appearance were first developed by means of hand drawings / sketches (Cook, Jonkhans), along with an explanatory text (Fournier). In order to gain a feeling for the free form, three-dimensional visual objects were then also made by hand, using various materials. It was only in a second step that the 3D database necessary for the construction process was

→ Skin 171) 176) 180)
→ design 034) 041) 154) 171)
↗ competition p. 269

↗ p. 39
↗ p. 41
↗ p. 81
↗ p. 83

The floating **Bubble**.
Sketch from the competition, Peter Cook

generated. This digital reproduction almost inevitably led to deviations, and thus to a lack of clarity. In any case, the appearance of the building would have been different if the design had been completed on the computer from the outset. As mentioned above, no commercially available CAD program existed for the digital construction of the **Skin**, which made digital improvisations necessary.[25] Improvisation was also involved in the production of the blue acrylic glass sheets. Although these were drawn on the computer and calculated in CAD, an impressively simple manual solution was found to achieve their curvature. The sheets were laid individually onto polystyrene cubes,[26] stretched down using glove leather and pushed into a kind of oven. The sheets were curved little by little and then allowed to cool down gradually, so that no cracks appeared.[27] Finally, they were attached to the lower construction using metal brackets. It became apparent during the course of construction that the lower structure was not always one hundred per cent accurate, so that manual corrections had to be carried out on site. Traces of this improvised, corrective treatment on site can still be seen in various parts of the **Bubble**.

→ design 174)

If you examine the Kunsthaus experiment, you will indeed encounter a highly unusual genesis. Building processes could not always be fully controlled – there were discrepancies between ideas and implementation, and constant modifications to the original plans. However, you will also find inventive improvisation and creative solutions like the ones described earlier. Basically, the entire project was tentative, searching and processual from the very beginning. This is underlined by Niels Jonkhans, who describes the Kunsthaus as 'a built and continually developing drawing.'[28] Because it was possible to continue drawing the sketch and writing the text, a playful approach to a complex undertaking could be adopted, with continual corrections along the way. However, this method quickly reaches its limits when time frames and budgets are (too) tightly calculated and too little attention is paid to practical research. Then the pragmatic, implementation-oriented approach simply begins too early and is inevitably shortened; otherwise, it is impossible to keep to the deadlines, and costs increase.

→ design 081) 084)

Why not a white exhibition space?

In *Curves and Spikes*, the catalogue accompanying the exhibition of the same name at Galerie aedes, Berlin, Colin Fournier writes: 'Without the restriction of having to adhere to strictly defined functions, there are two possibilities open to you: you decide on a striking, highly idiosyncratic form that passionately celebrates its iconic image, such as Frank O. Gehry's Guggenheim Museum in Bilbao, or you adopt a more reserved position and elevate it to the supreme principle of creating a flawlessly functioning, unobtrusive shell for the events that take place inside it.'[29] With this description, Fournier raises questions that have to be addressed in almost all discussions relating to new museum buildings:[30] to what extent is an architecturally ambitious, striking building suited to artistic programmes? Should art adapt to the museum, or the museum to art? Interestingly enough, Fournier sees the Kunsthaus Graz somewhere between these two poles: it was to be unique in its outer appearance, but its interior was to

→ reference 062)

design
→ 132)
↗ p. 79

Organic shapes. Sketches from the competition,
Peter Cook, Colin Fournier

allow curators and artists the greatest level of scope as far as spatial design was concerned. Opinions still differ today on how wide this scope has turned out to be, how 'impermeable' the shell really is and how suitable the building is for showing art.[31] Whatever the individual answer is, the Kunsthaus stimulates numerous discussions on the museum building and questions of exhibiting in general.

In his statement, Fournier touches upon another point: the fact that there has been a worldwide trend towards iconic buildings, which have become protagonists in themselves.[32] The Kunsthaus differs significantly here in that it actually combines two directions: the emancipatory design of spatial programmes from the late 1960s/1970s and the iconic architecture of the late 1980s/1990s. The former pursues the objective of stimulating a variety of activities in the building and activating the audience on as many levels as possible; the latter aims primarily at visibility, thus relying on the effectiveness of the (media) image. Therefore, it is hardly surprising that the positive image of its exterior predominates in the public perception of the Kunsthaus – basically, its iconicity. It fulfils contemporary expectations of such a building. However, this does not apply to its interior. Since the 1980s, expectations of exhibition spaces have undergone a strong shift in the direction of the 'white cube', whereas the interior of the Kunsthaus corresponds to quite another type of ideal space, originating from the 1960s and 1970s. At that time, the classical art museum with its white exhibition rooms and its air of sanctity and detachment had been transformed into a place of encounter, communication and production. It was to become open and lively, 'a place for experiments, for everything that bears the mark of creative renewal,' in keeping with Willem Sandberg's aspirations for the Stedelijk Museum in Amsterdam. The museum was no longer a consecration site, it was expected to 'open up to life,' become a commodity, so to speak, and to 'directly serve life in the present day.'[33] It was the task of architecture to provide the basis and the framework that would enable the museum to become an object of daily use. An important example of this approach, and probably the most well known, is the Centre Georges Pompidou in Paris.[34] A late echo of these ideas can also be found in the multidirectional spatial concept of the Kunsthaus. Its architects did not wish to create a representative container for rigid values and attributions, but a space for temporary and changeable settings. The space is conceived as an events space, promising unique experiences and encounters in the here and now.

→ friendly alien 001)

→ design 040)

In concrete terms, Cook and Fournier planned two exhibition levels, **Space01** and **Space02**. The height of the upper room, with its domed ceiling, intermittent light apertures and striking neon tubes, is 8.5 metres at its highest point. In contrast to this, and adding a complementary accent, **Space02** is laid out along an orthogonal grid with a room height of 4.80 m, a flat ceiling and neon tubes arranged in rows. The shell ('**Skin**') is dark grey on both levels.[35] In order to mediate between curatorial/museum-related and architectural concerns, the museum expert Dieter Bogner was brought on board. He proposed a presentation system based on a spatial solution by Frederick Kiesler for *The Art of This Century* (1942), Peggy Guggenheim's legendary gallery in New York. These displays, based on suspension points and wall mounts, work with thin, light wall panels or allow pictures to be hung directly in the centre of the room.[36] The suggestion

→ design 026)
→ Space01 140)
→ Space02 086)
→ Skin 087)

2017

(**Kunst**
(**Haus**
(**friendly alien**

Up into
the Unknown
→ 005)
→ 037)
→ 107)

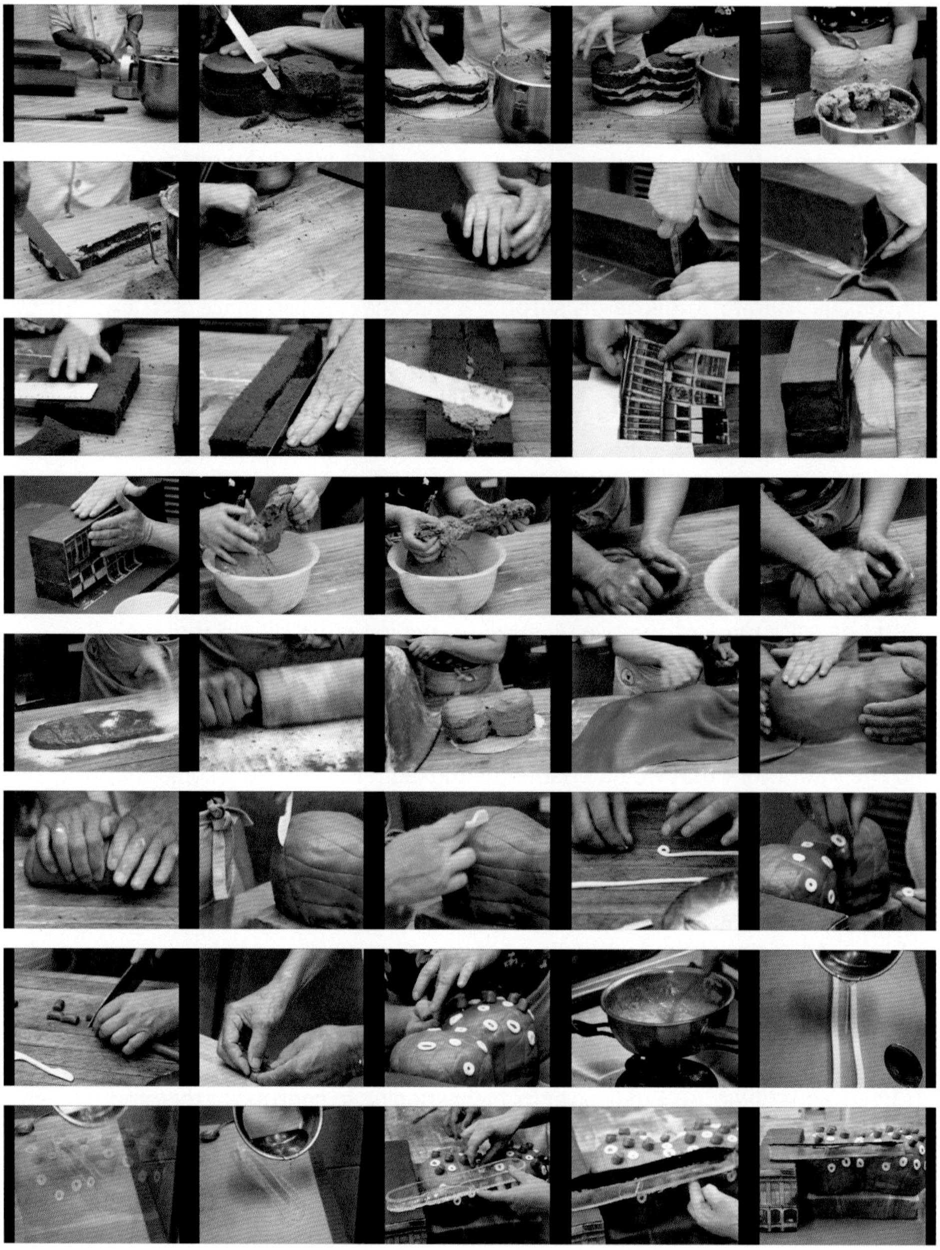

The Kunsthaus Cake (a remake), video stills

of realities:united, who won the tender for the 'media furnishing of the Kunsthaus' in 2002, followed a similar direction to that of Bogner. Technical infrastructures were to be accommodated behind the internal **Skin**, with telescopic bars for the presentation of art being mounted at the junctions of the triangular inner construction. In this updated version of Kiesler's cantilevers, their proposal was in line with that of the museum planner, Bogner.[37] Cook and Fournier themselves did not define the details of use and forms of presentation, but simply created technical prerequisites for displays, which could be activated as required. With suspension points in the ceiling and floor, they are based on a solution used by Archigram in the legendary London exhibition *Living City*, which was also planned for the interior of the *Bâtiment Public* in Monte Carlo.

→ Space02 091)
→ reference 031) 032)

Since its opening, the Kunsthaus has staged a number of spectacular exhibitions, finding unusual solutions for the specific spatial situation.[38] In this respect, the Kunsthaus fulfils the architects' promise to guarantee unique experiences on site.

No presentation is like any other. For **Space01** large artistic installations have been developed with the space in mind. Until 2016, both spaces also hosted group exhibitions of paintings or photographs presented in a traditional manner on white walls. In the meantime, the white, free-standing walls have been abandoned. Between 2016 and 2020, a series of practical tests were carried out, resulting in a modular, reusable, open system that will be implemented by studio itzo in 2021. It contains references to various historical displays, linking these with contemporary discourses on the subject of exhibiting. The proposed system remains close to the ideas of Cook and Fournier, but also takes into account economic and ecological considerations that played a minor role at the time when the Kunsthaus was built.

→ Space01 140)
→ Space01 115)
→ Space02 093) 095)

BIX

realities:united's initial assignment to 'supply media equipment for the building' applied only to the interior, but it was extended to include the façade. Through the use of media, a central idea from the competition design of the Kunsthaus was to be revived – the transparent, communicative façade.[39] A communicative outer skin was in fact created, the '**BIX light and media façade**', equipped with 946 conventional fluorescent lamps ('kitchen lamps').[40] The conceptual starting point for realities:united was a decision to use a technology that was already outdated at the time, based on the consideration that developments in the technical field are so rapid that any technology would quickly become obsolete. However, the **BIX** is not a low-tech project: the lamps are activated via a technically innovative ballast unit, developed by Swiss technicians. And the fact that each lamp can achieve any brightness level between 0% and 100% at the speed of a twentieth of a second is also the result of a sophisticated 'tuning process' using special hardware and software.[41] Because of these decisions, **BIX** deliberately overrides the usual standards of screen technology and expectations of media façades:[42] with just one colour (set by the manufacturer), the lowest resolution and technical limitations, the façade is attractive for artists, but uninteresting for commercial purposes. Furthermore, it is architecturally conceived, corresponds to

→ BIX 205) – 217)
→ BIX 208)

2019

Kunst
Haus
forecourt

forecourt
→150)

Forecourt, designed by Topotek1

architectural standards and establishes a synergetic relationship between architecture and medium. For Jan Edler from realities:united, the **BIX** represented 'a kind of fundamental research.'[43] It was to enable the Kunsthaus to carry out 'language research,' in order to collect the 'experience, semantics and grammar' required to deal with such surfaces.[44] To return to Peter Cook and a term he used in relation to the building of the Kunsthaus, **BIX** is also 'crap-tech' – functional, simple, easy to use, not high-tech but made of a mass-produced (kitchen) lamp available from IKEA, and yet highly sophisticated as far as the considerations and detailed solutions behind it are concerned. It is not the perfect media façade that can do anything, but rather the opposite – the possibilities are limited, in line with the conception.

The potential of the non-perfect

For Klaus Bollinger, the Kunsthaus has 'something human' about it, because it does not 'embody super-perfectionism' as a building.[45] Perhaps that is also the reason why many people quickly develop an emotional relationship with the Kunsthaus. They speak of the building as though it were a living being. This is revealed in the adjectives they use to describe it.[46] Additionally, and I am speaking from personal experience here, the non-perfect often has a huge attraction for artists and curators. This approach was deliberately chosen by realities:united with regard to **BIX**, but it seems to apply to the Kunsthaus as a whole.

→ friendly alien
005) 203) 220)

A building that is purposefully not perfect? It is not far from perfection to ideality, and there is a close connection between the two. In the context of the museum, particularly if we focus on the history of art and architecture in Europe, we are part of a tradition that has produced a wide spectrum of 'ideal museums'. But the ideal museum is independent of both context and time; it stands above social and everyday institutional perspectives. Political or economic constraints and seemingly banal but necessary functional requirements or everyday forms of utilisation are ignored. Ultimately, if we wished to avoid any kind of interference, built ideality would become autonomous, requiring neither visitors nor art. If it were any different, ideality and thus the ideal museum would be inconceivable. If, on the other hand, art institutions aspire to be part of the cultural life of their time, they react to specific social and artistic circumstances and (changing) demands, and thus lose their ideality. They are unable to maintain their perfection.

Cook and Fournier did not strive towards creating an ideal space; they anticipated changes and incorporated them in their concept. In this respect, the Kunsthaus follows the tradition of the *Fun Palace*, the Centre Georges Pompidou and the *Bâtiment Public*. But, of course, there are many details of the Kunsthaus that the architects themselves had envisaged as 'more perfect' – they would have realised them in a different way if they had had more time, more means and other technological resources at their disposal. However – and this leads us back to Klaus Bollinger's claim that the 'Kunsthaus is human'[47] – the building is no more perfect than human life itself. And *because* the Kunsthaus is not perfect, it neither upstages the art exhibited within its

2017

(**Kunst**
(**Haus**
(Space01

Up into
the Unknown
→ 005)
→ 035)
→ 107)

Up into the Unknown. Peter Cook, Colin Fournier and the Kunsthaus Graz

walls, nor sanctifies it. For this reason, it provides the opportunity for an encounter on equal terms – with art, but also with its visitors.
And yes, the construction of the Kunsthaus was an experiment. In central areas, the building is definitely not what it set out to be. But in my view, the visionary aspect did not 'shatter on the limits of earthly feasibility,' as the journalist Ute Woltron claimed in 2003, as quoted above.[48] We could also say: the visionary aspect well and truly grappled with the challenge of earthly feasibility. The Kunsthaus is and remains a building at a turning point. Ultimately its non-perfection distinguishes it from the high-tech, perfectly implemented buildings of the present day.[49] And that is precisely what makes it such a likeable building.

2003

(**friendly alien**

reference
→ 031)

Drawing by a pupil from BG/BRG Carneri, produced during the construction phase of the Kunsthaus

1 Ute Woltron, 'Space-Barbies Sarkophag', in: Der Standard, 18.09.2003.

2 Due to structural problems in the past, the flat roof had been converted to a gabled roof. The original design had a flat roof, which was now to be reconstructed. The idea of the penthouse was not pursued in the end.

3 Peter Cook, Colin Fournier, *Skin und Pin. Eine Projektbeschreibung*, 1999 (Kunsthaus Archive).

4 Dieter Bogner, Kunsthaus Graz AG (ed.), *A Friendly Alien. Ein Kunsthaus für Graz, Peter Cook, Colin Fournier Architects*, Ostfildern 2004, p. 27.

5 Colin Fournier, conversation with Barbara Steiner, 08.04.2017.

6 Colin Fournier, 'On Making a Building', in: *A Friendly Alien*, loc. cit., p. 100.

7 Loc. cit.

8 Peter Cook, loc. cit., p. 99.

9 Colin Fournier: *The Friendly Alien*, www.museum-joanneum.at/kunsthaus-graz/architektur/entwurf-renderings, (30.05.2020).

10 Peter Cook, in: *A Friendly Alien*, loc. cit., p. 103.

11 Colin Fournier, *The Friendly Alien*, www.museum-joanneum.at/kunsthaus-graz/architektur/entwurf-renderings, (30.05.2020).

12 Loc. cit.

13 In the planning, Price differentiated between small cells with a high degree of service function such as kitchen, restaurant, toilets, and large volumes with a lower service function such as auditorium, cinema and foyer.

14 The competition was won by Archigram. At the last minute, a decision was made not to realise the design.

15 Peter Cachola Schmal, *digital real. Blobmeister. Erste gebaute Projekte*, Basel 2001, p. 10.

16 Herfried Peyker, ARGE Kunsthaus, conversation with Barbara Steiner, 20.02.2017.

17 Gernot Stangl, ARGE Kunsthaus, conversation with Katia Huemer, 14.07.2017.

18 Sigrid Brell-Cokran, professor of individualised building production, RWTH Aachen, email correspondence with Katia Huemer, 29.08.2017.

19 Klaus Bollinger, Bollinger + Grohmann Engineers, conversation with Barbara Steiner, 17.05.2017.

20 Loc. cit.

21 Finally the budget was only exceeded by 2 %, which is extremely low compared with other museum buildings.

22 Even today, the '**Travelator**' has a chimney effect, in spite of the glass frontage of the ground floor.

23 One of the aims of the Kunsthaus was to encourage more intensive engagement with new media – also due to pioneering artistic achievements in Graz in the 1970s. For this reason, the main concept Included a platform for new media ('**Medienkunstlabor**' and 'media lounge'). In 2010, the '**media art laboratory**' and the '**media lounge**' were abandoned.

24 Peter Cook introduced this term in connection with the Kunsthaus. Peter Cook, conversation with Barbara Steiner, 19.01.2017.

25 For a detailed description of the construction process of the '**Skin**' see: Niels Jonkhans, 'A Friendly Alien – Kunsthaus Graz Austria', in: André Chaszar (ed.), *Blurring the Lines, Computer-Aided Design and Manufacturing in Contemporary Architecture*, Hoboken (New Jersey) 2006, pp. 172–179.

26 The polystyrene cubes had in their turn been CNC milled, loc. cit.

27 Herfried Peyker, loc. cit.

28 Niels Jonkhans, ARGE Kunsthaus, conversation with Barbara Steiner, 20.05.2016.

29 Colin Fournier, 'a friendly alien', in: Peter Cook/Colin Fournier, Klaus Kada, *curves and spikes. Kunsthaus und Stadthalle für Graz*, Berlin, Vienna 2003, p. 9.

30 See '**Museum architecture as a creator of possibilities. A conversation between Barbara Steiner, Pablo von Frankenberg and Sophia Walk**', in this book, p. 135.

31 For example the artist Mike Kelley, who exhibited in the Kunsthaus in 2009, was convinced that the architects of this building 'did not like art' and that there 'should be no exhibitions in it.' Mike Kelley, Kleine Zeitung, 21.05.2009.

32 See: Pablo v. Frankenberg, '**The attraction of the ambiguous. The museum as a source of friction for architecture**', In thls book, p. 99.

33 Willem Sandberg, *nu, midden in de XXe eeuw*, Hilversum 1959, p. 30; Willem Sandberg, 'Le musée ouvert', in. Ad Petersen, *Sandberg. Graphiste et directeur du Stedelijk Museum*, Paris 2007, p. 86.

34 See '**Museum architecture as a creator of possibilities. A conversation between Barbara Steiner, Pablo von Frankenberg and Sophia Walk**', in this book, p. 135.

35 It was considered whether the space behind the cladding should be painted white rather than grey. However, the installations behind the skin were not intended to be visible, and the cladding was to have a homogenous appearance. Gernot Stangl, loc. cit.

36 Dieter Bogner, consultant for museum planning, bogner.cc, Vienna, conversation with Barbara Steiner, 12.07.2017.

37 realities:united, Jan Edler, conversation with Barbara Steiner, 15.06.2017.

38 See Katia Huemer, **An extraterrestrial 'friendly organism'. A conversation**, in this book, p. 73.

39 realities:united, Jan Edler, conversation with Barbara Steiner, 15.06.2017.

40 **BIX** is a word creation derived from BIG and PIXEL.

41 The 'BIX-Simulator' was developed to test display options on the **BIX**. This programme is available to all artists via download.

42 realities:united, Jan Edler, conversation with Barbara Steiner, 15.06.2017.

43 Loc. cit.

44 Loc. cit.

45 Loc. cit.

46 See Sophia Walk, '**The friendly Alien Effect**', in this book, p. 219.

47 Loc. cit.

48 Ute Woltron, 'Space-Barbies Sarkophag', loc. cit.

49 An example of perfection: Beijing Daxing International Airport (PKX) by Zaha Hadid Architects (2019). The inner shell of the building is perfectly built, making full use of today's technical possibilities, and construction was completed in just four years.

2017

(**Favoriten**

Arthur Zalewski, selection from the series **Favoriten**
as part of the exhibitions **Graz Architecture** and **Up into the Unknown**.
Motifs: Glass Houses, Botanical Gardens at the University of Graz;
Kunsthaus Graz

Favoriten
→ 155)

giga
P
ZUGANG

Altstadt Mitte
Altstadt West
FREI

↗ p. 81

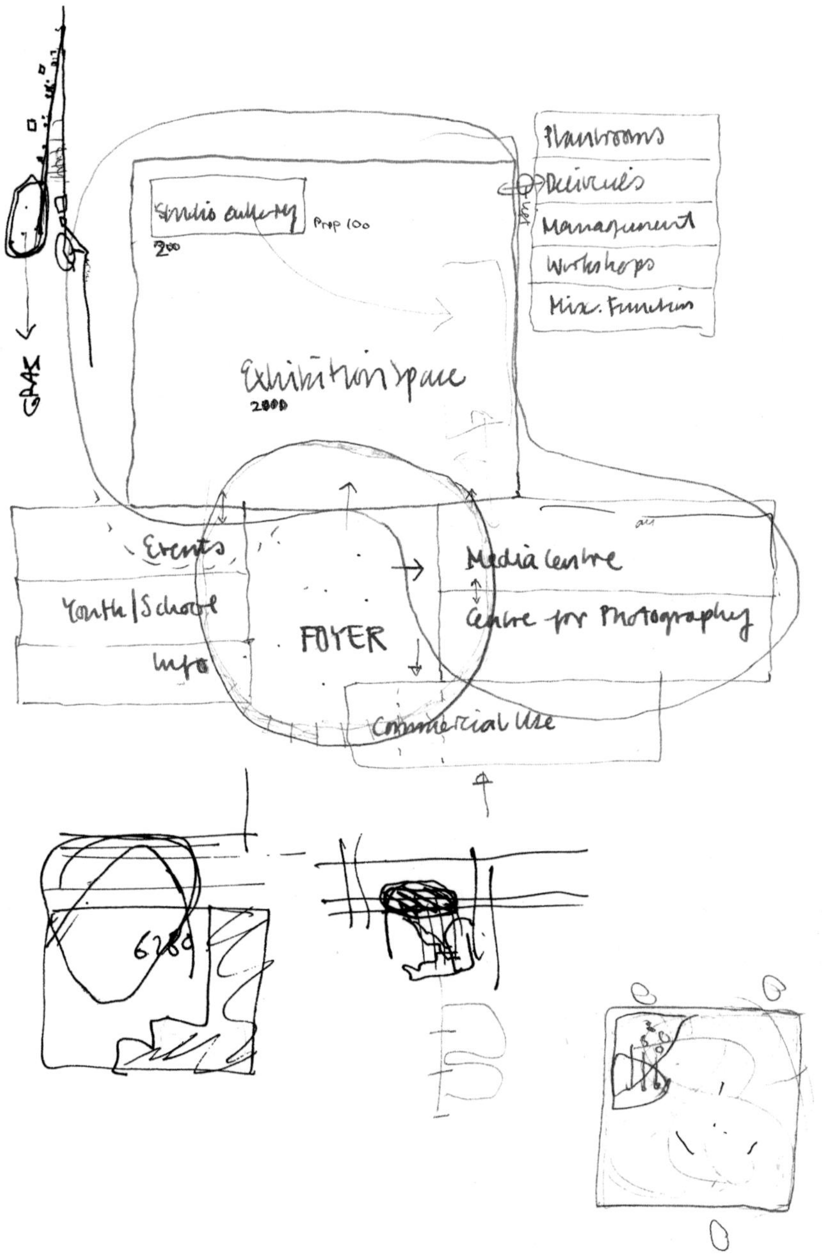

Distribution of functions. Sketches from the competition, Colin Fournier, Niels Jonkhans

An extraterrestrial 'friendly organism'. A conversation Niels Jonkhans, Barbara Steiner, Katia Huemer

26 September 2019, Vienna

2000

Haus
ground floor
design

↗ p. 83
↗ p. 85

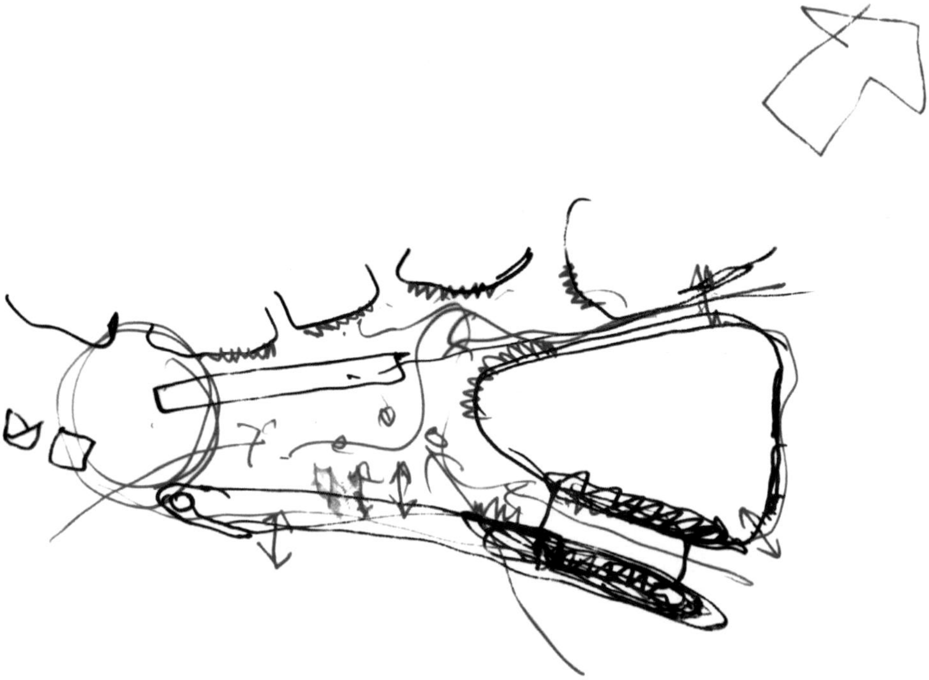

Floor plan variant of the open **ground floor**.
Sketch from the competition, Colin Fournier

An extraterrestrial 'friendly organism'

NJ **Niels Jonkhans**
BS **Barbara Steiner**
KH **Katia Huemer**

BS When you speak of the history of the Kunsthaus Graz, you do not use the usual narrative found in architecture, i.e. that of a linear development from concept to development. In your lectures on the Kunsthaus, you speak of the changes that took place during the implementation phase, and of the many ad-hoc decisions that had to be made along the way.

NJ For the technical implementation of a building with this extraordinary geometry, a huge amount of time is needed for research and development. You have to think not only in terms of solutions that deviate from the norm – they also have to be tried and tested, for example by using large-scale prototypes. And as there is rarely just one solution, many alternatives or variants of a solution are developed alongside one another, until one of them proves to be the most suitable. Because time played such an unusually significant role in the construction of the Kunsthaus, we often had to compromise as far as architectural or even functional demands were concerned. Because of this time pressure, the construction process had to begin in the development phase, which meant that we often had to change course at very short notice.

BS You once mentioned that a solution for the inner **Skin** of the Kunsthaus, i.e. the most visible part of the interior, was not found until the very last minute. That sounds very bold.

NJ Shortly before construction ended, we succeeded – against all odds – in finding a material that was viable in terms of time and budget, or what was left of our budget at the time. It was a cheap metal meshing used as a filter in sewage treatment plants, and we were able to refine its surface. You really can't get any cheaper than a sewage treatment filter! Without this solution, we would probably have had to leave the interior without cladding – an issue that came up in construction meetings again and again. It would have been a crazy idea to leave the ventilation system and the shell structure of a museum uncovered in the exhibition rooms! We did find a technical solution to extend this cladding to the ceiling lights, the so-called **Nozzles**, but unfortunately the client was not willing to provide the additional half a million euros this would have cost. So this part of the building actually remained without cladding. Along with its 'castrated' lighting, this remains a major subject of criticism to this day. There were also simple 'accidents' that shouldn't have happened, for example the exposed concrete was not of a high enough quality, especially for the **staircases**. But due to time constraints, we had no other choice but to say, 'We'll just have to live with it.'

→ Skin 087)
→ Nozzle 118)
→ staircase 181) 182)

Reconstruction phase, model for visually impaired people
and outward-facing light box, Lendkai

KH In response to the poor quality of the concrete, you changed the architecture of the whole **staircase**. How were the bannisters originally planned?

→ staircase 182) 184) 185)

NJ We wanted really light, glass handrails. The focus was supposed to be on the exposed fair faced concrete. In the end it became a continuous, unbroken white band. A construction of lacquered wood. Most visitors probably don't even notice it.

BS The Kunsthaus was an extremely ambitious undertaking right from the beginning. It broke new ground in many respects, and there were no role models to fall back on.

NJ Initially, the development of the project was highly abstract; for the most part, we worked verbally and using quick sketches. Before it finally became a building design, we had discussed the project in a very abstract way. We talked about how a new building would have to react to the surrounding context of this old city district with its myriad small details, how something new could be added without imitating the old and breaking up the scale of the environment. The term 'friendly alien', which was introduced later by Colin Fournier, actually describes it very well.

→ design 007) 034)

BS Of course, working in the abstract gives you a lot of leeway, but at some point you have to commit yourself.

NJ At some point, we had to give the building a concrete location and develop a specific form. This stage entailed more than a quick sketch; it was a process of moving forwards cautiously. Initially we tried to transform our ideas into an 'angular' building, there were even several versions of this. But we later moved away from this idea.

→ design 004)

BS One of the many qualities of the Kunsthaus is its ability to establish a connection with the historical urban landscape using contemporary means.

NJ As just mentioned, we didn't want to compete with the scale of the city and its many small details – all the ornaments, cornices, gutters, dormers and windows – we wanted to be in harmony with it, and yet create something completely new. However, as it turned out, that wasn't viable with the orthogonal or acute-angled volumes we were sketching. The site was simply too small for one large or several small right-angled volumes, which would have had to be built tightly to fit into the context. Ultimately, a flowing form that would effortlessly harmonise with the various angles, sizes and heights of the surroundings was the only logical solution. Before this 'completely new' element became tangible for us, many other variations had to be rejected, which is common practice in architectural design.

KH That means that you created a number of variations and then discarded them, made corrections ... how did you approach the subject of the **Skin**? It was one of the central design elements.

NJ Peter Cook referred to the shell of the building as a '**Skin**' quite early on – the Skin that 'covers everything'. In the competition, we didn't describe the structural design in detail – there was some talk of a composite structure made out of PET (polyethylene terephthalate) with an 'embedded supporting structure'. Some reference was made to a procedure developed by a company from the USA that was in the business of building sails. In the beginning, we discussed the appearance of the Skin, and the characteristics and effect it needed to have, in an abstract way. After a while, we actually had an organic role model. We built a latex model, jokingly referred to as

→ design 176)

↗ competition p. 269

2020

Haus
entrance
usage

'One of my duties is to unlock the Kunsthaus at 10 am and close it again in the evening. In the case of the revolving doors, which were made especially for the Kunsthaus, care must be taken to ensure that the mechanism is set in such a way that they don't turn too quickly or too slowly.'

Andreas Brandl, security

the 'ugly model' by Peter Cook, and tried to define the properties both formally and in a general technical sense. How could this **Skin** replace the 'classical window', which we were aiming to avoid, how could rain be drained (or absorbed) – these were some of the questions we discussed. The answers were mentioned in the competition, but not elaborated upon.

→ design 173)

BS The description of '**Skin**' already distinguishes it from other buildings.

NJ In architecture, the term 'envelope' is often used to describe both the wall and roof structures of a building. We continued using the name '**Skin**' to describe the building's envelope. Considering the organic form of the house, referring to it as skin was an obvious analogy. The concept of **Skin** was then immortalised in the official title of the competition entry, in which Peter Cook called the project 'Skin and Pin'. (editors' note: 'Pin' refers to the **Travelator**, the mechanical conveyor belt.)

→ Travelator 063) 081)

BS Didn't this description lead to misconceptions, too?

NJ Since a deliberate biological comparison was made, many of the people involved in the project, and also the public, imagined the **Skin** to be a soft, thin membrane that covered everything and could 'do anything'. Those who took the abstract idea of an organic skin covering the building too literally were extremely disappointed when the '**Skin**' became a 'shell', which was not thin all over.

KH So the central questions of construction were still open when you won the competition?

→ design 176)

NJ They weren't resolved in a technical sense, but they were as far as organisation was concerned. There were some plausible ideas on how to tackle the whole thing.
Some reference projects did exist, for example the BMW Pavilion by Bernhard Franken at the IAA in 1999. Volker Giencke's *greenhouses at the Botanical Garden* also served as a role model in some respects. Colin Fournier wrote a text based on an excellent piece of research on innovative materials in architecture. Adapted to our project, with additional explanations by an engineer from Ove Arup in London, this formed the basis of the technical description of the project in the competition.

→ reference 170)

↗ competition p. 269

KH Of course, it also aroused people's curiosity.

NJ Once we were given the commission, people were naturally curious about how it would be implemented. The first thing we needed was a team of architects and engineers. Once the team had been put together, after several attempts and avoidable delays, a decision was made to reassess the project's technical feasibility, taking the time lapse and the budget for individual parts of the project into account. It was decided that the constructive processes described in the competition were not viable, and an inevitable change of direction ensued. This did not come as a surprise – it had been foreseeable for some time. At this stage, I must say that none of the original ideas had been absolutely unrealistic – it was just the overly ambitious planning with regard to time and budget that made them unfeasible. So the plans were changed, but the general conditions remained exactly the same. In projects of such complexity, not only in a technical sense, but also in view of financial and time restraints, important decisions can only be made in a team with all the participants involved, right from the beginning if possible. Individuals are limited in their capacity to take action.

2018

Kunst
Haus
foyer

↗ p. 137
↗ p. 159

SUPERFLEX, C.R.E.A.M. Cash rules everything around me

KH Can you give us an example?

NJ The cooperation with Klaus Bollinger and his engineers, for example. It was only together as a team with Bollinger + Grohmann from Frankfurt that the structure of the entire building, particularly the building envelope, could be conclusively developed, taking all requirements into consideration. Naturally, this integrative development also resulted in changes being made to the shape of the building. In the first small model, it looked more like a used bar of soap or a boiled sweet – we referred to it as the 'lozenge' when we were sitting together in London. The first large model in the implementation phase was much more 'inflated'.

BS This process-oriented development is rather unusual and risky, particularly when such a large building task is at stake.

NJ In the competition, the initial focus had been on the right architectural answer to the question of how an enormous spatial programme could be embedded in a relatively small site that was difficult in a geometrical sense. A solution was found with regards to both function and urban planning. The process-oriented development was unusual, yes, but it was necessary, because at that time, back in 2000, there was nothing to fall back on. There was no database for details, which you now often have at your disposal as an architect. If you do something several times, you accumulate knowhow in the form of detailed solutions – not only in your head, but also stored as data. Our first task was to build the roads we wanted to drive along, so to speak. With the car fully loaded and the engine running. → design 040)

KH What was the first correction you made when it came to implementation?

NJ The first adaptation was actually the form of the building. We had decided not to regard the competition model as inviolable, not to subordinate all necessary technical decisions to the shape of it. The form was newly created, so to speak, in accordance with the construction and the changed spatial conditions, for example the room heights we needed. Of course, it was still based on the ideas and the building form of the competition design. The **Bubble** just became rounder, more 'inflated', because of the rise we required. When you draw a cross section through the transversal axis of the **Bubble**, the arc can't be too squat, otherwise the statics won't work. An unreasonably complex design would be required to prevent it from collapsing. So the arc had to be of a certain height to avoid the load of the shell becoming too high. This changed the building. The change in height wasn't enormous, we hadn't completely misjudged it in the beginning, but it made a visible difference. It had a positive outcome as far as the height of the rooms was concerned – they were higher in comparison to the 'flatter' bubble, which we intended. → design 076)
↗ plan p.346/347
Space01 → 137) 140)

BS The **Skin** was supposed to be transparent, and to continually change its appearance ... When was this idea abandoned?

NJ We had the shape and colour, and there was this idea that it would be transparent, but there was no technical solution for it, more of an image. It changed fairly early on, when the preliminary design was submitted and we had to provide a description of the technical feasibility, the plans and a cost proposal. We would have definitely needed materials and constructions that we didn't have at this point. So we made

Paju Book City. Current Architecture in Korea,
an exhibition by AedesBerlin

the first changes to the '**Skin**' because of time pressure. We went through several stages, for example we discussed a closed shell with a large number of small openings, similar to Peter Cook's drawing of the Lendkai view in the competition. It looked like a spaghetti strainer. Rather than going for this perforated shell, we then decided to transform the shell itself into a framework structure. This was architecturally correct and more efficient in terms of construction.

BS Could you have actually made the **Bubble** transparent?

NJ We could certainly have made the **Bubble** transparent, but it had to be possible to completely black it out when it was being used. And because our construction consisted of hundreds of triangles of various sizes, it was financially impossible to construct them in a way that allowed them to be opened and closed mechanically. We decided on a limited number of openings of this kind. The number was continually reduced, by the way, much to our dismay. The structural grid of the framework was based on various sizes, the most important being the maximum production width of plexiglass, the material we had decided to use for the outer shell. The stringency of the grid defined the order of all the components of the **Bubble**, and so the **Nozzles** also had to be placed in a more orderly manner, making them appear less playful. Little by little, the elegance of the original competition design faded, and the form became more bulbous and more accurately structured. The 'friendly alien' looked a little more austere than originally planned, and had a higher BMI.

→ Space01 047)

→ design 174)

KH There were massive additional changes in the ground floor area, too.

NJ The ground floor was conceived as a whole, like a public plaza – you were even supposed to be able to walk through the site diagonally from Kosakengasse to Lendkai. It was supposed to remain open, and as such be integrated into the urban space. We discussed the positioning of the café again and again. First it was supposed to be moved to the location of the original Café Meran, where Camera Austria is now, and then we considered the Needle. However, this was not possible for event-related reasons; it was also impossible to accommodate a kitchen there. Finally, the **café** was installed on the ground floor, towards Lendkai. The **Medienkunstlabor** and the **shop** were added. In the meantime, the **café** takes up the whole ground floor of the Iron House.

→ café 061)
→ Medienkunstlabor 014)
→ shop 015)

KH Was the **ground floor** meant to be glazed from the beginning?

NJ We had thin sheets of glass in mind. Actually just how it has turned out. However, a sun protection film had to be added to the glazing to minimise the heat input. This makes the glass lose its transparency in sunlight, and the **Bubble** almost looks as if it is sitting on a shiny silver base. This bothers us a lot, and it has led to justified criticism in the press. The transparent ground floor is often actually not transparent at all.

→ façade 190) 194) 195)

→ façade 043) 193)

BS It makes the Kunsthaus fall into two halves: a visionary top and a very pragmatic bottom. The transition zone seems abrupt.

NJ There wasn't supposed to be a door between the **ground floor** and the **exhibition**. A mechanical ramp, the **Travelator**, was to lead seamlessly from the public section to the upper area. This meant the air volume of the **ground floor** would merge with

→ usage 079)

2007

Kunst
Haus
foyer

↗ p. 87
↗ p. 89

that of the strictly regulated museum area, and as such it had to comply with certain regulations. At least in theory, because these decisions were made on paper before the building was finished. Due to time and budget constraints, it was not possible to commission a simulation of how the air would actually behave, and how the relatively small opening of the **Travelator** would affect it. So again, we had to take the safe option and give the glass the highest level of sun protection available at the time. I would have preferred a mechanical sun protection system – it wouldn't have been cheap, but you could have raised it at certain times of the day. The sun only shines on the **façade** in the mornings, as it lies to the east.

BS When you look at photographs of the Kunsthaus, they are mostly taken so that the trees on Lendkai optically block out the base, or the building is photographed from above so that you can't see the lower part at all. So the less successful elements are usually left out, at least in photos.

→ Kunsthaus 207)

KH If it had been possible to make the base transparent, wouldn't stickers have had to be put on the glass for safety reasons? That is partly already the case now. People even walk into the windows as they are. Other compromises would probably have had to be made.

→ façade 036)

NJ That's true.

BS Apropos image and media reception: the Kunsthaus is an iconic building, which stands in line with other iconic buildings constructed since the 1990s. Of course, in the context of the European Capital of Culture, the intention was to create a strong visual signal that radiated into the world. But it also follows another tradition – especially in the interior, it has a spatial concept that is very much oriented towards constantly changing usage. We know such concepts from the late 1960s and 1970s. So with regard to its architectural conception, the Kunsthaus is a hybrid. Let's talk about spatial concepts for the interior.

NJ The building is primarily based on an architectural concept of the museum interior. A specific underlying museum concept was defined by the organisers of the competition. In the crucial planning phase, however, no one was there to give specific curatorial directions or take responsibility for any deviations. The well-known museum planner Dieter Bogner laid the necessary foundations, and proved to be an important partner in the planning process. However, he had to ensure that the future director would still have the greatest possible freedom. And the person designated for this role was not in the position to specify his requirements and take responsibility for the risks involved, as he didn't join the planning process until it was almost over. The question of authorship must be addressed here. On the one hand it is defined in the competition project. On the other, additional experts who joined the process at a later stage rightly claim a part of the authorship. The important thing is that decisions have to be reached consensually, i.e. it must be possible to reconcile the various interests involved. It's a similar situation to the teamwork between architects, engineers and decision-makers I described earlier – to be successful, they all have to work hand in hand. Any additional interests introduced at a later stage, and changes that ensue, will always cause problems. The client always bears a large

2001

Kunst
Haus
Space01
foyer

Construction phase, (top) **Space01**
(bottom) access point from the **foyer** to the Iron House / **staircase**

share of the responsibility, and takes on a very specific role – in this case as a technically experienced participant responsible for the running of the institution rather than just as the representative of all interest groups, i.e. a mediator with no personal risks. You can never please everyone. So it is particularly true in the case of this project that the client was a member of the team.

BS That's an interesting point: the Kunsthaus began as a design with the classical authorship of two architects ...

NJ ... and that is how it should be – that is how the project originated. But the public and the architectural press often saw the famous visionary Sir Peter Cook as the single author, much to the chagrin of Colin Fournier. This was because he was so well known, especially as the co-founder of the Archigram group, which had produced projects that were immediately recognisable as prototypes. Peter Cook himself did not really share this view – he always referred to the team, he saw it as a multiple authorship so to speak. Anyway, after the project was born, it came to life. This applied not only to the development of the design and its realisation, but also to the time that followed. In a dynamic development, certain characteristics of the project turned out to be in need of improvement, either because of experiences during everyday use or due to external circumstances. In nature, evolution takes care of this. However, after it won the competition, many outsiders considered the design to be sacred. Less so the architects, Peter Cook in particular. As far as the 'DNA' of the building is concerned, I tend to agree with him on this. Development must be possible if the function of a building is to be improved – after all, the purpose of a building is to function.

BS The **ground floor** is a current example.

→ foyer 186)

NJ The original purpose was public accessibility. Over the years, the **ground floor** wasn't particularly popular. The **café** had very few customers, and the only part people really used was the **shop** in the corner of the building. During the course of the changes over the last few years, the functional areas have been moved around. You now have to walk cross the whole **foyer** to buy tickets, and the **ground floor** has become far more highly frequented. This is a change that brings us much closer to the original idea. All we have to do now is to get different glazing into the building and it would be perfect. Just a joke – or perhaps not.

→ shop 015) 059)

→ info 060) 065)

KH The requirements of a building change over time. Exhibitions are organised in a different way, there are other formats, other expectations – also on the part of the public. It's not different in the case of the Kunsthaus.

BS From this point of view, the platform idea is a convincing one, because it leaves a lot of options open. The building is defined by its use. However, and this is the downside, exhibiting can quickly become expensive, i.e. uneconomical, and also unecological. Many elements are built especially for exhibitions, and have to be disposed of afterwards. This is something we want to move away from in the future.

KH In the beginning, money was no object (laughs).

NJ That's true, but it only applied to exhibitions.

2004

Kunst
Haus
foyer

↗ p. 49

KH We had abundant resources at our disposal for exhibitions, even in terms of architecture. We can only dream of sums like that today. It gradually became less and less, and as a result there were fewer big architectural pitches. Practical decisions were required – and that is not only a bad thing, in my opinion. After all, these are public resources, and they have to be managed responsibly.

BS Interestingly enough, many visitors expect a white exhibition space. They soon come to the conclusion that our building is not suitable for exhibiting art. A view we don't share, of course.

NJ In my opinion, white orthogonal rooms don't work in the '**Spaces**' of the Kunsthaus.

BS Because they work against the logic of the architecture?

NJ Yes, it wouldn't make any sense from the point of view of design logic. But they could be capsules, like peas in a pod, I can imagine that. That is a solution that has been used in some of the past exhibitions.

→ Space01 112) 114) 119)

BS Katia, you have followed the development from the beginning. How were exhibitions at the Kunsthaus perceived in the first few years?

KH In the beginning, there was a huge sense of euphoria in the city. I think the discussions about the Kunsthaus began when people started questioning the exhibition programme in general, and then the spaces as a consequence. The criticism seemed to go hand in hand with what was being exhibited. As I see it, it was always about the programme as well as the spaces. People began to question whether it was possible to stage a programme in these spaces that fulfilled certain expectations of the Kunsthaus as an exhibition venue.

BS Apart from our specific case, there is a general point of criticism that could be directed at other 1990s buildings. It has been claimed that the architects were mainly concerned with the fulfilment of their own ambitions, pushing art into the side lines. In her book about the museums of the 1990s, Victoria Newhouse suggests that it was not only the architects who were to blame if the spaces seemed unsuitable for showing art – it was possibly also the fault of the people who organised exhibitions, who were not open to working with these spaces. In my opinion she is right.

NJ I really do believe that this building is a workshop that makes things happen. It offers a huge range of possibilities and variables. You can always surprise people with new spatial constellations. In the past, some have naturally worked better than others. Some of them deliberately competed with the space to create an interesting tension, while others played with the space, like Sol LeWitt's installation ***Wall*** or the group exhibition *Chikaku*. Another category of exhibitions simply said, 'We don't actually belong in here, but we don't care'. In this way, the building always became part of the exhibition. It is a huge task for exhibition organisers to find a way of dealing with it. And if someone really wants a white exhibition space, we have to remember that the Kunsthaus is part of the Universalmuseum Joanneum, a museum complex with plenty of other buildings and room types. That is the diversity of Graz's museum landscape.

→ Space01 108) 114)

BS We must also be clear and say that not everything can be done in the building, even though we are always coming up with new solutions – for showing paintings, for example.

2019

Kunst Haus foyer Cat-Tree

(Kunst
(Haus
(foyer
(Cat-Tree

Cat-Tree
→ 053)
→ 054)

The **Cat-Tree for the Arts**, was created by Oliver Klimpel specifically for this space. It has a modernistic architectural form which rises three metres into the air of the open Kunsthaus foyer. The softly shimmering and deep green epoxy object serves as a sculpture as well as a functional piece of furniture and display. As a presentation platform, it can be used in modules and creates options for exhibiting and presenting in the area near the entrance of the Kunsthaus – a vertical space that is home to artwork, objects and installations.

NJ You can hang paintings from the ceiling without using a wall as a background, you've already tried that out, or attach them to standing constructions that come out of the wall.

→ Space01 133) 134)

KH This solution could be seen in the Peter Kogler exhibition *Connected*. He made a direct reference to Frederick Kiesler's displays. Interestingly enough, realities:united, who are responsible for the concept of the **BIX façade**, had already suggested something similar.

→ Space02 091)

NJ I also find it interesting to lay pictures down – as we saw in Richard Kriesche's exhibition, he laid the pictures on platforms. And then there have been these really great installations that work directly with the space. I found Ernesto Neto outstanding. He created large net structures that seem to 'drip' from the ceiling. They were less impressive in the white rooms of other museums, where they had already been shown.

KH I found Katharina Grosse's exhibition impressive. The art installations, which were created especially for the space, were extremely powerful. Many artists make the space their own. They want to exhibit here precisely because of this building.

→ Space01 130)

NJ I've also heard from some people that they actually like the light-absorbing dark **Skin**, which could be seen as disturbing, because it makes the room almost disappear. In other museums, you would have to paint everything black.

BS I believe that what applies to artists is also valid on the curatorial side – you have to take a stance against the space. You have a strong partner in the architecture.

NJ And it can sometimes present a huge challenge to lenders who really want a white wall. For example for artworks where the hanging position, the colour of the background and the surrounding free space are defined down to the last centimetre.

BS Nowadays we say right from the beginning that we're not able to fulfil certain requirements. It's difficult when someone has never seen the space and wants to specify how something should look.

NJ That was part of the problem with *Videodreams*. There were some pieces that had to be installed in acoustically isolated boxes according to strict specifications. Luckily, not all the lenders were quite as strict, and it turned out to be a really good exhibition, in my view.

→ Space02 085)

KH It was a great exhibition! Really nicely done in an architectural sense. It was the first time we were confronted with the challenge of showing nothing but video works in an exhibition, without dividing the space into small cells. In my opinion it was a huge success, also because the presentation forms of the videos were so diverse – from peep-shows to cinema auditorium.

NJ You have to weigh everything up. How much can you expect of the artwork, how much can the room take? Of course, the work is more important. I believe that anyone who works in this building usually has a huge responsibility. If that is not what you want, you shouldn't attempt to do exhibitions at the Kunsthaus (laughs).

BS This spatial concept contrasts with another type of space that is very common, the space that suggests: 'I am not here'. But a white exhibition space, to return to this example, is very much there, it has a huge presence, a strong impact on our perception,

2017

(**Kunst**
(**Haus**
(foyer

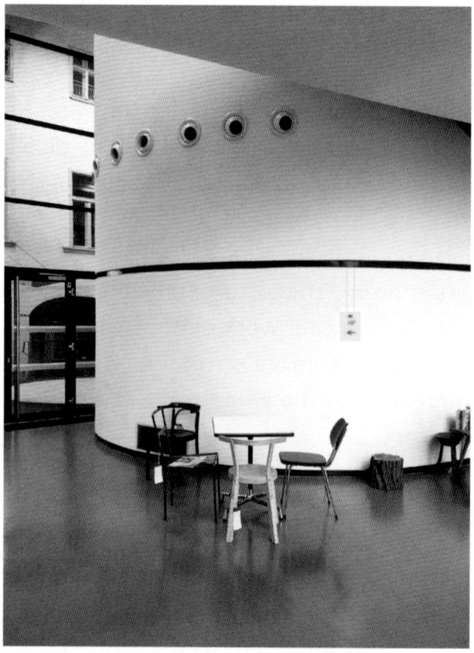

VIP's Union
→ 060)
→ 148)

Reconstruction phase; Haegue Yang. VIP's Union – Phase I

our encounter with the work of art. The Kunsthaus doesn't do that. It says with complete self-confidence: I am here! Pay attention to me, find out what's possible and what isn't.

NJ Yes. The architecture does the same thing with the city. On the one hand it adapts, on the other it is conspicuous and present. The building never retires into the background.

KH I think that classical exhibition spaces, i.e. white cubes, are less in demand at the moment. Expectations of such museums are changing, along with exhibition concepts, that is why people are trying to find solutions with fewer restrictions.

BS Niels, how much planning do you think is needed, and to what extent do you have to allow for changes? How much do you specify, how much is it even possible to specify? How much or how little has to be defined by the architecture to leave room for changes in the future – changes that are impossible to anticipate? In other words – how much do you actually have to plan? Where are the boundaries of planning? I'm asking you now as an architect.

NJ That's an interesting question. In this context I find the popular term 'multifunctional' rather meaningless. If you say that something is multifunctional, but you are not in a position to explain which parts of it work, and how, then it is an empty term. What I mean is that no space exists where everything can or must be possible. In planning, we speak of spectrums of usage – defined frameworks of possibilities that can be tried out in scenarios. We went through the same procedure for the exhibition spaces at the Kunsthaus. The only given was the shape of the spaces, which was determined by the outer shape of the building. We ran through various display possibilities with realities: united and Dieter Bogner, and also with the future director, Peter Pakesch, and his team. We spoke about additional structures that could be added as physical information carriers, large and small. We referred back to examples including Frederick Kiesler's displays, and even to larger, performative structures like his *Raumbühne* (Space Stage). realities:united suggested a 'subskin', an adaptable supporting structure that could be mounted over the inner shell of the building – something similar was even realised. We then defined additional points that could take particularly heavy loads, either standing or hanging. Appropriate design precautions were taken for this.

→ reference 091) 103)

BS Defining points and zones leaves a lot of room for manoeuvre, but it gives structure to the space and the possible usage of the space.

NJ The points and zones were intended to define possibilities, from the statics to the electrical planning, which specified where data or electricity was available. You could compare it to vocabulary that specifies the range within which things can be described.

KH It also works quite well, as you can add or remove certain zones – light surfaces for example – and there are points on which more load can be placed. It is a repertoire we can rely on.

NJ Exactly, you could summarise it in a kind of manual – an instruction manual that describes how the building works and, conversely, how it might not. For example, if

With **untitled (Project Space)**, sculptor Heimo Zobernig and artist/architect Eric Kläring collaborated on a sculpture whose interior held an exhibition space scaled down to roughly 10 square metres. This was placed in the **courtyard** of the Kunsthaus and, because it occupied as much of the available space as possible (under compliance with all security standards such as keeping exits accessible), had an asymmetrical shape. Over the period of a year, various young artists each presented their thoughts on contemporary sculpture.

Project space in the **inner courtyard** by Heimo Zobernig and Eric Kläring someone wanted to use a mixer to curl hair, it wouldn't be mentioned in the manual, so they would have to think twice. If they wanted to try it out anyway, they wouldn't be able to blame the mixer when it went wrong.

BS I really like this kind of concept. Because it describes potentiality. You can activate it or not, as you wish. You can get annoyed about the building or you can say 'hurrah'!

KH Or you can ignore the given circumstances. That's what artists have done again and again.

NJ Experiments are possible, but they are inherently located in a field of tension between success and failure, and should be evaluated beforehand. But there is always room for manoeuvre, which has to be explored. The Kunsthaus is an object that has to be used. You have to give it a lot more thought than you would give to a white space.

BS It was only when I started to work with the Kunsthaus in a curatorial capacity that I realised how unique it is in many ways. That is why, in spite of all its imperfections, or perhaps even because of them, it has been such a success.

NJ I think in some ways a building like this can be compared to an organism. An extraterrestrial 'friendly organism'. In a friendly way, it adapts to things that change in the course of time.

BS But it remains rebellious. A little bit of an alien. It's not totally amenable as a partner, and that's what I like about it. It still has a will of its own.

2019

Kunst
Haus
foyer
Cat-Tree

Cat-Tree
→ 049)

Barbara Edlinger. Fields

2020

Kunst
Haus
foyer
Cat-Tree

↗ p. 147

Community. Visible

1950

(**reference**

↗ p. 101
↗ p. 153

(top) Although today in harmony with the glass and steel architecture of neighbouring buildings, when it was first built MoMA's pioneering style stood out boldly from its historical surroundings. The Museum of Modern Art, New York City
(right) Some lines in the net that stretches between the museum and iconic architecture. Drawing: Pablo von Frankenberg

The attraction of the ambiguous. The museum as a source of friction for architecture

Pablo von Frankenberg

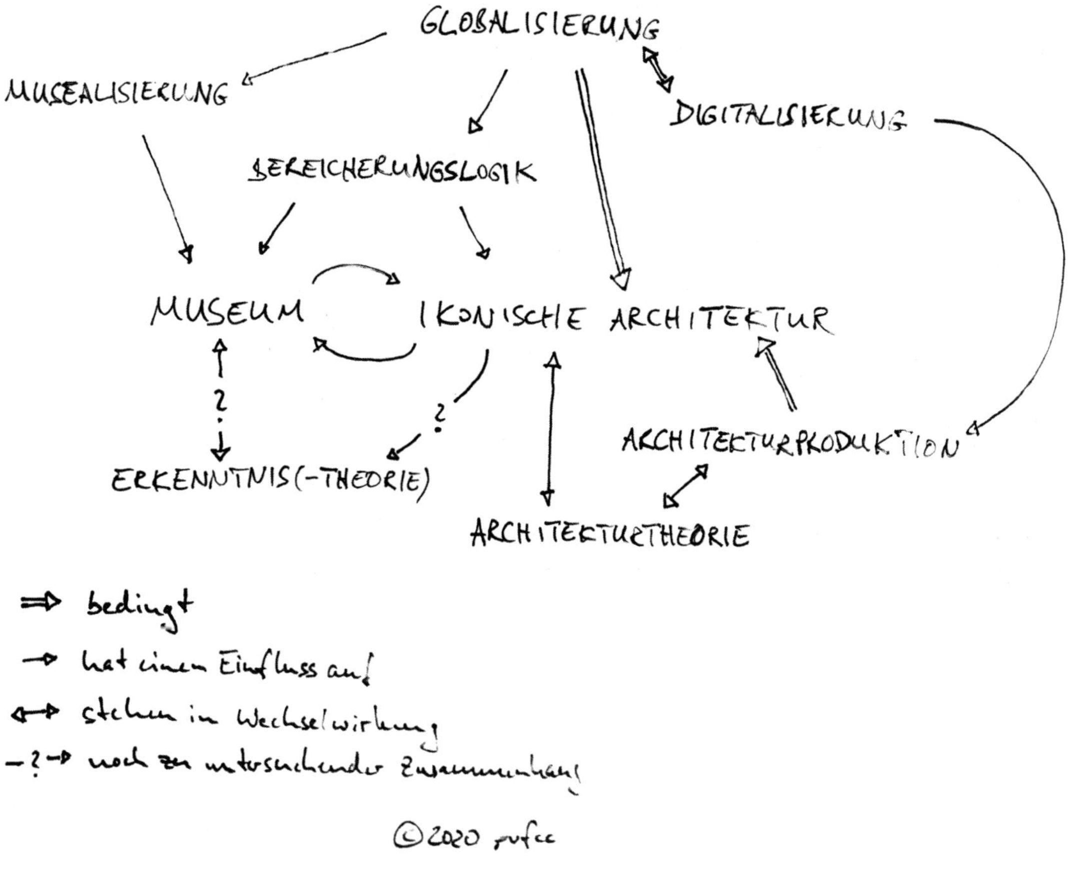

2019

Haus
foyer
façade

foyer
→ 049)
→ 186)

Reconstruction phase in the **foyer**, lightbox with section for the location of projects in the **Kunsthaus**

The attraction of the ambiguous
The museum as a source of friction for architecture

The museum architecture of the 19th century mainly conformed to existing architectural styles and directions, referring either to the origin of the collections – the palaces of rulers – or to classical antiquity as an educational ideal.[1] With the opening of the Museum of Modern Art in 1939, designed by Philip L. Goodwin and Edward Durell Stone, there was a fundamental change in the relationship between the museum and architecture. In 1939 MoMA, built in the *International Style*, formed a striking contrast with its historicist surroundings in a way that we can hardly imagine as it stands today, in an environment made up almost entirely of smooth glass surfaces. The museum building was a trendsetter. All other types of building in the neighbourhood seemed to follow on from its example. From now on, the building of a museum was linked with the possibility of achieving new and controversial architectural settings.

→ reference 055)

In the early 2000s, the architectural theorist and critic Charles Jencks proclaimed the age of iconic architecture.[2] The museum entered into an alliance with iconic architecture that had a radical impact on the institution of the museum, the exhibits, the surrounding urban space and architecture itself. Little research has been conducted on this subject up to now. This essay traces some of the lines of the network resulting from the alliance between the museum and iconic architecture. As we shall see, the connection between them is by no means accidental.

→ reference 056)

Iconic architecture and art

According to Jencks, one characteristic of iconic architecture is its proximity to contemporary art – 'The iconic building, when successful, puts architecture on a par with the best contemporary art to explore freely the possibilities of open-ended creativity.'[3] The strength of iconic architecture lies in a contradiction – on the one hand it can hardly be categorised in terms of its formal language, but nevertheless it serves as a logo. It generates a recognisable, clear, unmistakable image that appears to be without precedent. It thus generates a broad repertoire of possible interpretations. This is reflected not least in the richness of the metaphors used by architectural critics to describe it.[4]

However, this diversity of interpretation by no means leads to indeterminacy. In spite of diffuse attributions of meaning, every iconic building is so distinctive that it serves as a landmark and an emotional point of reference.[5] The visibility of architecture, especially public buildings, provokes a reaction. While art itself hangs in the clearly separated area of the *white cube* or, far more frequently, slumbers in the depots of large museums out of the public's sight, the museum as a building stands in the overwhelming diversity of the urban space. It is not only seen by museum visitors and curators. It is possible to avoid the contents of a museum, whether they be old masters or abstract paintings, dinosaurs or steam engines, coins or minerals. Avoiding museum buildings is more difficult – with the exception of highly segregated cities.

2020

Haus
foyer
usage

'The first tactile guidance system was developed in 1965 by Japanese inventor Seiichi Miyake to make life easier for a visually impaired friend. The tactile paving provides haptic cues, offering safety and navigation and, like all measures to improve accessibility, makes the Kunsthaus Graz an exhibition centre for all!'

Eva Ofner, visitor management, accessibility contact

The public domain of a work of art is governed by its canonisation, in which many parties are involved, including art historians, critics, the art market, collectors and museums. But even a canonised work of art is not necessarily accessible to the public, for example if it disappears into a private collection, is not included in the current exhibition, or if its presentation in the museum is associated with financial and/or social thresholds.[6] From the beginning, the public aspect of museum architecture is defined in a different way to the contents that are exhibited inside it.
However, the genesis of iconic museum architecture differs significantly from that of a work of art. Even though there are artists who work together in a team in a similar way to architects, creating their works of art with the help of employees, the development and design of architecture is generally less free than art can be. In contrast to artists, who can also of course be subject to existential economic pressure, and sometimes even political influence, architects are dependent on a whole range of external factors that are often predetermined (e.g. building regulations), as well as on clients, experts and stakeholders (political decision-makers, structural engineers, urban planning offices, fire prevention experts, private developers, property market developments, etc.) Architecture, especially the architecture of public buildings, gains its importance not only through its reception, but above all through its use, i.e. through social interaction. Social interaction can certainly arise from a work of art, but it is a fundamental component of architecture. By using a piece of architecture, walking through it, meeting others in it, getting a feeling from it, finding refuge in it, seeing it in the context of a city or a landscape, one attaches importance to it.[7] Its importance is never limited to its worth as a showpiece – it is also defined by its utility value.
When we think about the connection between iconicity and museum architecture, then, we should not restrict ourselves to the imposing character of its design. It is more helpful to consider why a museum building is so important for architecture itself, and to acknowledge the fact that political and economic interests are associated with it. We can use two guiding questions to trace the lines of the network in which the iconic museum architecture is located: What socio-economic developments are negotiated through iconic museum architecture? And what significance does this kind of architecture have for the possibilities of the museum as an institution that stores, generates and imparts knowledge?

The attraction of the ambiguous

Since the turn of the 21st century, there has been a significant increase in the number of new museum buildings worldwide,[8] including more and more iconic buildings. These building projects are generally equipped with a large budget and have a high prestige factor, which makes them attractive for international architecture firms. The attraction rises with the unclear formulation of the building task, which gives architects a great deal of freedom. With a few exceptions,[9] this freedom is not intentional, but results from a lack of knowledge and experience on the part of everyone involved. Because a museum is not an everyday building, little is known about all the things that

2020
(**Kunst**
(**Haus**
(foyer
(shop
(info

shop
→ 070)
info
→ 065)
↗ p. 49
↗ p. 83
↗ p. 87

Shop, design by Oliver Klimpel

need to be considered in terms of technology, air conditioning, visitor flows, the handling of exhibits, safety, didactics and other requirements, which are, on top of that, often contradictory. During the course of their career, museum directors seldom have the opportunity to create a new building or extension, let alone to acquire the practical knowledge that comes from being involved in two or more large building projects. In general, people who work in museums are specialists in dealing with space, but not in creating it from scratch. This means that the wishes they formulate for a new building are often ambiguous. 'Flexibility' is certainly one of the most frequent words found in the tender specifications for museum buildings published over the last 20 years, with no further explanation of why this flexibility is required and how it will be used. Public building authorities are also rarely confronted with museum building projects. If they cannot rely on the employees of the museum or museum advisors with specialist knowledge, they generally focus on the outer appearance of the architecture. In view of the investment they are making, they are generally looking for a charismatic landmark. The fact that the building should also contribute to the efficient running of a museum often seems to be a secondary consideration. If there is no clear information on the museum programme, or in some cases even on the collection that is to be exhibited,[10] the (external) design is often the criterion that dominates all discussions. Private patrons also act with similar intentions. Functionality and charisma do not have to be mutually exclusive, but planning the interior in line with the complex task of operating a museum quickly runs into difficulties if there are no clear specifications. This is especially true if the priorities of the public or private authorities funding the project are at odds with those of the architects.
The planning architects often also lack the specialist knowledge required for this particular building task. There are comparatively few architectural firms worldwide with more than two museums in their portfolio. And even that is not necessarily enough to give them sufficient knowledge on the requirements of an art museum compared with a museum of cultural history, for example, or a technical museum compared with a natural history museum. As a result, the clients outline the construction task of the museum fairly openly in their tenders, while architectural teams, confronted with relatively few specifications, see an opportunity for self-realisation. This means that very different aesthetic, cultural, political and economic interests can be invested in a museum building.[11] In the following, an analysis will be made of the interaction between the aesthetics of museum architecture, influenced by digitalised design and presentation methods, and the economic interests attached to it.

Aesthetics and technology

The commercial and large-scale use of Internet and digital photography began at the beginning of the 1990s, although both technologies had been developing for decades. The global rise in the construction of museums coincides with the digital production and global, individual dissemination of images. Of course, no causality can be deduced from this coincidence. However, it certainly had a favourable impact on the high concentration of iconic architecture designs for museums: visiting museums had become

2017

Kunst
Haus
foyer
info

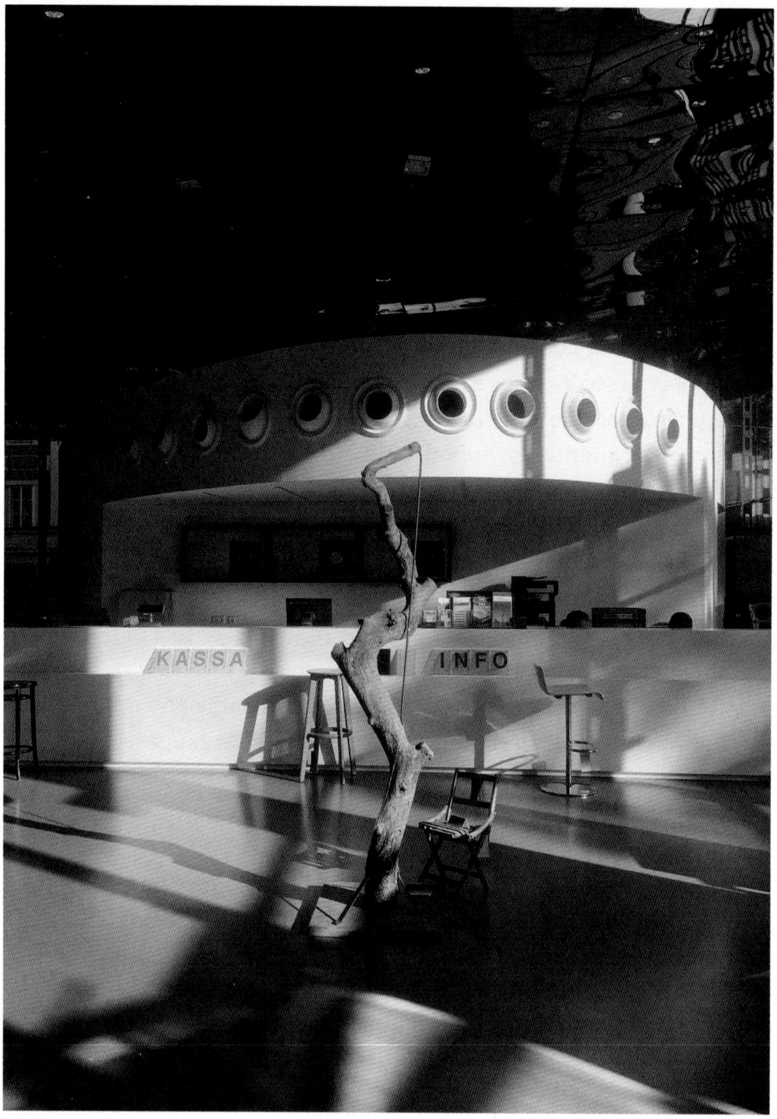

foyer
→ 050)
→ 051)
usage
→ 065)

Temporary labelling of information counter;
foreground: Haegue Yang. VIP's Union – Phase I

part of a leisure economy, and this was reflected in the creation and distribution of highly distinctive images on social networks.[12] This, on the other hand, increased the economic advantages of financing architecture that was of as spectacular a nature as possible. Through their unique design vocabulary, iconic museum buildings are highly marketable – they attract tourists, and the sharing of photos on social networks makes a significant contribution to the marketing process.

At the latest since the emergence of the so-called 'Bilbao effect', iconic museum architecture has generally been considered particularly profitable. The iconic forms of newer museum architecture became an important economic factor for cities around the world even before the Guggenheim Bilbao was built, but this project also influenced the status of (museum) architecture in other ways. In order to calculate the design vocabulary of this museum, which was revolutionary at the time, Frank Gehry's architectural office used *Catia*, CAD software from the field of aircraft construction originally designed to simulate the entire production process of (aircraft) parts. In co-operation with Frank Gehry's office, the software manufacturer developed the program to enable the parametric modelling of buildings.[13]

This step enabled the production of digital images through so-called render programs in addition to digital photography and the processing of images using digital cameras and Photoshop. The three-dimensional simulation of buildings made it possible to visualise architecture beyond ground plans, sections and views from any perspective at the push of a button, so to speak. Since then, a huge amount of architectural photography has been enhanced through enormous quantities of digitally generated renderings that make local mayors and private patrons dream of creating a monument to themselves.

Aesthetics and economy

The Guggenheim Bilbao focuses on a specific function of museum architecture – it acts as an aesthetic, artistic, cultural, urban planning 'image booster' for the city. It has made other cities fantasise about achieving a social and economic upturn through a new museum building, even though they are unable to afford an additional extensive infrastructural programme like Bilbao, or are not involved in a larger marketing concept like the Kunsthaus Graz during the Capital of Culture programme in 2003. This does not only apply to art museums and publicly funded institutions. In the last 20 years, private donors or firms have funded a whole series of new museums that are often named after them. These buildings obey the principles of iconic architecture – in Europe as well as in the USA, Asia and the Arab world.

→ reference 062)

Here, museum architecture belongs to the structures of 'enrichment' analysed by Luc Boltanski and Arnaud Esquerre. They examine new economic instruments that feed into the processes of capitalist accumulation, focussing on the interaction between areas such as 'the fine arts, culture, the antiques trade, the foundation of trusts and the creation of museums, the luxury industry, patrimonialisation and tourism'.[14] Rather than adding value through the production of new goods, the logics of enrichment

2003

(**Kunst**
(**Haus**
(foyer
(café

info
→ 059)
→ 063)
↗ p. 49
↗ p. 83
↗ p. 137

Former café Les Viperes

suggest that profits are generated through 'the exploitation of the past'. This works by relating things that already exist to the past, thus making them more valuable.[15]

For Boltanski/Esquerre, museum architecture is an important example in their argumentation. They use Frank Gehry's museum building in the *Parc des Ateliers* in Arles, France, as an example. The complex is built entirely from the proceeds of a fortune inherited from a pharmaceutical company. The project speculates explicitly on the Bilbao effect[16] – i.e. it aims to upgrade not only the newly founded museum, but the entire region. This project also implicitly underlines the authority of the financial donor as a patron of the arts and culture, thus strengthening her influence in cultural policy and the artistic field. The fact that this does not pay directly into the account of the pharmaceutical company from which the money ultimately came is irrelevant, since the cultural capital, generated in the form of reputation, can be converted into economic capital and/or political influence by the heiress.

While the enhancement of cities or regions through new museum buildings is usually accepted without question, little research has been done on how this constellation works and, above all, on the distribution of the added value it generates and the objectives of its profiteers. However, the fact that the museum in Arles is, like other museums, privately financed, and that these museums are sometimes associated with the names of brands or individuals and used by companies for representative purposes, corresponds directly to the enrichment principle described by Boltanski and Esquerre.

These mechanisms are by no means new. They were already exemplified in the first iconic museum building, the Guggenheim Museum New York, built in 1959. Frank Lloyd Wright had not planned the economic exploitation of his architecture, but he was aware of it even before construction was finished. In 1954, Wright wrote to his nephew expressing the concern that the museum's new director, James Johnson Sweeney, the successor of Hilla von Rebay, the initiator of the project who had fallen from grace after Solomon Guggenheim's death, would make a 'museum business' out of the building.[17]

Museum architecture gives art and culture, which is visually effusive and constantly changing, a distinct, permanent image that is easy to market. What role the emergence of iconic museum buildings plays in the development of the global art market, however, is more difficult to ascertain. The fact that the price of a work of art rises once it has been exhibited in an important museum, or the origin of an antique is considered more secure and its value rises, cannot necessarily be attributed to the architecture of the museum. Nevertheless, the significance of a museum can increase through new architecture, and this can have an indirect impact on the art market.

Even if architecture plays its part in this logic of 'enrichment', it is not the only effect it has. As a public place, a museum building can have far more diffuse connotations.[18]

Nonetheless, it is no coincidence that contexts of economic exploitation are particularly related to the architecture of a museum. Since the Guggenheim Museum in New York, museum buildings have been creating landmarks in a reliable way. They have become easily distinguishable icons that symbolise an institution, a city, or a company, and can be marketed accordingly.[19] This formula seems to work on an international scale, and is one of the empirically proven reasons for the boom in museum building, even in countries with no tradition of museums.[20]

→ reference 062)

For the work Cuestión de Pasta by the Italian artist Fausto Grossi (based on an idea by M. Victoria Lasheras Penã), lawyers from the Guggenheim Foundation tried to obtain an injunction for alleged copyright infringement against the artistic pasta production. 'Pasta' can also mean 'money' in Spanish.

Design in transit

The internationalisation of museum architecture not only defines itself through the global dissemination of its images and its attractiveness, even in countries with no museum tradition, but also through a certain group of architects who are responsible for many of the museum buildings that have received worldwide attention. These architects (mostly male) sleep in hotel beds far more often than in their own. They travel back and forth between various clients, offices, construction sites and biennials, hardly ever taking more than a couple of days' holiday a year. They often design their drafts 'on the move', in Business Class on a transatlantic flight, in video conferences between different time zones, between the desks of an open-plan office or over lunch, because every project manager has to seize the opportunity if the 'master' (extremely rare: the woman master) is in the office for half a day. This way of working only succeeds through the maximum exploitation of a work force that is willing to compensate for inadequate organisation structures by working through the night and taking certain substances to enable them to do so. Precarious employment contracts, hordes of trainees and a team organised in a strict hierarchy, i.e. focussed on a single individual, are the ingredients of international architecture production.

If the so-called star architects indeed spend most of their time in transitory places – hotels, airport lobbies, stations, conference rooms – it is of course not far off the mark to say that the museum buildings of the last twenty years, which were mainly designed by these architects, resemble Baudrillard's 'space debris'[21] or Jinping's 'weird architecture'.[22] It is tempting to link the international effectiveness of museum buildings with the international context in which their creators move. But this view ignores the difference between architecture and art, as outlined above, which not only highlights the widely regulated process of the development of museum buildings in particular, often accompanied by public discourse, but above all shows the different social demands behind the usage of architecture and art. The significance of iconic museum buildings can therefore be found not (only) in the way their designers live and work, but in social, bureaucratic, economic and technical interdependencies, which are far more clearly defined for architecture than they are for art.

There are certain basic starting conditions for the creation of iconic museum architecture that are similar across the world. This, however, most decidedly does not lead to a similarity or interchangeability between designs; it demonstrates instead that globalised architectural production is shaped by digitalisation and mobility. Here, globalisation in no way means enforced conformity in the sense of a 'universalised world culture'.[23] Within this, capitalist principles such as growth or even 'enrichment' would not work, because it would level out precisely those differences that are the basis of capitalist exploitation. Local diversity and differences are significant 'innovators' and sources of profit for the globalised market.

Even the Guggenheim museums, whose business model has often been criticised, are proof of the fact that museum architecture lives from diversity, in spite of globalised production conditions. The museum franchise system, developed by the former

2017

Kunst
Haus
foyer
Travelator

↗ p. 43

Reconstruction phase of **foyer** and reception desk

Guggenheim director Thomas Krens, relies on the various different contexts of the new buildings. The symbolic profit for the brand of the museum and the financial growth in the founding capital does not come from enforced conformity, but from the exploitation of differences. The important thing is that each place has a new architectural design (Bilbao, Abu Dhabi) or simply the promise of one (competitions for Salzburg, Guadalajara, Rio de Janeiro, Helsinki, etc.) In this way, the franchise creates a locally anchored image for expansion, which at the same time represents the reliability and high artistic standards of the brand and communicates its connectivity in just about any context.[24] The murmur that goes through the world of art and architecture whenever any kind of possible expansion is announced pays off for the Guggenheim brand. If it also pays off for the cities and regions in which the building is situated, this is usually because the new museum is only part of a far larger intervention in the infrastructure. This was certainly the case in Bilbao and in Abu Dhabi. In both cities it could even be assumed that not only the iconic museum architecture, but also the publicly funded expansion of roads, bridges, neighbourhoods, public transportation, and so on, contributed to the brand and balance sheet of a privately run cultural institution, as did the licence fees charged by the Guggenheim Foundation and the public contribution to the operating budget.

Digitalisation and architectural theory

Just as iconic museum architecture cannot be reduced to the conditions of its origin in a globalised and digitalised production setting, neither can it be broken down to contexts of economic exploitation, even though both are important features of its appearance at the end of the 20th century. A far more fundamental prerequisite for the success of iconic architecture is the relationship between the digitalisation of architectural production and architectural theory.

In 2001, the editors of the German architecture magazine Arch+ stated that 'theoretical architectural debate has been exhausted (for several years).'[25] More than ten years later, Rem Koolhaas followed suit and took the theory several steps further: '[...] if you plot architectural publications, you will see a timeline that suggests Europeans and Americans were incredibly active in terms of producing architectural manifestos and architectural thinking, but that our thinking stopped in the 1970s.'[26] Looking back 40 years later, Koolhaas places the book *Learning from Las Vegas* by Robert Venturi, Denise Scott Brown and Steven Izenour from 1972 at the end of the productive era of Western architectural theory.

One of the greatest changes in modern architectural history coincides with this lack of theory: the mechanisation and digitalisation of architectural production, which provides architecture with completely new tools and means of expression. The discrepancy between the decline in theoretical perspectives concerning these technical possibilities and their proliferation is also reflected in the fact that, in attempts to produce theoretical versions of CAD, BIM and parametric modelling, the tools themselves are idealised as theory, i.e. the use of the tool is mistaken for reflection on it.[27]

2019

(**Kunst**
(**Haus**
(foyer
(Travelator

foyer
→186)
→187)

Travelator with functional artwork **Soft Intervention** by Hannes Priesch and Herta Kramer-Priesch

There is a specific reason why digitally generated images and parametric design possibilities lead to confusion between theory and tools, or why they may be mistaken for one another. They bring in a new time dimension for architectural production – the immediate future. While drawings and plans always require mediation and interpretation, and it always takes a certain amount of time to create or copy them, renderings and 3D models not only seem 'evident', but once the 3D data has been created, the respective models can be adapted in next to no time. The changes are shown immediately. Renderings and 3D models do not represent architecture, but simulate it. Simulation blurs the boundaries between drawing and built architecture, planning and implementation, thinking and doing.[28]

Before the possibility of parametric 3D modelling existed, changing a design involved completing new drawings, which took a relatively long time. Now the design can be adapted immediately by changing the parameters (if the model is already in place, in just a few clicks). It is also immediately visualised in the same step. This aspect of immediacy lures us into trusting the programs and the visualisations they create more than our own thoughts on the building task at hand. As fixed systems, the programs seem to include their theoretical explanation right away. The simulation of the existing urban space that surrounds an object, for example, seems to render a site visit obsolete, or even the greater mental effort involved in imagining the design in the context of real urban space. In this way, thinking about architecture can quickly become a system that only allows outside influences that can be digitalised.

The new programs give rise to new formal languages in architecture, the limits of which seem to be determined by progress made in programming[29] rather than the manifestos and theories that precede the programming. This neither says that CAD or algorithm-based designs are not creative, nor that thinking was only possible in the predigital era. However, it is reasonable to assume that immediacy and obviousness, which are new in the architectural design process, can more easily escape theoretical and critical analysis.

The lack of theory in contemporary architecture is not only expressed in the confusion between theory and object. One of the main contributing factors is that architectural theory, methodology and philosophy have been pushed into a marginal position in architectural study programmes, both at universities and at universities of applied science, at the latest since the so-called European Bologna Process that aimed at standardising the higher-education system. Priority is given to the learning of technical skills (particularly CAD, BIM, project management), which would actually be more suitable study content for an apprenticeship than for a university course.[30]

This starting point – digitalisation in the absence of theorisation – appears to be fruitful for the ever newer forms of iconic architecture. As with any innovation, all its (technical) possibilities are exhausted before it is taken down from the pedestal of novelty to find its place in everyday life. The technical possibilities of visualisation and parametric modelling and the digitalisation of the interface between planning and implementation have opened up an entirely new range of possible forms in architecture. Iconic forms have suddenly become far easier to conceptualise, portray and realise

info
→ 060)
café
→ 061)

'What I like about the reception desk is that it serves – much as it did in its previous role as the café counter – to create relationships. At a bar you hand over the drinks, whereas at the information desk, it's information; the familiar character of the "sympathetic bartender" ideally has the same communication skills as the person at the museum information desk.'

Sabine Messner, foyer management

than was the case in Frank Lloyd Wright's day – which still did not stop him from creating an iconic museum building that continues to explore the possibilities and impossibilities of exhibiting art today. Digitalisation is not a *conditio sine qua non* of iconic architecture, but it does have a significant effect. This can be seen in the example of the Kunsthaus Graz – Peter Cook first designed it using pen and paper and classical models, but then had it digitally modelled using standard programs and completely digitally transferred into the detailed design stage.[31] The Guggenheim Museum in New York and the Kunsthaus in Graz both show that iconicity is by no means dependent on the digitalisation of architecture, but that digital design possibilities facilitate iconic design language. The time required for the complete planning and construction process of the Kunsthaus was around three and a half years, while the Guggenheim Museum took 16 years.[32]

→ design 173) 174)

Revival of the museum

The loss of theory in architecture, along with the emergence of its new technical possibilities, coincided with a revival of the museum that had been imminent for some time. In Germany, for example, history museums had been losing importance, but with the onset of deindustrialisation in the 1970s and 1980s, history exhibitions now attracted unprecedented numbers of visitors. The major attractions at that time were the national exhibitions on the Staufer dynasty in Stuttgart and on the Prussians in Berlin.[33] The renaissance of the museum was by no means limited to the German-speaking world. In the Anglo-Saxon world it was reflected not only in the increasing number of new museums being founded,[34] but also in a shift towards broader mediation methods aimed at introducing people with no in-depth education in the humanities to history museums.[35]

From a business perspective, this change in the 'institutions in the 'business' of making aspects of heritage available' was seen as an important factor in the development of 'heritage marketing'.[36] In the 1980s, mass tourism was accompanied by the emergence of the leisure economy.

Deindustrialisation not only resulted in mass unemployment in some areas, but also led to the 'elevator effect' as far as income was concerned.[37] Mass tourism and the leisure sector reinforced the importance of the marketing of history, which is the starting point of the enrichment analysis carried out by Boltanski/Esquerre. Museums and their buildings became important again, albeit without one or the other being clearly defined in terms of its nature and significance, its functions and its requirements, as outlined above.

Still, the museum is an instance of cultural self-assurance and reflection. The museum has a sovereignty of interpretation in fields of knowledge, aesthetics and history, which in the best case makes itself available in a reflective sense. In this way, the museum provides a source of friction – also for architecture. Once described as the 'playground'[38] of architects, it is in reality unknown territory, for which neither architects nor the people who work in it have a map. In many ways, designing a museum

'For my work, which focuses on the people who visit the building, this open and bright atmosphere is a crucial factor that positively shapes their first impressions and our communication. Glass walls surround the **ground floor** both towards Lendkai and towards **Space04** and the **inner courtyard**, allowing a view of Esther Stocker's **mural, No. 19**.'

→ 067)
→ 068)

Thomas Kirchmair, foyer management

is like finding your way without a compass. The fact that this exploratory procedure frequently results in iconic museum buildings is not only due to contexts of economic exploitation or digitalised and globalised design processes, but also to the museum itself – it provides a platform for social, cultural, aesthetic and scientific discussion, a platform that seems to have been lost to architecture as a discipline.

Museum architecture as an experiment

The museum is a place of discourse that generally works in close cooperation with certain scientific disciplines. Art museums – whether they are contemporary, modern or dedicated to the Old Masters – usually recruit their personnel from the field of art history. The catalogues of their exhibitions thus obey scientific standards, even in cases where the target audience is not only made up of specialists. Technology museums are often run by engineers and technology historians. Museums of natural history and their specimens still serve as scientific research facilities. Even history museums not only organise exhibitions, but also carry out research according to the standards of their (specialised) discipline. Even if the museum cannot be defined solely by its rational/scientific frame of reference, it is a characteristic that museums all over the world have in common. Museums are places that offer the possibility of addressing various scientific views of the world – or at least this is the aspiration on which they are based. Since the Enlightenment, scientific research has been the view that defines the world. The museum progressed from the Chamber of Art and Curiosities in the Renaissance period to become an independent scientific institution during the course of the Enlightenment. Once this transformation was complete, it became a building task of its own.
Far more significant than this development – which was also reflected in museum architecture – was the fact that, with the increasing scientification of the world and differentiation between academic disciplines in the 18th and 19th centuries, the importance of philosophical epistemology was called into question. The German philosopher Jürgen Habermas states that epistemology dissolved with the specialisation of the sciences into the theory of science and the methodology of individual disciplines.[39] From now on, epistemology was the teaching of how sociology or astrophysics, palaeontology or entomology, experiments, researches and generates new knowledge. But Habermas is critical of the advance of scientism, in which knowledge of the world can only be gained through the findings of special scientific disciplines, and in which Kant's question 'What can I know?' is only seen as a question for individual disciplines. Scientism replaced philosophical epistemology (which for a long time had hardly been separable from theological epistemology), which until then had been a guiding force in the exploration of the conditions of human perception and knowledge. What is recognisable, what is not, and in what way, was now limited to the self-reflection of each individual specialist field and its specific methodology. According to Habermas, the unique characteristic of philosophy – the fact that it addresses the conditions of knowledge in a way that encompasses all areas of human life – seemed to be disappearing.[40]

↗p. 49

Space04 with a view of Esther Stocker's mural Nr. 19

This development was quite problematic for architecture, as its methodology was not particularly well developed.[41] This is partly due to the modern self-conception of the subject, which does not necessarily see itself as a researching science.[42] Architecture was once understood as a universal discipline that sought methodological inspiration from its neighbouring disciplines (essentially philosophy, but also sociology, engineering, physics, etc.), but the more it concentrates on its technical skills and practical competence, the more its capacity for theoretical and methodological self-reflection declines.

Highly complex in terms of content and function, the museum, as a poorly defined construction task, shakes up the realm of architecture with its recent lack of theory and methodology and digital upgrading. At the same time, architecture, with its practice-oriented design approach, its ability to reduce complexity through visualisation and its radically subject-alienated external perspective, shakes up the spatial and institutional reflective competence of the museum, which is often non-existent or far too entrenched. Due to this starting position, recent museum architecture must be seen on many levels as an experiment that can give rise to heated controversy both before and during the planning period, as well as after completion.

The Kunsthaus Graz, this 'calculated uncertainty',[43] is a good example of this. As the embodiment of a historical architectural utopia (Archigram), it not only explored the relationship between theory/utopia and practice in a new way; the approach to the UNESCO World Cultural Heritage site in the old town of Graz also had experimental characteristics. For the interior, the description 'anti-white cube' is rather an understatement. The exhibition space certainly poses a challenge to the curators' experimental creativity.

The Guggenheim museums in New York, Bilbao and Abu Dhabi are also examples of the source of friction that architecture can become for a museum, and conversely, the museum can become for architecture. The ramp at the New York museum creates new perspectives on the connection between art and space. The museum in Bilbao is the first serious attempt to create a new business model in the cultural field; additionally it provides spaces with dimensions that can accommodate large sculptures, which could otherwise only be exhibited outdoors. The branch in Abu Dhabi, on the other hand, broadens the experimental expansion approach to a region that has no museum tradition.

The experimental aspect of iconic museum architecture is not only limited to art museums, as the example of the Mercedes-Benz Museum in Stuttgart reveals. Its underlying double-helix structure not only broke new ground in terms of construction and statics, but the way in which it interweaves museum storytelling and architecture was unprecedented. The Musée du Quai Branly in Paris is another example that created something new through its special combination of architecture and the approach to exhibits, which influenced museum discourse on a permanent basis. The Ruhr Museum of Cultural History in Essen, on the other hand, rebalanced the relationship between monument protection, the presentation of exhibits and structural change through the conversion of a disused colliery building, featuring Rem Koolhaas' iconic luminous

In the exhibition **Bonheur automatique**, Hanspeter Hofmann explored the question of how quasi-mechanical intersections between humans and their surroundings can be used creatively. To this end, Hofmann operated a week-long print shop in **Space04** – which is usually reserved for events. Every day, new information and new images were integrated into the work process and superimposed on a pre-produced graphic using a printing press on location.

Hofmann applied the resulting images to the walls of the room, so creating a constantly evolving process of artistic entrenchment and intergrowth with daily realities, and at the same time addressing fundamental questions about the generic distribution of artistic work categories between printmaking, painting, performance or installation.

Hanspeter Hofmann. Bonheur automatique

escalator as its point of access. New architecture often leads to a process of museological rethinking that no temporary exhibition or reorientation of a permanent exhibition could ever achieve.

Conversely, for architecture this means that it can scarcely avoid clear statements and critical debates regarding the museum, even though it no longer has a systematic and theory-building influence in other areas, such as critical discourse on living and working, urban coexistence, learning or health and safety. Even though the client's interest in profit and securing the next contract may generally have more impact on an office's design than the nature of the building task at hand, the museum is dissociated from such considerations in spite of the logics of enrichment, especially since it remains a rare building task despite the museum boom. We can therefore assume that explorative and experimental approaches can be found in every iconic museum building (project), which in its turn allows conclusions to be drawn on both the social position of the institution of the museum and the status quo of architecture.

The museum offers spaces for analysing our perception of the world. As an institution of knowledge, the museum is a mediator of and between world views, a space where encounters between different views can take place. It invites us to pause, to take a critical stance. Accordingly, the construction of this space must address the question of what constitutes the conditions of our perception. Iconic architecture seems to be a perfect partner for this. The extent to which architecture affects the epistemic processes vin the museum, and thus contributes to associated subjects, remains to be investigated. What is certain, however, is that the connection between architecture and knowledge can be analysed precisely on the basis of the source of friction the museum provides for architecture.

In the dance performance **ONÍRICA**, Marta Navaridas created a physically intense and visually compelling play between three performers, in which emotional and physical states manifested themselves as live sketches.
The dancers moved within a choreographically and spatially defined frame that had been installed in the event space, continuously painting the walls, floor and ceiling with blue Edding crayon.

ONÍRICA. A dance installation by Marta Navaridas

1 The museum is a comparatively recent building task. If we assume that independence, accessibility to the public and purpose are the fundamental criteria for the building task of the museum, the Dulwich Picture Gallery (built in 1817 by Sir John Soane in south London for two private collectors who donated the museum to Dulwich College) was the first museum ever. The Fridericianum in Kassel (1776) is often claimed to be the first museum building (e.g. Maximiliane Mohl: Das Museum Fridericianum in Kassel: Museumsarchitektur, Sammlungspräsentation und Bildungsprogramm im Zeitalter der Aufklärung, Heidelberg 2020, 99–100), but its public character is doubtful. The owner, Landgrave Friedrich II, was able to use the museum as his private study without being disturbed by the public at any time. Although it had an outside entrance, like the Düsseldorf Picture Gallery (1714) before it, public access depended on the goodwill of the ruler.

2 'A specter is haunting the global village – the specter of the iconic building. In the last ten years a new type of architecture has emerged. Driven by social forces, the demand for instant fame and economic growth, the expressive landmark has challenged the previous tradition of the architectural monument. In the past, important public buildings, such as the cathedral and the city hall, expressed shared meaning and conveyed it through well-known conventions.' (Charles Jencks, *The Iconic Building. The Power of Enigma*. London 2005, p. 7). The term 'signature architecture' is related to iconic architecture, but is used in more of a pejorative way.

3 Loc. cit.

4 On the meaning of metaphor for (iconic) literature, see the contribution by Sophia Walk in this volume. p. 219.

5 The association between emotion and iconic architecture is made by Anselm Wagner, who considers it to be inseparable from what is reported about this architecture: 'which emotions a popular *iconic building* [can trigger], which uses all the means of (neo-) romantic staging and also has an accompanying media echo'. (Anselm Wagner, 'Architektur und Emotion. Eine Skizze', in: *Archimaera*, 8/2019, pp. 9–32).

6 This also applies to other kinds of exhibits, of course, even if some of the economic structures are different here. An Eames chair in a museum of applied art always has an advertising and thus a value-enhancing effect, even if the chair on display is not subject to capitalist exploitation. Before its museum career, an archaeological exhibit is most likely to have been traded on the antiques market, which is similar to the contemporary art market, although it is dominated by other actors and areas of knowledge. See also the *Rubbish Theory* by Michael Thompson, particularly the performative elements that play a role in the cycle of value being attributed to things (Michael Thompson, *Rubbish Theory. The Creation and Destruction of Value*, London 2017, p. 113).

7 See Umberto Eco, *Einführung in die Semiotik*, Munich 2002 [1968], p. 300.

8 See Pablo von Frankenberg, *Die Internationalisierung der Museumsarchitektur. Voraussetzungen, Strukturen, Tendenzen*. Berlin 2013, pp. 1–2.

9 An example of such an exception would be the Danish Architecture Centre in Copenhagen, which houses a museum as well as fulfilling other functions. The briefing for the entire building was drafted in cooperation with the team of architects from OMA, which then served as a binding and accepted basis for the planning and construction process that followed.

10 See Frankenberg, 2013 (as in note 8), pp. 116–120.

11 See Frankenberg, 2013 (s. note 8), p. 244.

12 The structural conditions of this principle were examined by Pierre Bourdieu and Alain Darbel in the pre-Internet era. The results of this empirical study can also be seen as a basis for understanding the mass posting of museum buildings and works of art on Instagram and similar platforms. The *Love of Art: European Art Museums and their Public*. Palo Alto 1991.

13 See Gunnar Eliasson: *Advanced Public Procurement as Industrial Policy: The Aircraft Industry as a Technical University*, New York 2010, p. 221; Nikola Marinčić, *Computational Models in Architecture*, Basel 2019, pp. 98–99; Timothy Lenoir, Casey Alt, 'Ströme, Prozesse, Falten. Überlagerungen zwischen Bioinformatik und zeitgenössischer Architektur', in: Henning Schmidgen, Peter Geimer, Sven Dierig (eds.), *Kultur im Experiment*, Berlin 2004, pp. 37–81, here: 59–62. The museum's website still proudly mentions this innovative technology transfer: www.guggenheim-bilbao.eus/en/the-building/the-construction (17.03.2020).

14 Luc Boltanski, Arnaud Esquerre, *Bereicherung. Eine Kritik der Ware*, Berlin 2018, p. 15.

15 Loc. cit., p. 16.

16 Loc. cit., p. 85, see also www.monopol-magazin.de/arles-maja-hoffmann?slide=2 (18.03.2020).

17 Leslie Sklair, 'Iconic Architecture and the Culture-Ideology of Consumerism', in: *Theory, Culture & Society*, 27 (5), 2010, pp. 135–159, here: 155.

18 See e.g. the role of the museum in the creation of public spaces in the Arabian Gulf, Frankenberg, 2013 (see note 8, pp. 127)

19 It is difficult to gauge the value of such a landmark. An internal analysis by Daimler AG (formerly DaimlerChrysler) shows that it greatly exceeds the costs of building the museum. The company offset the coverage of the Mercedes-Benz Museum by UNStudio against the advertising costs that would have been due for the same amount of space in similar media. According to this calculation, the construction costs had paid for themselves in just a few years. The Guggenheim Museum Bilbao is also extremely conscious of its value. When the Bilbao-based Italian artist Fausto Grossi made pasta in the shape of Gehry's building, he immediately received a letter from the museum's lawyers: 'cease production of the noodle or prepare to be sued', see Andrea Fraser, 'Isn't This a Wonderful Place?

2020

Haus
shop
usage

shop
→ 059)

'The bookshelf, designed by Vito Acconci for the Walther König bookshop on the occasion of documenta IX in 1992, establishes a connection here in Graz with the Murinsel, which Acconci also designed. The shelf opened up a place in the building that was not visible to the visitor in this form before.'

Claus Sondergelt, shop manager

(A Tour of a Tour of the Guggenheim Bilbao)', in: Alexander Alberro (ed), *Museum Highlights: The Writings of Andrea Fraser*, Cambridge 2005, pp. 233–260, here: 244. The market value of museum architecture is thus considered to be higher than the artistic value of macaroni.

20 E.g. in China and in the Arabian Gulf, see Frankenberg, 2013 (see note 8).

21 'Architecture in its ambitious form no longer builds anything but monsters, in that they no longer testify to the integrity of a town, but to its disintegration; not to its organic nature, but to its disorganisation. They do not give rhythm to the town and its exchanges, they are dumped on it like space debris fallen from some unknown disaster.' (Jean Baudrillard, 'The Indifference of Space', in: Francesco Proto (ed.), *Mass, Identity, Architecture. Architectural Writings of Jean Baudrillard*, West Sussex 2006, pp. 71–80, here: 77).

22 A remark made by Chinese President Xi Jinping at an official symposium on art and literature in 2014, which became a directive of the Chinese government in 2016 (www.nytimes.com/2016/02/23/world/asia/china-weird-architecture.html, 18.02.2020).

23 Ulrich Beck, *Was ist Globalisierung? Irrtümer des Globalismus – Antworten auf Globalisierung*, Frankfurt/Main 1997, p. 87.

24 An interesting side note here is that more and more property magnates make up the board of trustees of the Guggenheim Foundation www.nytimes.com/2005/04/27/arts/design/a-museum-visionary-envisions-more.html (03.03.2020).

25 Hans-Joachim Dahms et al., 'Neuer Pragmatismus in der Architektur', in: *Arch+*, 156/2001, p. 26. The entire issue 156 of Arch+ is dedicated to an attempt to establish the extent to which (mainly American) philosophical pragmatism could provide guidelines for a new theory of architecture.

26 Rem Koolhaas, 'Preservation Is Overtaking Us', in: Jordan Carver (ed.), *GSAPP Transcripts*, New York 2014. Quoted from the online version: www.arch.columbia.edu/books/reader/6-preservation-is-overtaking-us (20.02.2020).

27 E.g. Patrick Schumacher, 'Parametricism. A New Global Style for Architecture and Urban Design', in: *AD Architectural Design*, Vol. 79/4, 2009, pp. 14–23. A good example is also provided by Lenoir/Alt, who in their essay identify Peter Eisenman as one of the few architects who used CAD at the turn of the 21st century not only as a tool, but to newly define architecture. At the same time, the following sentence reveals how little this approach relies on a theoretical foundation or contributes to creating one: 'In contrast to his previous works, in which he was inspired by the works of Derrida, Eisenman was now disillusioned with deconstructivism and turned to Deleuze for interesting approaches to his own work.' (Timothy Lenoir, Casey Alt, 'Ströme, Prozesse, Falten. Überlagerungen zwischen Bioinformatik und zeitgenössischer Architektur', in: Henning Schmidgen, Peter Geimer, Sven Dierig (eds.), *Kultur im Experiment*, Berlin 2004, pp. 37–81, here: 65). In this view, architects instrumentalise philosophical works as a source of inspiration that changes periodically, and not as a means of founding their own theories, which in this case unfortunately also applies to the attempted theorisation of CAD.

28 'If architecture loses the idea of representation, how will buildings acquire meaning?' (David Ross Scheer, *The Death of Drawing: Architecture in the Age of Simulation*, London/New York 2014, p. 13) This fatalistic question does not arise as long as tools and theory are not confused.

29 Jeremy Till suggests that the problem of technical determinism in architecture probably already begins with the training of the architectural profession (cf. Jeremy Till, Architecture Depends, Cambridge/London 2009, p. 15).

30 See also Pablo von Frankenberg, 'Architecture as Science: Add on or Autonomous', in: Juan Almarza Anwandter et al (ed.), *Vom Suffix zur Agenda. Forum Architekturwissenschaft*, Berlin 2020.

31 The complex shape of the building was modelled using Rhinoceros 3D und Microstation, and the detailed design was then produced with the help of AutoCAD.

32 The longer planning and construction time of the Guggenheim Museum New York was due to a series of factors including the end of the Second World War and the inflation that followed in America, the death of the patron and conflicts between the initiator Hilla v. Rebay and the descendants of Solomon R. Guggenheim. Nevertheless, even a layman can imagine what a challenge the manual calculation of the building was, which would have been far easier to handle as a computer model, especially in its execution. Nowadays, this possibility makes planners and builders far less afraid of exalted forms. A computer-aided simulation of the structure also makes it easier not only to present the building in the design stages, but also to directly visualise every smallest change on the way to completion.

33 See Anke te Heesen, Mario Schulze, Vincent Dold (eds.), *Museumskrise und Ausstellungserfolg. Die Entwicklung der Geschichtsausstellung in den Siebzigern*, Berlin 2015.

34 '[...] in the 1970s in the United Kingdom, a new museum opened every second week' (Allan Hepburn, *Enchanted Objects: Visual Art in Contemporary Fiction*, Toronto/Buffalo, London 2010).

35 This was at least the aim of Philip Coombs, the first American Secretary of State for Education and Culture under J. F. Kennedy, see Philip H. Coombs, *The World Educational Crisis: A Systems Analysis*, Oxford 1968.

36 Shashi Misiura, *Heritage Marketing*, Oxford 2006, pp. 3–5.

37 Which means, according to Ulrich Beck, that all social classes go up a level, although this had a different meaning for each different class and tended to promote social individualisation.

Photo by Georg Weinseiss

(Ulrich Beck, *Risikogesellschaft. Auf dem Weg in eine andere Moderne*, Frankfurt/Main 1986, p. 122). It is not surprising that history exhibitions were in vogue again during this period of social change. The achievement status attached to visiting a museum is connected with the search for one's own roots, especially in the case of a Prussian exhibition in Berlin or a Staufer exhibition in Stuttgart.

38 Vittorio M. Lampugnani, 'Die Architektur der Kunst. Zu den Museen der neunziger Jahre', in: Vittorio M. Lampugnani, Angeli Sachs (eds.), *Museen für ein neues Jahrtausend: Ideen, Projekte, Bauten*, München, London, New York 1999, pp. 11–14, here: 14.

39 See. Jürgen Habermas, *Erkenntnis und Interesse*, Frankfurt/Main 1968.

40 See also Jürgen Habermas, *Auch eine Geschichte der Philosophie*. Vol 1: *Die okzidentale Konstellation von Glauben und Wissen*, Berlin 2019. Here Habermas pursues the question of what the task of philosophy consists of if, by specialising in the sciences, it wishes to avoid becoming a service provider for the cognitive sciences or a mere administrator of its own history.

41 See also Georg Franck, „Die Architektur: eine Wissenschaft?', in: Der Architekt, 1/2009, pp. 28–35. 'Eine Wissenschaft im Sinne der Wissenschaftstheorie ist die Architektur gewiss nicht', Franck writes here (p. 28) and takes this statement as his starting point for a differentiated consideration of the scientific ambitions of architecture.

42 This is revealed not least in the fact that it has been possible for a 'network of architectural studies' to develop between several German universities, which is certainly willing to understand 'architectural studies' as an independent discipline alongside architecture. See also Juan Almarza Anwandter et al. (ed.), *Vom Suffix zur Agenda. Forum Architekturwissenschaft*, Berlin 2020).

43 Cedric Price, blurb, in: Peter Cook, Colin Fournier, Dieter Bogner (eds.), *Friendly Alien. Kunsthaus Graz*, Ostfildern 2004.

2020

Haus
freight elevator
usage

usage
→ 201)
→ 202)

'The **freight elevator** is the most important channel connecting the various levels. I mainly use it to transport catalogues, tools and consumable supplies. But it is also used for transporting art. The **freight elevator** is the most important point for all transport and routes between the stores and the exhibition area.'

Arnold Stickler, building management

2019

Kunst
Haus
freight elevator

bridge link
→175)

More recently, the Kunsthaus programme has been marked by an increasing interest in creating intersubjective situations for visitors through performance formats – either actual performances or the conscious creation of human interactions through various artistic means. With its performative architecture for staged encounters, the Kunsthaus Graz is the ideal location for such events.

The series **Perfomance Now**, which began with a packed weekend of performances, aimed to stage activities throughout the building. **'I don't think I am trying to commit suicide'** used the phase of exhibition set-up – always a period of transition and change – as well as areas such as the delivery zone, or the **freight elevator**, which are usually inaccessible to visitors.

Magdalena Kosch and Viet Anh in the framework of
'I don't think I am trying to commit suicide'. Performance Now

2020

Haus
third basement level
usage

'The most important machines in the Kunsthaus are on the **third basement level**, 15 to 20 metres underground. They are what actually keep the entire building running. When you go into these rooms, it almost feels like you are in a spaceship.'

Michaela Hofmann, cleaning service

2020

Haus
third basement level
usage

Kunsthaus
→ 204)

'Once a week I operate each wheel to test the sprinkler system. I like the look of the sprinkler system technology – the red wheels make it look exciting.'

Peter Rumpf, in-house technician

intersection
↗ p. 346
↗ p. 81
↗ p. 83

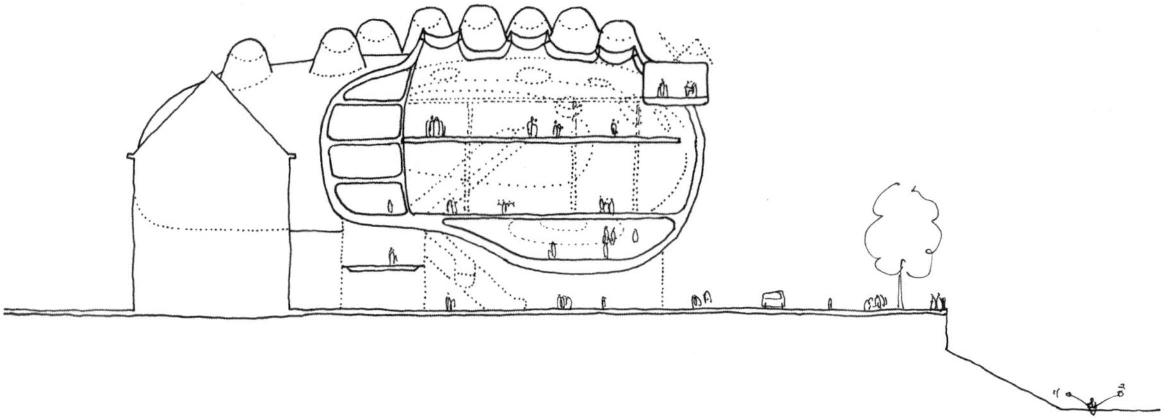

Cross section of the **Bubble**.
Sketch from the preliminary design project, Niels Jonkhans

The latent potential of museum architecture. A conversation about border demarcations, accessibility, flexibility versus change, the public museum
Pablo von Frankenberg, Barbara Steiner, Sophia Walk
20, 21 and 22 September 2019, Graz

1997

(**reference**
(design

reference
→ 106)
↗ p. 39
↗ p. 45
↗ p. 295

The Tongue, design drawing, Peter Cook, Colin Fournier

The latent potential of museum architecture

PvF **Pablo von Frankenberg**
BS **Barbara Steiner**
SW **Sophia Walk**

Border demarcations

BS Demands and discussions on the topic of border demarcations can be observed in almost every social sphere today. However, drawing a border can quickly lead to delimitation, or even exclusion. In other eras, there was a desire to cross borders, whether they were of a categorical, disciplinary or spatial nature. Peter Cook and Colin Fournier were architects of a generation that strove to overcome borders intellectually, but also in a purely practical sense. The **ground floor** of the Kunsthaus shows this quite clearly. The original intention was to leave it completely open – even dispensing with glass walls. However, it proved impossible to make this concept a reality, mainly due to climatic reasons.

→ design 041) 151)

SW The architectural historian Wolfgang Pehnt once put it this way: the best kind of museum is one that you enter without realising it. Here he refers first and foremost to the opening up of museum buildings to a wider public, but ultimately it still applies today, linked with the question of what architectural means can be used to achieve it. You have returned to this idea. The visual axes have been opened up, more points of access have been added and fixtures removed. In the previous situation – when the **café** was still where the **ticket booth** is now – the **ground floor** zone with the connection to the **Iron House** was not so visible, because it was too cluttered and narrow.

→ café 015)
→ info 059)
→ courtyard 052)

BS We want to open up the **courtyard** in the future, too. We are working on that with our neighbour, *Haus der Architektur*. However, I have noticed that our visitors don't always appreciate this gesture of opening up the museum towards the urban space, and the multiple points of entry. They find it confusing. So there is an interesting reversal – what was once thought of as a gesture of emancipation, i.e. not patronising people, but encouraging them to find their own personal point of entry and discover the building in their own way, is now seen as something of an imposition. Most people want clarity, clear instructions on how to enter the museum or get from A to B, how to move around in the building.

SW In the 1960s and 1970s, defying architectural and spatial barriers also meant overcoming social borders. This is an extremely important matter for the museum, and we should have been clearly aware of it, at least since the publication of *The Love of Art* by Pierre Bourdieu and Alain Darbel. This empirical study on habitus and distinction in the art space was published ten years before Bourdieu's book *Distinction*.

BS It also became obvious that overcoming spatial barriers does not automatically mean overcoming social ones. From today's perspective it seems a little naive. If

↗ p. 231

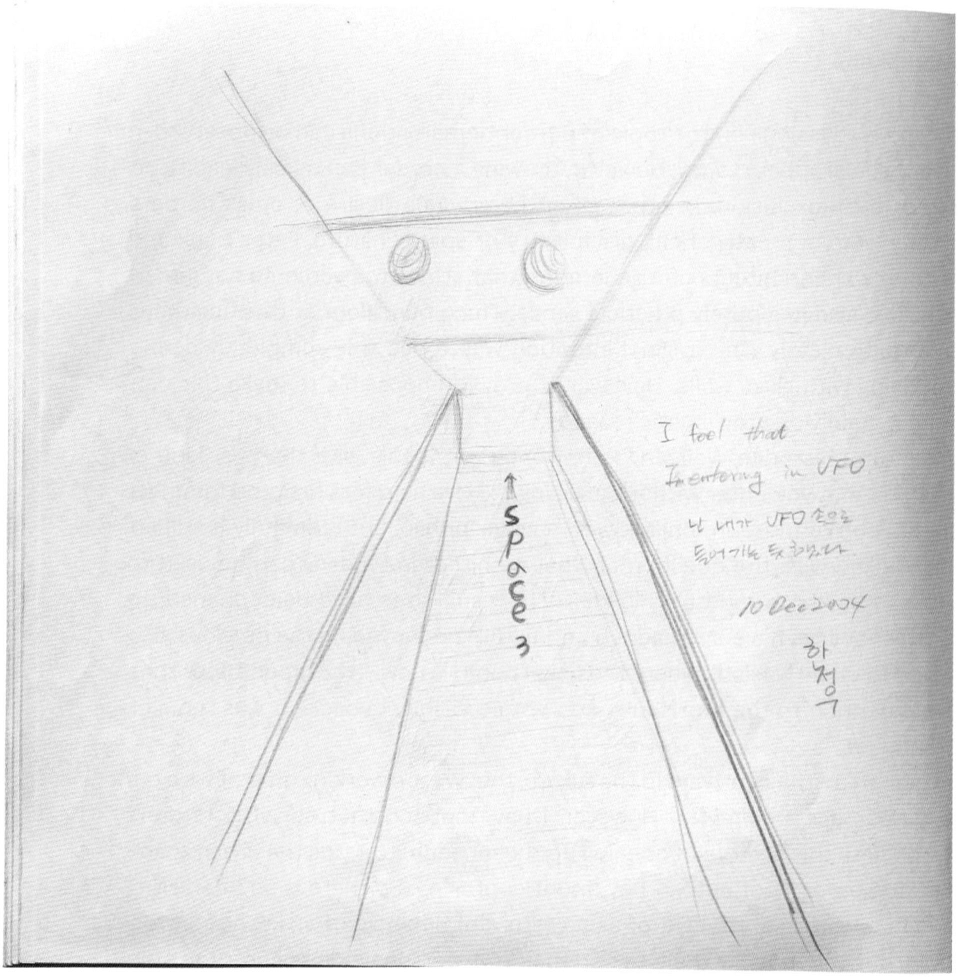

Extract from the visitors' book

I bring the street directly into the building, an idea that was literally put into practice the first time the Sprengel Museum in Hanover was built, it doesn't initially mean that people will follow. But at that time it was an important gesture of opening up. The original part of the Sprengel Museum, whose architecture I greatly admire, is now a listed building. If you consider how the museum is perceived today, it is usually the new part of the building that people admire. Its exhibition rooms are clearly separated from the exterior, white spaces lined up in a row – basically, it is an updated version of an enfilade. In my view, it represents a step backwards from the first building.

PvF But it has to be said that the exterior of the Sprengel extension stands out because of its unusual surface. And it makes interesting references to its surroundings – the Maschsee lake for example. Inside it, you walk through wonderfully proportioned volumes of space. The rooms are slightly tilted in the floor plan. As a visitor you hardly notice, but it does have an effect. The actual exhibition rooms are designed as classical white cubes. There is a break here in comparison with the exterior, which can certainly be interpreted in different ways. In any case, they have an air of exclusivity.

BS Exactly. And suddenly the boundary that was so clearly removed in the original building is back again, almost programmatically.

PvF At the opening of the Sprengel Museum extension, just a few artistic installations were shown in the rooms. For example, Pierre Huyghe tipped coloured dust – paint scraped off the walls of the Centre Pompidou, the Museum Ludwig, Cologne and the Los Angeles County Museum of Art – into the exhibition hall. As a visitor you walked through it, spreading particles of coloured dust wherever you went. The new museum was marked with the history of other museums. Apart from the symbolic initiation rite, the message for me was this: we have to bring more life into this museum, because otherwise it is completely dead. As an architect, I can perhaps take pleasure in this pure spatiality. But this kind of spatial experience does not necessarily have anything to do with the museum as a constantly changing place, and the art that is shown in it.

SW It is important to think of the museum in terms of its use. In many cases, far too little attention is paid to this.

BS It strikes me that there is an increasing tendency for museums to be divided up into unconventional shells (outside) and extremely conventional spatial programmes (inside). This can be seen quite clearly at the old and new Tate Modern.

PvF The only thing that isn't conventional at the Tate Modern is the Turbine Hall itself. And it works quite well as far as borders and demarcations are concerned – in my opinion, it crosses boundaries in quite a wonderful way.

BS It is also a kind of sluice, almost like a road leading inwards, but not in quite such a literal sense as the entrance of the old Sprengel Museum.

PvF Absolutely, all kinds of people go through it. Of course, that is not only down to the existing architecture, but also very much because of the new Millennium Bridge over the Thames – i.e. the surrounding urban architecture. This footbridge has made it

2000

(**Haus**
(Travelator
(usage

design
→ 081)
reference
→ 077)

'The moment you step onto the **Travelator** is an exit from everyday life. Before you are even halfway up the conveyor belt, you have left the city twice as far behind you. Up the escalator, through my trap-door and up into art, après nous le déluge.'

Markus Gugatschka, visitor and art collector

far easier for people to access the great hall, bringing them into contact with art. It is worthwhile to think of the museum in terms of its connections with the urban space, reinforcing its public character.

BS The Tate Modern's spatial programme for the collection and temporary exhibitions was classical from the very beginning, and the interior of the new annex is the same. From the outside, it makes quite a different impression. And in fact it has something else in common with other newer buildings – you find the same thing in Hanover. The so-called side rooms, where you can sit and look out of the window, or perhaps leaf through a few catalogues, are separate from the works of art. At the most you might find the occasional video on a small monitor there. Here is the art. Boundary... ... and here is everything else. Here is the shop, the café, the quiet rooms, there might be study rooms, mediation rooms. The areas are not thought of as a whole. This is different to how it used to be.

PvF In1988, Nathalie Heinich did some empirical research on the Centre Pompidou. She found that this idea of opening up the boundaries between various areas didn't work. The concept of connecting the library, the public areas, the museum and all kinds of other institutions wasn't viable from the user's point of view. People went there to use the library, visit the museum, make music or meet one another. The building was used, i.e. everyone found their own personal use for it – for some it was a library, for others it was the front terrace – everyone had their own Centre Pompidou. Very few visitors were interested in the mixture and combination of uses that were originally planned. Thus the vital question is this: how can you succeed in making a building really permeable, not only in the sense of crossing the boundaries of the building itself, but also breaking up the divisions in how it is used?

BS Nowadays there is another problem that didn't exist up until the 1980s: the commercialisation of the ground floor area. Often it is no longer even accessible to you as an artistic director. It was the same at the Kunsthaus when I arrived here – it took a long time and a great deal of persuasion to reclaim the area for art and non-commercial purposes. I found it interesting that historical models hardly play a role at all in the conception of new museums. For me they are certainly worth a second look, especially when it comes to making the building come to life. Although it must be said that the multipurpose approach and permanently changing spatial programmes that were introduced back then no longer work today.

SW Cedric Price once said that a house is not, or should not be, so much a building but a network of services and information. But things are different in reality, because of course a museum building has at least a kind of constructive delineation. The intention was to move away from the idea of the façade as such – the Centre Pompidou did not have one, at least not in the planning stages. The idea of the ground floor zone flowing into the street area or urban space, creating a public space situation, where can it be seen to have worked?

BS At the Centre Pompidou it was security concerns that prevented it. The considerations of Renzo Piano / Richard Rogers were never put into practice, or at least only very selectively. Where the concept actually did work, in the sense of people using

Travelator
→ 076)
↗ p. 85
↗ p. 297

Narratives. –35/65+. Two generations, installation by Martin Bricelj on the **Travelator** the facilities it offered, was in Marxist cultural concepts. By the way, the Pompidou was also conceived in this tradition, through André Malraux. He was involved in the initial considerations. The *Maisons de la culture* he initiated in France are also designed to have a mixture of functions. This is why the *Kulturhaus* is named as it is, a cultural house, rather than a *Kunsthaus*. There is a completely different social relevance behind it. These concepts have entirely disappeared from our range of perspectives, perhaps because they immediately make most people think of the Eastern Bloc. Apart from the *Maisons de la culture* there is the *Kulturhuset* in Stockholm, which is still well frequented today. Its essential aim was to provide an extended concept of culture.

SW Why do you think we have lost sight of these concepts today?

BS I believe the main reason is that we were not prepared for these concepts, and the expectations of a Western public were different. It has a lot to do with the history of the modern age, with museums being separated into different types. People still have this idea firmly in their heads.

SW And that means we have internalised completely different types and forms of use. You could say that the way in which the museum is 'used' is generated by the type of museum it is. But just as the architecture supposedly defines the way we approach the building, our own attitude as we enter a museum is also significant. And in addition to that, spaces with multiple codes, i.e. spaces with different uses, also create additional work when it comes to the organisation of their use. It seems that certain attributions of use are needed to provide clarity and orientation for the users, both internal and external. More unspecific, open types of use mean that we must continually adapt to them. And people are creatures of habit.

BS Right up to the present day, certain spatial programmes fail because they do not conform to visitors' expectations of an exhibition. What people do expect is unfortunately becoming more and more standardised – the white exhibition hall. Even at the Kunsthaus, most visitors are convinced that you can only have a good exhibition in a white space. It is simply not enough to design and build a spatial programme. The use is essentially a result of what is already in their heads – their mindset – whether people can imagine using what is offered. In the case of houses of culture, it probably has a lot to do with the fact that the bourgeois concept of the museum in the West was extremely powerful, and Marxist houses of culture were seen as an ideological threat – people felt the need to distance themselves from them. I think that internalised conventions were totally underestimated for several decades when it came to new types of building and usage.

PvF I would like to take a step backwards, to Cedric Price and the theme of the network. When you say that attempts like the Centre Pompidou have fallen victim to the classical categorisation of modernity, and that it would therefore be impossible to achieve cultural permeability, I ask myself the following question: How can we define a use that works? What does it mean when we say it works, or it doesn't work? In principle, the Centre Pompidou worked incredibly well right from the beginning. It was a huge success with the public. It triggered the first major wave of gentrification

2000

(Travelator
(design

usage
→ 110)
Space01
→ 107)
↗ p. 83
↗ p. 235

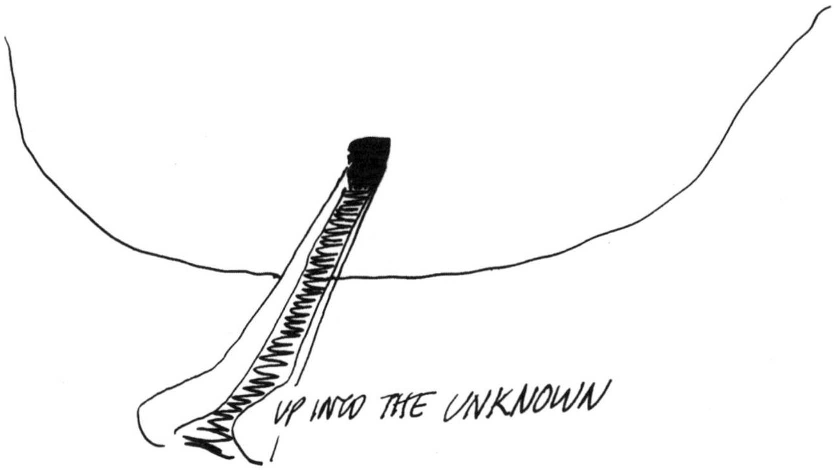

The **Travelator**. Concept sketch from the competition, Peter Cook for the urban quarter surrounding it. So perhaps it didn't work in terms of permeability, but it did in many other respects. If you see the building as a network, it is in fact true that a network works not only when all of its synapses are fully connected, but also when the pathways through the network all function latently. Then everyone can find his or her own way through it. In that sense, the Centre Pompidou provided a network that could be used either way. Perhaps it just wasn't used in the way the creators of the network intended. Does that mean that it doesn't work at all?

SW Of course you are right in what you say about the function, i.e. the use. Something is created and is perhaps used in a completely different way – yes. You could say that is a good thing, because it means that there has been an appropriation of space and an adjustment to the environment. And because the architecture allows it – precisely because it provides a network.

BS Nevertheless, I do regret that it wasn't possible to realise some of the original bold ideas at the Centre Pompidou. Fifteen entrances, films produced in its own workshops that you could watch on the exterior of the building, coming out of the metro with your shopping bags and encountering a Picasso behind glass – wonderful!

SW So we can say that conventions are more likely to be found in the exhibition space. As far as the outer shell of the building is concerned, they are apparently less present, because otherwise you could just put cubes on the lawn. But that doesn't happen, because a special kind of exterior is expected.

BS That is an interesting paradox. Unusual things are expected of the outside, but not of the inside.

PvF I think the aspect of representative culture could offer an explanation for this. The Kunsthaus Graz does not only define itself through its visitors, who actually go into the building and see the exhibitions. Rather, it lives very much from this image of the Kunsthaus, the way it stands in this exact context and looks the way it does. And you can't create an image like that with a perfectly air-conditioned warehouse. It has to be an iconic sign. Iconicity is important, so that you can say, 'even though I've never been to Kunsthaus Graz, I know that some pretty crazy things happen there. And somehow it is modern art, contemporary, it's not my thing, but it's there.' Friedrich Tenbruck would describe this effect as representative culture.

BS But the reputation of an institution relies on a little more than that. The media machine is enough to promote the iconicity of the architecture and the image it reflects. But if you want to enable other spatial experiences, other forms of encounter with art, you need a good programme.

PvF It starts to become a problem when museum buildings appear and everything else disappears behind their architecture. There are building projects where no one is interested in what kind of exhibitions are to be shown in the museum, or which target audience is supposed to visit them. The crux of the matter often lies in the architectural tenders, especially in the art field ... These tenders often don't even mention the collection, the art.

BS That is partly because, these days, the people who work in museums are rarely directly involved in tenders for large building projects. External consultants are used

↗ p. 149
↗ p. 297

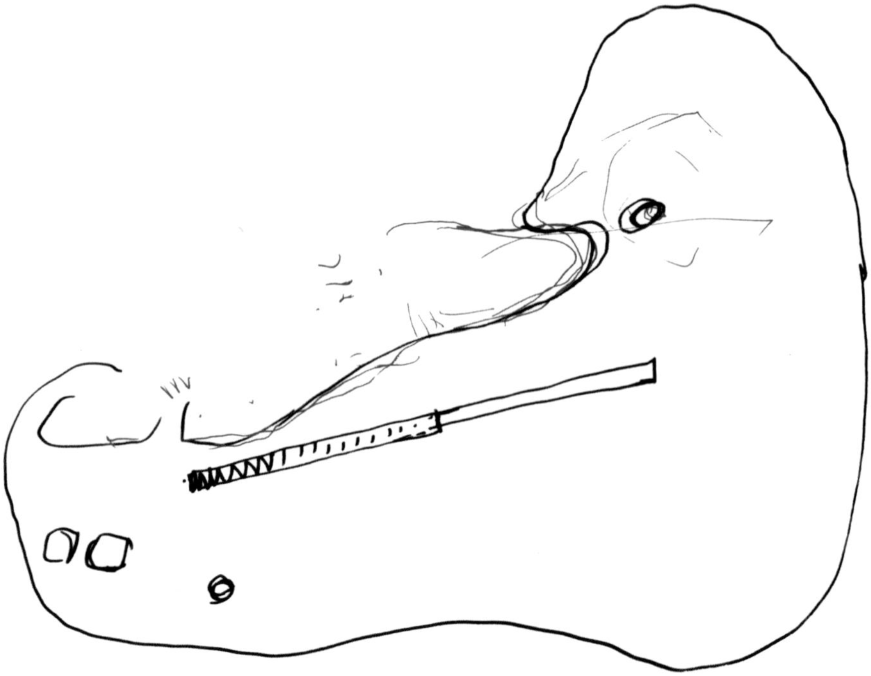

Exhibition level. Sketch from the preliminary design, Colin Fournier instead. I have nothing against museum consultancy, but the problem is that questions relating to contents and strategy are dealt with by external advisors. That is why I think that there is a lack of clarity concerning what is supposed to happen in these buildings in the future, because the people responsible for it are not included in the process. They have no say in the matter until later, when the building is finished. This was what happened at the Kunsthaus, by the way. Even though there are some exceptions, museum consultancy tends to be concerned with global solutions. Because the concepts have to work in the same way wherever they are. That is why the buildings that house most art institutions lack an element of specificity, something that makes them unique. A convincing model for me would be an amalgamation of external and local expertise.

PvF Absolutely. Nevertheless, you can't measure the entire museum consultancy sector by the same standards. Of course there are the large, efficiency-driven players. But then there are others with a very specific expertise. A museum couldn't afford them permanently, but they can be hired on a temporary basis. There aren't many museum directors like you who work with architecture in such an intensive way. And if architects are not really challenged by museum teams, certain internal concerns can quickly recede into the background during the planning stage. It's great if you have someone who speaks the language of the architects as well as that of the museum.

SW In the planning stages, it is helpful to involve people like security officers, technical services and cleaning staff. It's important to ask these people for their opinions. As far as I know, this never happens. Although these are the people who use the building on a daily basis and have knowledge that no one else has access to.

Accessibility

SW There is a *display object*, the **Cat-Tree for the Arts** by Oliver Klimpel, in the **foyer** of the Kunsthaus. You have experienced difficulties because people use it as a play object, or put their cups and rucksacks on it, with no respect for the art on display on it. In response to this, Oliver raised the height of the plinth, because there wasn't enough of a threshold before. The new one is now considerably higher. It would be different if the **Cat-Tree** were upstairs in the actual exhibition rooms.

→ Cat-Tree 049)

BS I'm not so sure about that – the public doesn't even necessarily behave reverently towards the art in our exhibition rooms. It's because of the nature of the space. It would be different in a white exhibition space, where the aura of the space encourages a different kind of behaviour. I don't necessarily mean humility towards works of art, but there really is a kind of 'sanctity' that stops people behaving too inconsiderately. We don't have that here. That is why people don't behave the same way here as they would in a white space. Many people see the rooms in the Kunsthaus as an adventure playground, and treat them accordingly. In this respect, the emancipatory message the architects had in mind was successful. However, it sometimes goes hand in hand with extreme disrespect for the exhibits.

↗ p. 79

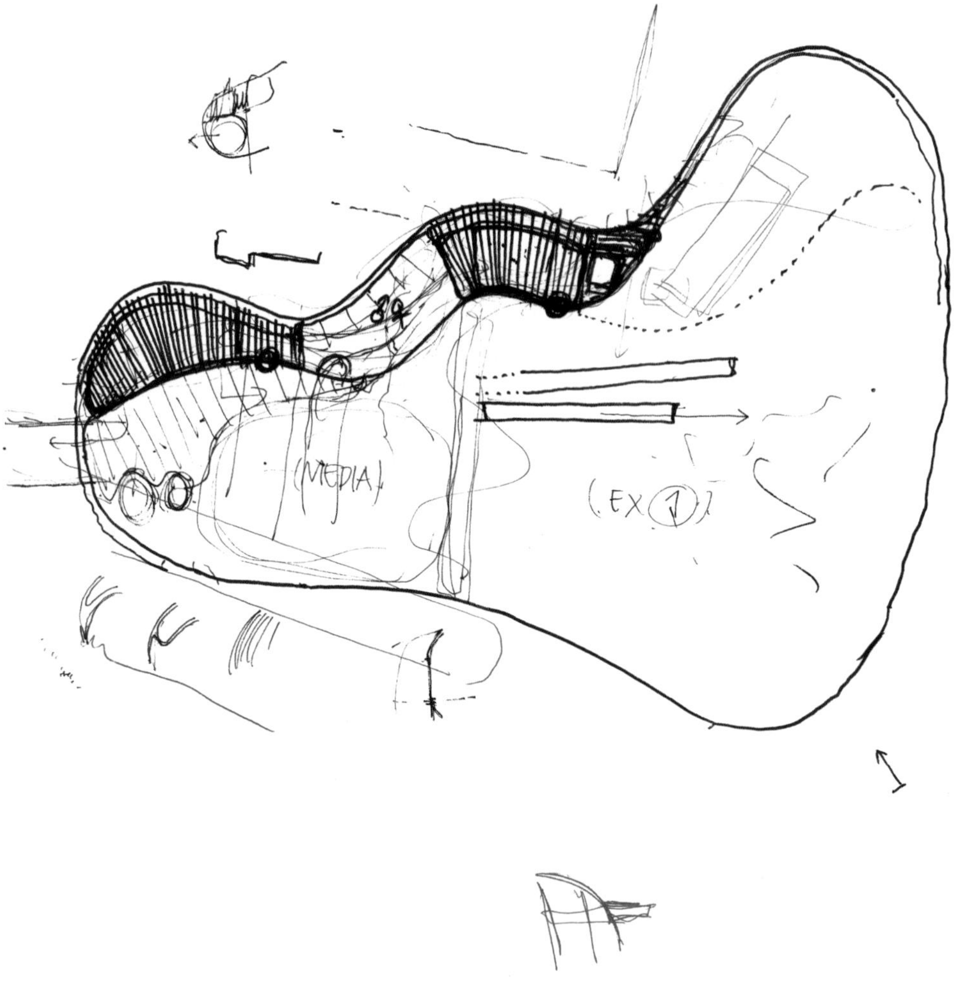

Exhibition floor. Sketch of floor plan, preliminary design phase, Niels Jonkhans

PvF That makes sense to me when you consider that the **entrance** to the Kunsthaus, i.e. to the exhibition floor, works more or less without thresholds. Gliding into the building on the **Travelator** is like a rite de passage. I don't even really see the ticket inspector. I might even forget to show her my ticket. I flow into the building. In this respect, the shifting of boundaries really works at this point. Does that lead to a lack of respect for art? Do visitors touch the exhibits?

→ Travelator 079)

BS Wanting to touch the artworks would be the least of my worries. I can understand that. If something attracts you in a tactile way, you want to find out more about it, that is something I really do understand. What I mean is that some people ignore the fact that it is an exhibition. Art has been torn from its pedestal – the great challenge of the 1960s and 1970s has been met. But it hasn't necessarily led to a rapprochement with art. Today we have to talk about why people can't come in to the exhibition with an ice cream cone, a dog or an umbrella, and deal with their indignation if we don't allow them to. Please don't misunderstand me – this is not a plea for the re-auratisation of art or its spaces. I would just like more appreciation to be shown for art.

PvF An aura doesn't necessarily convey a boundary, but more of a vibe, a presence. Can I find a way to present an object – whether it is an art object or a cultural artefact – in a way that gives it a direct, obvious presence? And even that doesn't necessarily create a boundary, in my opinion. It may create a boundary that I can then apply to the object, but the object itself and the way it is exhibited do not have this boundary.

BS An aura charges a work of art, and I wonder how much auratic charge is required to make someone keep their distance? That would create a boundary around the object. But I also see a boundary that lies within the object itself. Because auratic objects are not approachable objects. And so the boundary moves back to the work of art. In this context I find it interesting that strategies of auratisation have begun to succeed – not only in the art context, but also in the luxury retail sector.

PvF On the other hand, you could argue along the lines of Roland Barthes' *punctum* – '… the element which rises from the scene, shoots out of it like an arrow, and pierces me' – i.e. it touches me. I need something that works for me, speaks to me, and then I can engage with it. In this sense, an aura can also be seen as an invitation to overcome boundaries.

BS Perhaps it's splitting hairs, but for me this sense of being touched comes from aesthetics. Insight through the senses – you recognise something that cannot be verbalised.

What bothers me is the absorbing aspect of the aura, the 'sanctity' that resonates from it. Aesthetics is more than just a message passed on to the senses – it is insight through sensory perception. It also bothers me that the white exhibition space suggests it has always been there. A given fact, something that simply exists and you can never question it. But for a long time, the white space was just one of many possibilities. It didn't really become established until the late 1980s.

PvF I have the feeling that even if I am working against it or with it, I reinforce its inherent lack of utopia. My focus is not on myself, but on the white exhibition space, rather than being productive in other ways. It seems to me that it has no emancipatory power.

floor plan
↗ p. 345

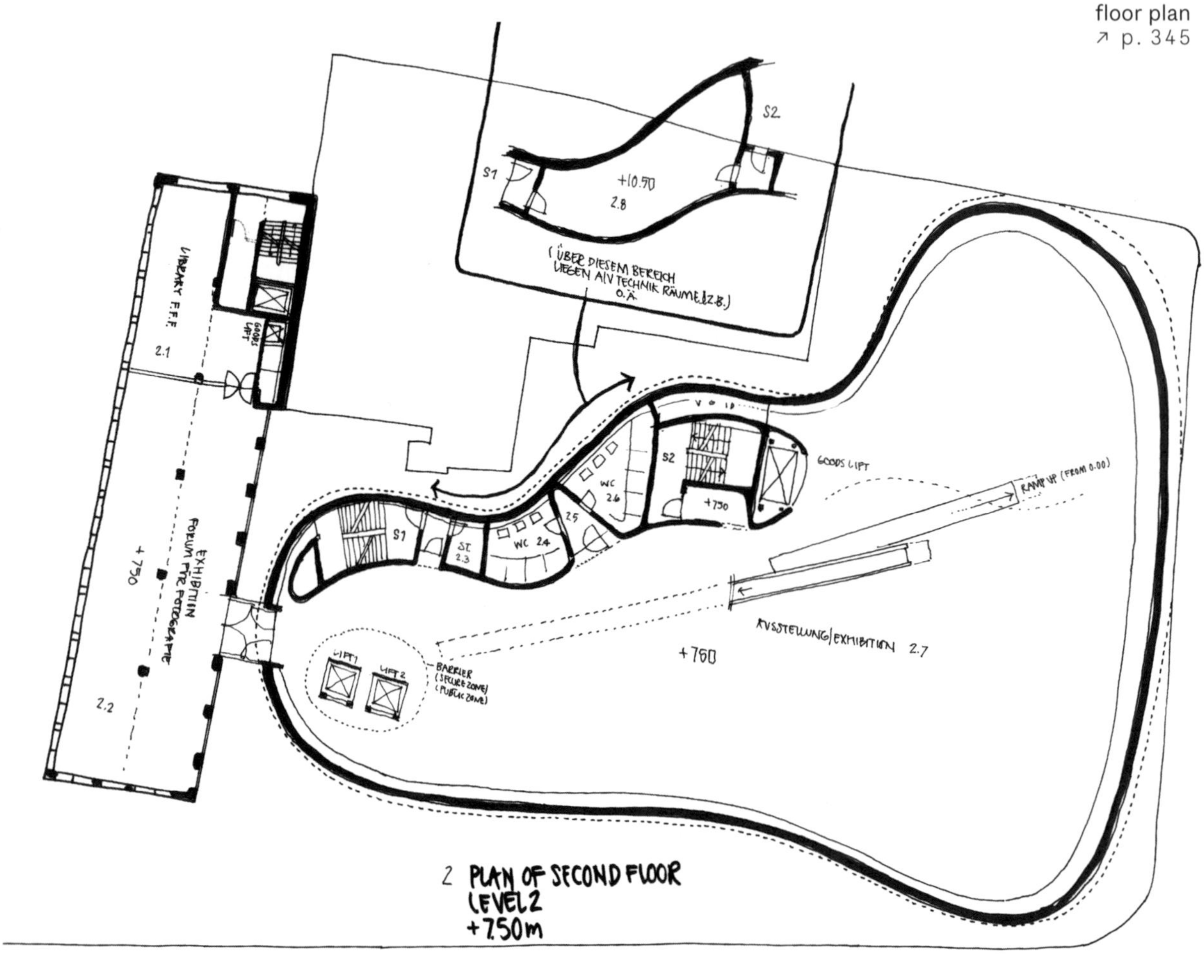

Exhibition floor. Floor plan,
preliminary design phase, Niels Jonkhans

BS Interesting that you should mention a lack of utopia in this context. From today's perspective, what you say is absolutely correct. At the time of its genesis, it was exactly the opposite – in the 1930s, Alfred H. Barr saw it as a utopian space because it disallowed political instrumentalisation. Nowadays we are concerned with a completely commercialised space.

SW We have spoken of disciplinary, spatial and social boundaries, and also of accessibility. But the question is also – where do these three types of boundary play a role together, perhaps especially in a museum?

PvF A positive example for me is the Brooklyn Museum. It was built as a classical historical museum, a temple with a large flight of stairs leading up to the most sacred area on the top floor. In Brooklyn, this flight of stairs has been removed and the entrance relocated to the ground floor. So you start off with the basics, as you can see in the ticketing area. So when you come out of the subway, rather than having to go up another flight of steps to pay homage to art, you are pulled directly into the building. This fits in with the museum's programme, which is strongly rooted in the local community. The universal museum also hosts street art exhibitions with artists from Brooklyn. That's what the crowds come for. So here the social boundary is removed programmatically, but also in an architectural sense. How would this work at the Kunsthaus?

BS It already works extremely well at the Kunsthaus in an architectural sense. People flock into the building for all kinds of reasons. However, in contrast to the Brooklyn Museum, although we are part of the Universalmuseum Joanneum, we are active in the field of international modern and contemporary visual art, with regular excursions into the performative. We begin in the 1960s. That is a set part of the programme, on the one hand because Graz was an important city for the avant-garde movement in those days, and on the other because the other museums of the Joanneum cover earlier periods. I would like to collaborate more with other parts of the Joanneum, but it's not so easy, not least because our rooms often don't have the right climatic conditions. We do work with the local community, but not to the same extent as other actors in Graz, and any community work we do is related to global developments. I think that contemporary art already has many connections with people's lives as far as contents are concerned, but you have to open up other avenues beyond this. Along with art mediation, I am interested in the Kunsthaus building as a tool to introduce people to contemporary art exhibitions. Being facetious, I would say that the building is our Klimt frieze. A lot of people go to the Secession building in Vienna – not because of contemporary art, but because of Gustav Klimt, and perhaps also because of Olbrich's architecture. In our case it's the building that attracts people.

SW It really seems to be the case that many architects who come to Graz (I know this from my own circle of acquaintances) want to visit the Kunsthaus because they are interested in the architecture, because they know the architects, because the image of the architecture is well known beyond the boundaries of Graz. Of course they notice the exhibitions then, but always as a kind of foil through which the architecture

2004

Kunst
Haus
Space02

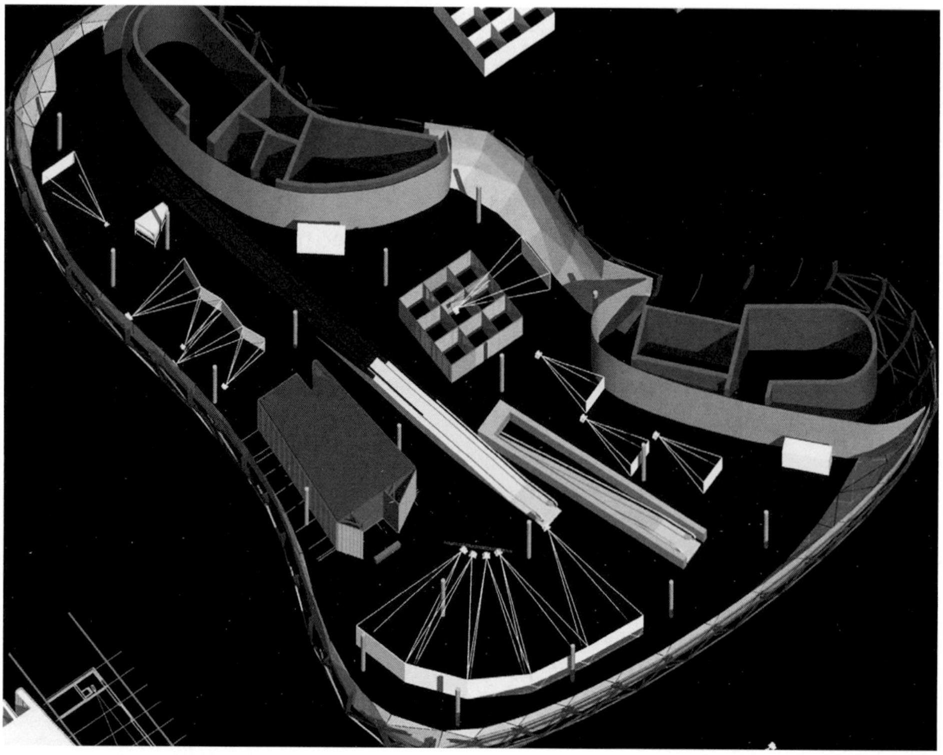

In curating the exhibition **Videodreams**, Adam Budak made use of the obvious theatricality of **Space02**, whose absence of daylight makes it an excellent space in which to present media art. The atmosphere between dream and staging created by the content of the works on display was magnified by the various different forms in which the videos were presented – from a screen-like canvas (Aernout Mik) to an object-like peep-box (Joan Jonas) to the classic black box with cinema seating (Teresa Hubbard/Alexander Birchler).

Videodreams. Between the Cinematic and the Theatrical, design drawing for the exhibition, Niels Jonkhans is viewed. At the Kunsthaus, the presence of the construction plays a crucial role in the perception of art.

BS And we make use of that to the extreme. The building is a magnet and a mediation tool.

→ friendly alien 035) 218)

PvF The advantage of the iconicity of a building like the Kunsthaus Graz is that it enables multiple attributions to be made. Because it is so open to interpretation, a far larger public can relate to the building. If you look at Schinkel's *Altes Museum*, you have to have some kind of previous education to understand what it's about. It's easier to appreciate it if you have this kind of understanding.

BS And it's enough for someone to say the Kunsthaus Graz building is cute.

→ friendly alien 002) 005)

PvF Absolutely. In fact, that applies to any iconic building. It's one of the best things about this kind of architecture. You can criticise iconic architecture in general, for example by saying that it lacks context. You could certainly say that the Kunsthaus does not rely on the historical centre of Graz. It could work just as well elsewhere.

SW And as such you could say that it's an ideal museum – because it is without context, so it can be thought of regardless of its location.

BS But the Kunsthaus is not without context.

PvF It changes the context and it changes because of the context, that is true. But there are certain buildings that only work within a certain context. It's different with iconic architecture. One of the best examples of this is the MoMA in New York. When it was built in 1939, it was a complete alien. In historical photographs from the 1940s, MoMA really stands out in the context of the historical buildings on 53rd Street. And now? You can hardly tell MoMA apart from all the other modern glass and steel constructions. This museum building has influenced its surroundings to such an extent that the environment has adapted to the museum rather than it being the other way around. Do we perhaps find the same thing happening with the Kunsthaus Graz?

→ reference 055)

BS The Kunsthaus has also adapted to its surroundings to a large extent. I think that should be acknowledged. It inscribes itself into the roofscape and provides a fitting contrast.

→ Kunsthaus 205)

PvF There is other iconic architecture that can't be accused of standing in a vacuum. But I think this building could have developed its iconic effect elsewhere. The iconic effect stems from the fact that it is so open to interpretation. And as such it doesn't really matter whether I know anything about Graz, or come here with no historical knowledge whatsoever.

BS But even though the iconic effect could arise anywhere: the moment you arrive here in a physical sense from wherever you come from, you will find yourself in a specific situation. The iconic qualities can be seen and disseminated by means of photos. But if you are on site you will see these surroundings, the relationship of the building to this specific environment.

→ friendly alien 001) 010)

SW I would say that anyone who comes to Graz and wants to see the Kunsthaus already has a certain image in mind, and this image is largely void of context. Once you are here, you see the roofscape, the city ...

BS ... and meet people. You arrive, enter the city, look for the place, go into the building. This entire process feeds into the impression you have. It is the 'iconic image' that spreads its fame. When I was in Korea, people had never heard of Graz, but they knew about the Kunsthaus. The mechanism works in the remotest of places. And still it is true that something changes significantly the moment you arrive in the actual place.

SW Uses also become specific to a place, and make a place specific. This is often underestimated. How you use a building is strongly related to the circumstances – what are you doing in this place, in this museum, who is with you, how long will you stay here, where were you before and do you have to find your way around, get your bearings, once you are inside the Kunsthaus. All in all, a picture arises during this process, and as such it is not interchangeable. We all know the phenomenon – when we are travelling, we like to take certain types of food home with us from all over the world – but they never taste like they do when we are on holiday. Because all the things that make a place specific are missing.

BS Still it seems to me that precisely this specificity is becoming more and more disturbing. It's a little like global chains such as McDonalds – you expect exactly the same standard wherever you are. A similar trend can be observed in the landscape of art institutions – in relation to whatever is being exhibited as well as to the way in which it is exhibited. I saw a Rauschenberg exhibition at the Tate Modern and was disappointed, because it seemed completely interchangeable. Even though it was an artist whose work was fundamentally concerned with specific questions related to exhibiting. That is to say, just like architecture, the art scene is increasingly generating a contextual void. Whether we are concerned with buildings or exhibitions, they all look as though they have come off a production line, although they claim to be extremely special. More than anything else, it is usually the marketing departments that produce this 'specialness'.

SW Particularly in the case of exhibitions here at the Kunsthaus, however, they are not perceived as being unrelated to the architecture that surrounds them. You inevitably ask yourself how the building affects the exhibition. And how the exhibition affects the building. A lot more thought is given to this than in other museums, for example the ones that adhere more closely to the ideal of the white cube. At the Kunsthaus, you are more or less forced by the architecture to include it in your ideas on forms of presentation. There is no white wall you can hang something on, you have to think about what a particular wall looks like, or even if it is actually a wall at all. It could be cantilevers à la Kiesler, as we saw in the Kogler exhibition *Connected*, or metal panels like the ones used in the exhibition *Graz Architecture*.

→ Space01 119) 129)

→ Space02 091) 093)

PvF So does the Kunsthaus avoid this kind of marketing of contemporary art?

BS Nothing can completely avoid marketing nowadays, but let's put it like this: there are barbs and spikes. And that's what I like about the building, it's a hybrid between the emancipatory ideas of the 1970s and the branding architecture of the 1990s, which came into vogue with the European Capital of Culture. Perhaps one of the reasons I admire the building is that its very conception is inherently ambivalent. It actually

2007

(**Haus**
(Space02

The artist Werner Reiterer focused on the building as 'individual' and in this context explored the personification of space. During his solo exhibition **Eye Sucks Wold** in 2007, a mere A4-sized piece of paper affixed to the wall invited visitors to **Space02** to scream as loudly as possible (Breath, 2007). Those who flouted social conventions and rose to Reiterer's challenge were rewarded with an instant reaction: The room started to breathe both visually and audibly. Once a certain decibel level was reached, the light in the room started to turn on and off to the rhythm of breathing, while speakers broadcast the sound of the artist's breath.

Werner Reiterer. Eye Sucks World

consists of rival concepts that are brought together. And that is why it is so fascinating to work with the building, in these rooms.

PvF An international exhibition company would have no chance at the Kunsthaus, because you can't make money with it. Although this kind of company often produces travelling exhibitions of a high quality, they are customised for standard museum spaces. It is more complicated and time-consuming to develop specific solutions for spaces like the Kunsthaus. So in spite of its iconic marketability, in a certain way the Kunsthaus Graz is immune to developments in the art market. Was that the original intention of the architects?

BS That was probably not their intention, because this situation didn't exist back then. Cook and Fournier dreamt of curators creating specific situations again and again. But time has caught up with our architects, because they couldn't know what type of exhibition business we would have today.

PvF It is the usage that makes the building specific – you state quite clearly, and I completely agree with you, that no matter how iconic the building is, as soon as it is there, as soon as it opens its doors, it is no longer the architecture alone that counts – you have to deal with people, with trams going past, with the postcard shop, with the ice cream parlour around the corner. Can you take all these things into account as an architect? Can you succeed in planning a museum building that works – even in the sense of how it is used for the next ten years?

SW That depends on how much you deal with the location as an architect, with the actual building site. For Cook and Fournier, Graz was not unknown territory. They were in touch with Günther Domenig, Volker Giencke, Klaus Kada, Michael Szyszkowitz and Karla Kowalski, and Fournier was teaching at the TU (TH at the time). But of course it is true that architectural planning can only anticipate social processes up to a certain point. Just thinking about how the urban space might be changed by a new museum building is a highly complex task.

→ reference 162)

Flexibility versus change?

BS I think that Cook and Fournier were actually pursuing the idea that the Kunsthaus building could be appropriated again and again. They didn't intend for too much to be defined in advance – that is why it consists of platforms rather than small spaces. This is very much in keeping with the thinking of the 1970s. You find it at the Centre Pompidou, too. In many ways, Piano and Rogers had similar thoughts. They also thought in terms of platforms.

PvF. And networks that could be used in different ways.

BS You build potentialities. Architects don't anticipate a specific use, but they do anticipate many possible specific uses. They can't know what these specific settings will be, but they anticipate the potential in the sense that it could consist of multiple, very different possibilities. The *Bâtiment Public*, planned by Cook and Fournier in the 1970s in Monte Carlo, is an important example of this way of thinking. In principle, what they had in mind was a popular cultural centre with a theatre, a circus, art

→ reference 031)

2006

Kunst
Haus
Space02

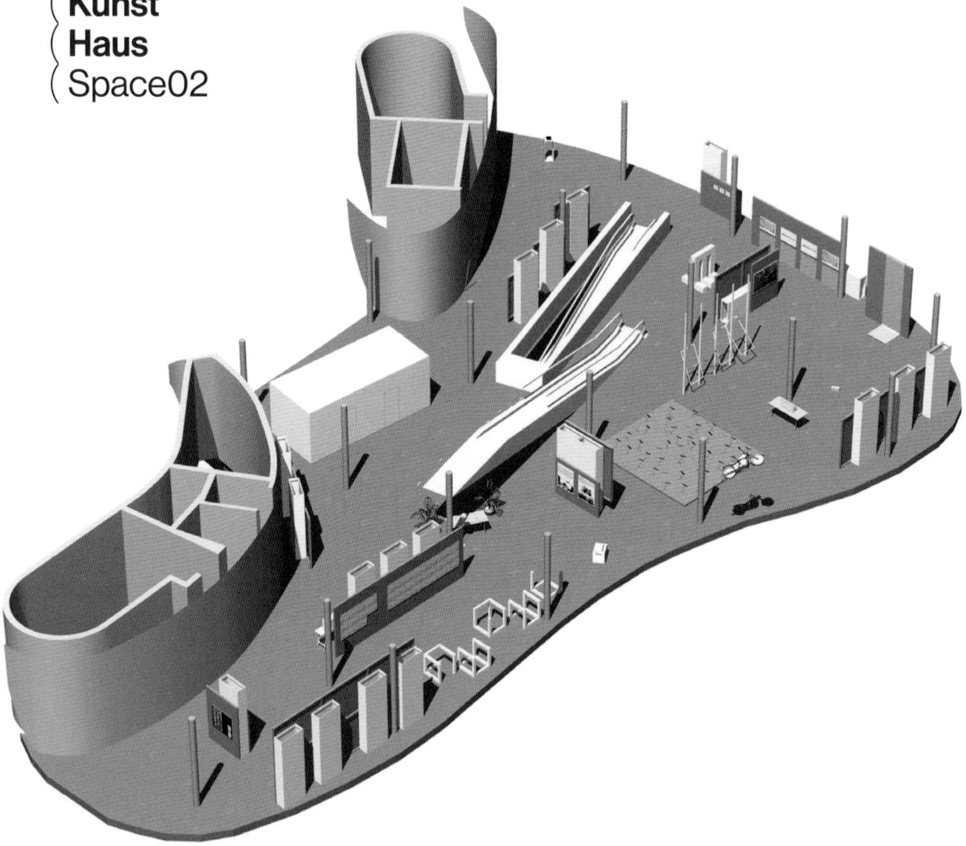

Annick und Anton Herbert's collection is focused on Minimal Art, Concept Art and Arte Povera and pursues a concept that calls for a special form of exhibition architecture. In collaboration with Niels Jonkhans, artist Heimo Zobernig created an unconventional presentation, which highlighted the character of the Kunsthaus as a temporary laboratory. The design concept stipulated the use of existing moveable wall panels from the inventory of the Kunsthaus and rearranged them in new ways. These 'recycled' walls were paired with supporting sheets of laminated fibre, unfinished and installed in standard sizes. These building blocks were the base for the spatial installation of art works in the exhibition spaces. The contrast between space, material and surface created tension as the installations harmonised with the Kunsthaus in some locations and clashed with it in others.

Inventory. Works from the Herbert Collection

exhibitions, classical concerts, a go-kart track – all these things potentially in one place, in a constantly changing space. A fantastic idea! Unfortunately the question of economics immediately arises – all this continual rethinking and rebuilding is rather expensive – and ultimately also unecological.

PvF What you are saying could be a possible definition of museum architecture – thinking in potentialities or latencies. When I begin a design as an architect, it is always utopian, because I am thinking in terms of a future that is not foreseeable. That is even the case if I am planning a detached house for a family – I don't know whether the family will have children, whether the parents will get divorced, or whether someone will die.

SW Basically, a design is always a hypothesis that is put forward, and it cannot be verified until the building is finished and in use. → design 081) Function and use are not the same thing. Functions are always specified in spatial programmes, defined in the number of square metres and room sizes. Use is what begins when the building is finished and people move into it. Function is related to the typology of the building, whereas use is concerned with how it is actually used, you could also say it is what happens in everyday life. Function specifies the *what*, and use the *how*. → usage 109)

PvF When I build a museum, the functions that I have – the use is not so important at this stage – are fairly open in many areas. I have to be able to exhibit, so I need climate control, but how I exhibit inside is not defined at all. And that brings us back to current art discourse, which can be extremely heated in this area. We don't know what kind of art will be produced in the next five years, or what kind of buildings we will need to accommodate it.

BS We need spaces with as many sources of potential as possible.

PvF A large number of contemporary art museums have old structures, they were not built for their current usage. We are not only talking about exhibition rooms but also (semi-) public rooms, lecture rooms, catering, shops. These areas have to function → design 040) today. It is a tableau that I have to build as an architect, even though I cannot be sure whether it will work, or how. I have no idea how it will be used later. Even if the founding director sits in the committee of the architectural competition and says: this is my understanding of art, and this will be my collection. Five years later, the management will change, and the rooms will be used in a new way. You also inherited this house and made something new out of it.

BS Actually all I did was to clear it out. In the course of time the **ground floor** had become more and more cluttered, so I emptied it and tidied it up – but sure, in a way that meant it had to be restructured. → foyer 186) The topic of spatial structures has accompanied me for a long time. When I was the director of the GfZK (Museum of Contemporary Art) in Leipzig, I worked with *as-if berlinwien architects* to create a building that provided a possible answer to the spirit of flexibility from the 1960s and 1970s. We said: the building is not flexible, but changeable. Flexible was what the 1970s wanted to be. We asked ourselves how can something be changeable without us having to constantly rebuild it? Every time I visit the museum I am surprised by the curatorial and spatial settings that arise there. To this day.

2006

Kunst
Haus
Space02

Protections was the title of a performative exhibition about the discrepancy between a desire for a maximum degree of individualism anchored in our modern society and a need for protection at the same time. The artist duo Elmgreen & Dragset created the spatial structure for this interpretation. Their concept included two 'single-family homes' which, positioned on two exhibition levels, not only completely ignored the spatial conditions of the Kunsthaus, but even confronted the architectonically dominant space head-on with their insularity.

Protections. This is not an exhibition

SW In other conversations you have emphasised that the construction of the GfZK was equally concerned with consciously placed architectural limitations, i.e. with a regulated level of changeability.

BS Yes, the conception equally depends on limitations. *as-if berlinwien* addresses transparency, but at the same time opacity – you can sometimes see in or out, and sometimes not. The rooms are designed as flowing zones with upper and lower openings, more like spatial zones. So you can sometimes even see other visitors' feet. We were always concerned with the question: what can you see and how do you envision your position in the room. What you can't do there is to close a room off. Basically it is a relational architectural system. Most artists still love this building today. It doesn't suggest you can do anything you want. There are a lot of things you can't do, but it does offer you a great deal of possibilities. The building encourages you to explore them.

PvF People are always saying that the white cube is flexible. But it is actually the most inflexible exhibition space I know. It is simply a built ideology that I either have to follow or resist. This duality rules out a lot of possibilities.

SW The white cube strongly influences our perception, which most people hardly notice. There is little consideration of what this white cube is, how it works, how it defines use. It is not the architecture that is in the foreground, but the exhibits.

BS The fact that the focus is on the artworks is the main argument put forward by advocates of the white cube. I consider this to be a mistake. You naturalise the type of room as though it had always been there. But it is an extremely ideological construct, as Pablo says. Many people forget this. Of course it influences our perception and conception of art, as well as our encounters with art. It makes a difference whether you immerse yourself in the contemplation of a work of art, or a picture literally shoots towards you, like a Frederick Kiesler. Or whether you can pull the images to eye level like you could at Peggy Guggenheim's The Art of this Century Gallery in New York or in El Lissitzky's Abstract Cabinet in Hanover. It's a completely different approach to art.

→ Space01 091)

PvF Is the difference between changeability and flexibility of a temporal nature, then? Do you just change the rooms around for a certain period of time and then do something else afterwards? Flexibility is intended for a shorter period of time. Here you have to be able to do anything all the time.

BS Potentiality is built into the structure of *as-if berlinwien's* building. It even applies to the building technology, which can be turned on and off as required. Generally the building is climate friendly and ecologically planned and built. It relies on natural climate systems and materials. It is divided into various climate zones. There is a core zone where the best climate conditions can be created if necessary, for certain loans for example. The outer zones have windows from floor to ceiling, so nature literally floods into the interior, creating light and shade on the walls. Usually this would be distracting, but in this building it is intentional. The artists work with it.

PvF Does this mean that, if I want to plan changeability, I have to consider use? And if I want flexibility, I have to consider function?

usage
→ 104)

'During my work at the Kunsthaus, my full attention is focused on the floor. There are electrical cables and sockets in every floor outlet, which helps me a lot in my work. The Kunsthaus is a beautiful building, it is an honour to work here.'

Aziz Tadrous, cleaning services

SW You mean whether changeability becomes clear through use and flexibility through functions? In my opinion, functions are less flexible, because they have to be predefined more than uses. Usage happens as soon as a building is 'in use'. But functions come beforehand, they are inscribed into the building before use begins. Changeability is revealed more through use than through function. In the sense that you can inscribe a certain changeability into functions. Flexibility can only arise from usage, it comes when the building is in use. Maybe function, and therefore flexibility, is something that is predetermined, while use and changeability are something that is 'lived', something that develops over time. Perhaps the term potentiality combines the two – the part that can be planned, and the part that arises from it. The designers and the planners can influence the flexibility of the functions, but the users shape the changeability of the usage.

The public museum

BS The most important question for me is this – what constitutes a public institution, what does it show, for what reasons, and for whom? I expect a museum to work on making corrections. At least it should break through the mainstream. And I expect it to take a different stance to private initiatives, private collections. A museum should not be a subcontractor for private collectors, but enter into a constructive dialogue concerning where the strengths of the public museum lie and what private individuals can achieve. That also means making a commitment to public discourse.

PvF Which finally leads us back to architecture, i.e. to the public mission of the museum. Does the art museum fulfil this mission? What role does the art market play? I am convinced that one of the most important aspects of building a museum is to fulfil the needs of the public, which ultimately finances it. That is what makes the building task so complicated. If you build a museum, you have to take the public into account.

BS Yes, but which public? The problem is that the public has become extremely multifaceted.

SW This idea of the public goes back to the developmental history of the civic museum. In those days, the public sphere was certainly considered to be far more homogeneous. The royal, stately context opened up, first for researchers, then for a certain public.

BS Today we are in a far more complex situation, there are several publics to address on various levels.

PvF As an architect, it is important to be able to answer the exact question you just asked – with the help of the museum team, and in some cases even with the help of external experts and specialised museum consultants. This means the museum always becomes a utopian project, because you can never know how concepts of the public sphere will develop in the future. However, the building has to be planned for this future and these concepts of the public sphere. And it is usually left exactly as it is for several decades, or even centuries.

Kunst Haus Space02

Space01
→129)

Peter Kogler has been working since the 1980s as a media artist between computer graphics, film, collage and architecture. For his exhibition he used the Kunsthaus as the stage for a large-scale production: his computer-generated projections transformed **Space01** into a limitless, pulsing cosmos, while moving images with an impressive mechanical orchestra at the centre created a feeling of constant motion one level below, in **Space02**. Kogler integrated three of Frederick Kiesler's cantilevers developed for the gallery **The Art of This Century** (1942), and which held images.

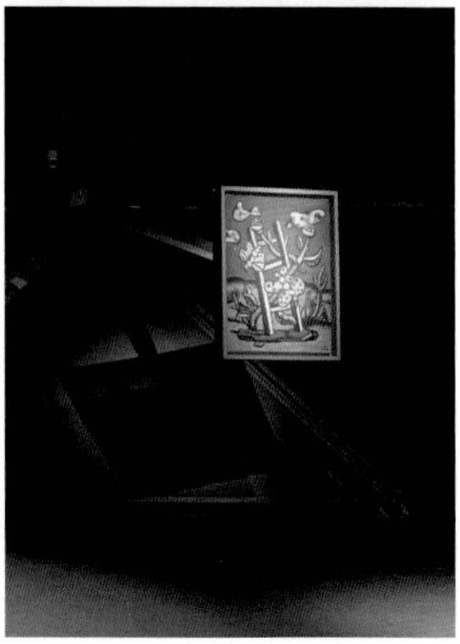

Connected. Peter Kogler with ...

SW I think that architectural planning is primarily about incorporating the present day. Having a feeling for the present day and its cultural forms of expression through music, art, fashion and literature. Jacques Herzog said as much in a conversation with Jeffrey Kipnis (in the El croquis edition on Herzog & de Meuron): Creating architecture has something to do with being integrated in the present day. This doesn't mean that the past doesn't play a role, or that current planning will not be valid in the future. We are concerned with layers (of time or influences) that are superimposed.

BS You sketch, design something that you cannot yet place in a precise location.

PvF Exactly. And with that we are back to the idea of the potentialities and latencies of museum architecture. Here we are concerned not so much with flexibility as with changeability. As an architect, how can I succeed in planning something which – in the case of a museum we are usually talking about five or ten years – will retain its validity from the first sketch, the first competition and the time when it opens in around ten years? In reality I have to plan for the next twenty years at least, so that the building will work for a future generation, even if I have no idea what this generation will be like. How can I succeed in providing a platform that can not only be used, but also represents a challenge and helps to form society or the public sphere.

BS Yes exactly – to form. Museums also generate publics. Even that is hardly possible today, because since the late 1980s, when museums became independent and began having to earn money, we have been working with certain 'target groups' in mind. That means fulfilling existing expectations to the maximum. No one speaks of art being challenging any more. But it has to be able to make unreasonable demands, at least in a measured way. Of course it's not about alienating the visitors.

PvF Would you say the museum is per se a place that dissolves the barriers of time and space? I'm referring to the heterotopic character of the museum that superimposes various times, thus making the boundaries to the future porous.

BS Shouldn't we be thinking in terms of simultaneity instead? Dissolving time and space – yes. Dissolving past, present, future – yes. But at the same time we are always directly in the middle of the present, in a specific time period.

PvF ... to enable any kind of critical discourse.
When we go to a museum, we can at best hope to deal with what our society was two years ago, or two hundred, or two thousand years ago. But because we can do that, we can begin to consider what it means to think in terms of the future of a public sphere or a society.

BS Yes, and at the same time we can ask ourselves: where do we stand now?

PvF But that only works because there is fixed architecture. If we hold an exhibition in someone's private house, the aspect of time and space is less significant than if it is shown in fixed architecture that will probably still be there for the next twenty years. The museum can offer transformative experiences. Through these transformative experiences we can encourage people to think about the public sphere they are in. That is what makes the task of building museums so special.

2005/06

Kunst
Haus
Space02

Space01
→ 119)

M City. European Cityscapes

SW The time/space aspect of the museum relies on the presence of people and social groups. It doesn't work without visitors. In a museum, I am in the present, in the here and now, but I am exposed to a past that is shown to me – also through the presence of other visitors. And through my position in the museum, in a certain place at a certain time, I have a place within the society that is shaped or depicted by the museum.

PvF Should the white cube also be seen as something that distinguishes itself from other types of museum? Is it there to create further boundaries in the discipline of modern and contemporary art? To prevent anything else from entering this kind of museum? The laboratory character of the white cube would then be not only aseptic, but also cleansing in a preventive sense. If this were the case, we might have to consider it as emancipated from the history of museum building, which is based on universalist approaches. In the early stages of museum architecture, the aim was not to provide optimal light for art or optimal climatic conditions, but to open up spaces to an undefined or increasingly undefined audience. The white cube creates distance on several levels – in terms of content, architecturally and socially.

BS That is an interesting theory. But before the white exhibition space asserted itself in the course of the 20th century, art museums had already been through a history featuring a reduction in artefacts and a change in how they were presented. In my opinion, the break occurred towards the end of the era of the encyclopaedic museum, in the last third of the 19th century. The focus of the civic art museum was on aesthetics. In fact various different types of space existed side by side, all of equal standing, until well into the second half of the 20th century. It is just that any alternatives to the white exhibition space have more or less disappeared today.

PvF When I look at contemporary museum architecture, it seems that the default button of museum architecture is the white cube. It doesn't even seem to matter whether you are building a contemporary art museum or a history museum – if in doubt, it will be a rectangular room with white paint on the walls. That is why, right at the beginning of the planning process, it is so important to involve people with expertise in both museums and architecture. These people are not always the curators.

BS I would say that the majority of clients rely on the white cube. During a discussion at the Hamburger Bahnhof in Berlin, I once asked Ascan Morgenthaler from Herzog & de Meuron why they show so little ambition when it comes to developing alternatives for the interiors of the museum buildings they design. The answer was: because that is what the clients want. The white exhibition space is simply what is expected in the context of art.

SW They think it might provide greater flexibility. But in fact the white cube is even more of a restriction, it dictates far more than you think. For example – through its uniformity it has a global recognisability, and because of its orthogonality it only allows for certain curatorial possibilities. Presumably most people might think of a building like the Kunsthaus as being much more restrictive, with far more limitations. But that's not my impression. Here the exhibition architecture has to be considered to a larger degree, it is more of an issue. Whereas the mechanisms of the white exhibition space are invisible. → Space02 093)

Graz Architecture is the perfect example for the use of Kunsthaus space with a large number of two-dimensional and sometimes very small exhibits without the help of free-standing walls in **Space02**. Developed by Rainer Stadlbauer and Anna Lena von Helldorff, the starting-point for this display system was the orthogonal grid of ceiling anchors originally placed by architects Cook and Fournier. Seemingly hovering in mid-air, the horizontal and vertical aluminium and perforated tin modules were suspended from these anchors. They served as a spatial and visual separation between the various objects on display, although the perforated tin did create visual connections along contextual lines. Large, colourful acrylic glass panels facilitated navigation of the space. These displayed biographical details as well as information on the objects themselves.

Graz Architecture. Rationalists, Aesthetes, Gut Instinct Architects, Democrats, Mediacrats

PvF That takes us back to the space of potentialities. You have to build a space that is challenging. But what does potentiality mean, what does challenging mean in this context? There is no general guiding theory for museum building. At least not anymore. It was a theme that was repeatedly addressed in the 18th and 19th centuries, or even in the 20th century.

BS There have also been many museum reform movements, which have influenced not only the theory but also the practice of building. Not to mention artists, who have greatly challenged the ideas of the museum and exhibiting in general, and formulated it in a new way. Of course you could now come to the conclusion that the museum is no longer being newly formulated today. Neither the architecture, nor the museum and its contents.

PvF In terms of both theory and built space, 'The Delirious Museum' by Calum Storrie occurs to me when I think of an ideal or utopian museum. It dissolves boundaries and says – actually, everything is a museum. All you have to do is go through a city, for example, and pay as much attention to your surroundings as you would to the walls of a museum. This experience could be seen as the ideal museum.

BS However, in the case of the city your example also shows us that ideality, however it is conceived, crumbles in the face of reality. And that also applies to the museum and museum architecture.

PvF You would have to succeed in newly formulating the institution of the museum and the practice of exhibiting. Why do these utopian museums no longer exist?

BS The ideal museum is free of context and time. Basically just like the white exhibition room. That's the problem I have with it. No account is taken of the constraints and conditions you have to work with. Otherwise you wouldn't be able to think in terms of ideality. I am interested in the precise circumstances under which I can work, along with the artists and the curators, and I want to work with them, making them the subject of my work and integrating them into the programme.

PvF Sophia sent me your essay 'Mögliche Museen' (Possible Museums) in preparation for today. And I am slowly beginning to understand why you use this description. You don't mean utopian museums, possible museums of the future, but possibility-museums. And that is intriguing – what is actually possible WITH museums? It is a pragmatic perspective, or to use the words of Ernst Bloch – a concrete utopia.

SW You could also say that the ideal museum is related to utopia. And this utopia is not characterised by the fact that it can be implemented exactly, but that it makes us want to improve things, to identify problems perhaps. Utopias contain concepts of the ideal that make us think in terms of possibilities. You also wrote this: possible museums are conceivable museums.

PvF And this means: I can think in terms of museums. Or I can think with them. Working on the institution itself, however, is something I can only do IN the institution. This is where architecture comes into play again. In order to look at the conditions involved in the production and reception of art, and to observe the institution, I need a building that has been built solely for the purpose of showing art. It must be built in a way that allows discourses to take place there, discourses that change and are changeable. That is what makes museum architecture so wonderful and so complex – it has to build potentialities.

2019

Kunst
Haus
Space02

Space01 → 137)

This exhibition explored the relationship between the arts and traditional crafts from the perspective of contemporary art, placing both within a larger societal context. The meaning and value of craftsmanship as an essential part of material culture, cultural identity and sense of community was linked with the social and economic realities and production processes in a globalised world. Eight artistic positions, of which several works and workgroups were on display, unfolded as four solo exhibitions each with two specific displays on two floors. In this manner, the presentation became part of the artistic practices on show.

ARTS ↔ CRAFTS. Between Tradition, Discourse and Technologies.
Installation by Johannes Schweiger

This group exhibition presented the legendary founding years (1970–1980) of the California Institute of the Arts (CalArts), which includes many renowned artists among its alumni. Multiple perspectives on the school (for the first time, the show brought together the parallel trends from concept art, feminism and Fluxus, as well as the school's radical pedagogical concepts) were reinforced by the appearance of transience in the exhibition architecture. Free-standing wall segments that were partially covered with planks allowed views of the show's various sections and reinforced the connection between the various art practices.

Where Art Might Happen. The Early Years of CalArts

2020

Haus
Space02
usage

'After working in this building for 17 years, there are a few things that haunt me. Whenever you want to get into the equipment rooms, you first have to look for a mobile door opener on the exhibition level. Unfortunately, for architectural reasons, so that the curve would be a homogeneous wall, no door opener was fitted.'

Erik Ernst, facility management

Hollerer/Marte. ‘Do we need to have an accident?’

Sofie Thorsen also worked with the spatial conditions of **Space02** for her exhibition **Cut A-A'**. Thorsen is focused on culturally influenced forms and their political, social and historical context. Her ability to create different perspectives on architectural forms through her artistic work was obvious in the exhibition design. Photographs of playgrounds that caught the artist's eye with their sculptural qualities and modernistic architecture were suspended from the ceiling and through cut-outs creating visual corridors that allowed glimpses of colourful poles mounted horizontally between ceiling and floor. Suspended projection surfaces and a concrete slab that seemed to hover above the ground, serving as a painting base, opened up the possibility of new associations with the space.

Sofie Thorsen. Cut A-A'

The Paradise the Downfall. Hartmut Skerbisch – Media Works

Curator Günther Holler-Schuster approached the formal language of graphic designer and artist Karl Neubacher, one of the pioneers of avantgarde and concept art in Graz during the 1970s, with an artful exhibition design. Various architectural elements such as hanging surfaces reminiscent of poster walls, suspended between floor and ceiling, created tension between formal playfulness and conceptual precision.

Karl Neubacher. Media Artist, 1926–1978

James Benning. Decoding Fear

2010

Kunst
Haus
Space02

Artist Tatiana Trouvé's exhibition morphed into a psychological experience of the Kunsthaus space. With walls that connected to the existing architecture, with windows and metal mesh, Trouvé created – inspired by the post-apocalyptic landscapes of Dino Buzzati's science fiction novel *Il Grande Ritratto* – a form of 'anti-space,' a space, so to speak, in which the borders between inside and out became blurred. Trouvé included the columns which dominate **Space02** in her concept for the space by adding additional columns and thereby disrupting the strict architectural grid.

Tatiana Trouvé. Il Grande Ritratto

↗ p. 53
↗ p. 93

Frederick Kiesler, Raumstadt (City in Space),
Exposition internationale des Arts Décoratifs et Industriels Modernes,
Paris 1925 (coloured glass slide)

2020

Kunst
Haus
Space02

Space01 → 133)
Nozzle → 122)

The exhibition **TOMORROW** developed over two floors of the Kunsthaus. Although they might have appeared different at first glance, the forms of presentation addressed the singularity of the individual work, while at the same time placing it in relation to the other works and the architectural space.

In **Space02**, a multi-section yellow wall zigzagged its way through the room. This created dynamic combinations of the view and sequence of the works on show. Because the individual walls jumped back and forth, some pictures 'vanished' in and through movement, while new contiguities and perspectives constantly emerged.

In **Space01**, several huge, abstract canvases were mounted on ceiling-high metal supports, giving a structure to the space. Here too, new perspectives, images and spaces opened up unexpectedly as you moved through the show. From certain positions, each painting could be observed individually. However, the works also formed ensembles or were fragmented, depending on how you moved in the space.

Herbert Brandl. TOMORROW

'A well-designed floor is the basis for any good exhibition. Its organisation and use allow us artists to tell stories, to create conceptual links between the works on show, and to steer visitors through the exhibition.'

Azra Akšamija, artist

1997

(**reference**
(design

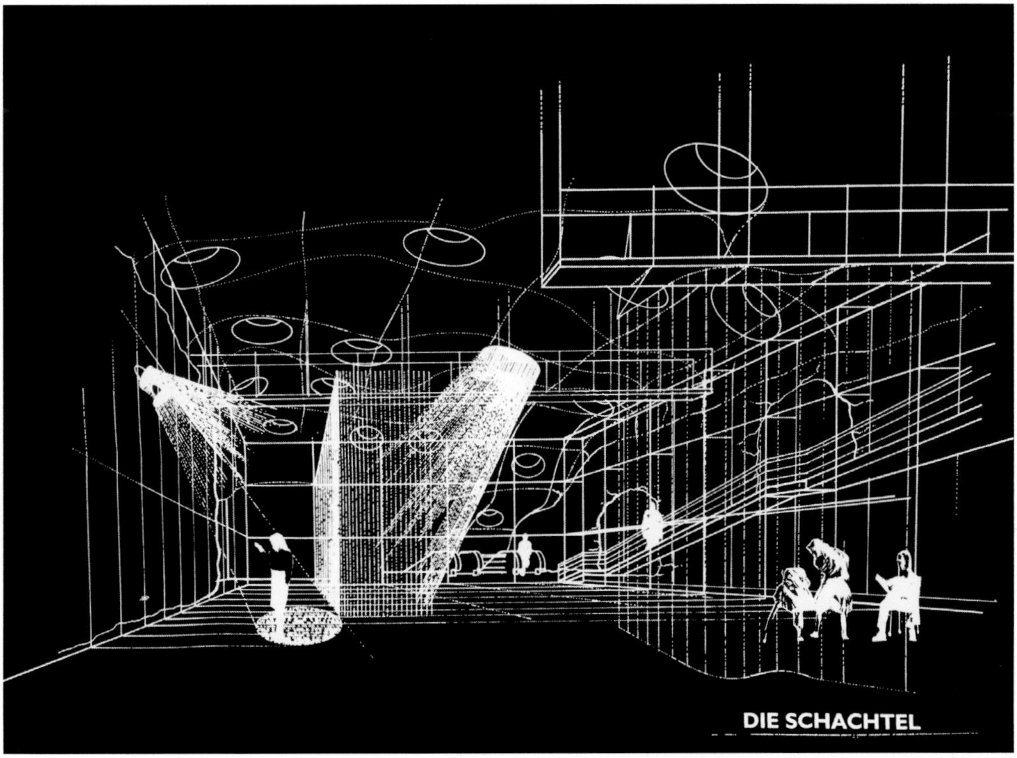

reference
→ 077)
↗ p.45

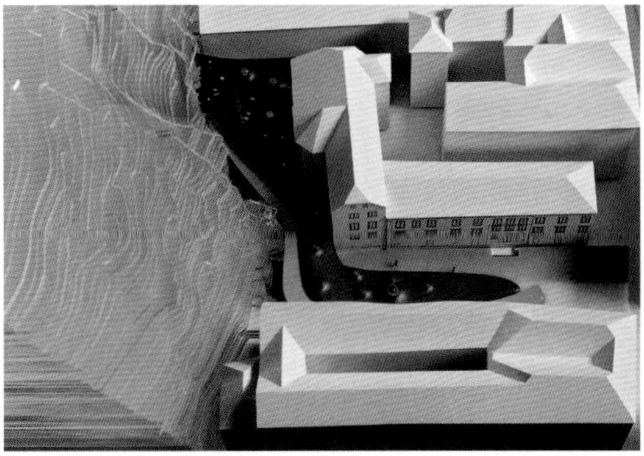

The Tongue (top) design drawing,
(bottom) photo of model, Peter Cook, Colin Fournier

Up into the Unknown
→ 005)
→ 030)
→ 037)
design
→ 081)
reference
→ 029)
↗ p. 293

Up into the Unknown – the title is also a quote by Peter Cook – focused on the architecture and the building process itself. It was designed by Niels Jonkhans, who was a partner of Cook and Fournier, and has always acted as a consulting, and to some degree executing architect for exhibition displays and changes to the building. Together with Anna Lena von Helldorff, he developed a system of table displays and text plaques with a colour scheme that defined specific project phases. Colourful strings that connected various areas across the room revealed thought processes and created contextual associations outside of chronological lines.

Up into the Unknown. Peter Cook, Colin Fournier and the Kunsthaus Graz

2004

Kunst
Haus
Space01

usage
→ 109)
Space01
→ 116)

The first major foray into the reflection on the amorphic structure of the Kunsthaus was undertaken by one of the leading advocates of Minimal Art, the concept artist Sol LeWitt (1928–2007) with his project **Wall**. Using over 140 tons of lightweight concrete blocks, the artist shaped a structure that wended its way in a free form through **Space01**, reacting to the organic 'dome' of the Kunsthaus. Although Sol LeWitt considered the possibility of an open-air presentation once the exhibition had ended, thus emphasising the autonomy of the three-dimensional sculpture, the artist did essentially embody the architectural conditions of the exhibition space in creating this piece.

Sol LeWitt. Wall

2020

Haus
Space01
usage

Space01
→ 108)
usage
→ 090)
→ 105)

'On the floor of **Space01** there is a clearly visible trace left by Sol LeWitt's **Wall**, from the second ever exhibition. Such traces inscribe particular events or even just everyday use into the building – a bit like the marks measuring a child's height in the playroom doorway at home.'

Katia Huemer, curator

2010

Kunst
Haus
Space01
usage

design
→ 081)
usage
→ 079)

'Heads are what appear first. The visitor's head. How do visitors navigate the space after they get off the **Travelator**, when they arrive in **Space01**? Curious, questioning looks, working out which direction to take. Then comes the decision. The visitor turns around. This is followed by a look that takes in the exhibition space looming before them.'

Gabriel Johannes Zisler Kratochwil Bianchi, visitor service

2012

Kunst
Haus
Space01

Space01
→108)

In 2012, sculptor Michael Kienzer's solo exhibition demonstrated that **Space01** seemingly encourages sweeping sculptural gestures.
'In my opinion, it is difficult to stage an exhibition here which does not react to the space in any way. [...] It is a unique space which almost demands an answer that would probably not have arisen elsewhere,' said the artist in a conversation with curator Katrin Bucher Trantow for the exhibition catalogue. Industrial pipes were welded together and wove their way through the room in random formations, like a three-dimensional drawing.

'With one dimension more than LeWitt, basically in 3D,' (Katrin Bucher Trantow) Kienzer measured the room with a sculpture (*Sich*, 2012) that used as many dimensions as the space allowed.

Michael Kienzer. Logic and Self-Will

In her solo exhibition, painter Antje Majewski created a small universe of various viewpoints and cultural narratives through the use of seven different objects and by incorporating the works of numerous other artists connected with her. Didier Faustino translated this concept into spectacular exhibition architecture. A spatial structure grew like a flower in the heart of the biomorphic structure of **Space01**. Walking through the rooms, one ambled through the maze of **The World of Gimel**, entrenched and interwoven like the narratives which grew from the central objects.

Antje Majewski. The World of Gimel. How to Make Objects Talk

Rock – Paper – Scissors. Pop-Music as Subject of Visual Art.
Installation by Mike Kelley

Kunst
Haus
Space01

For the group exhibition **Chikaku**, which examined the contemporary art world in Japan, architect Makoto Sei Watanabe developed an elaborate spatial concept, which aptly traced the numerous labyrinthine paths of artistic expression. A screen-like fabric band that assumed the shape of the room wended its way through **Space01** and opened up new spaces, blocking certain views while creating new fields of vision elsewhere.

Chikaku. Time and Memory in Japan

2003/04

Kunst
Haus
Space01

For the very first exhibition at the newly opened Kunsthaus, Niels Jonkhans developed a system of moveable walls which provided surfaces where two-dimensional art could be hung. These free-standing walls with rounded edges could be positioned anywhere in the room and were adjustable lengthwise. They were also used for numerous future exhibitions.

Einbildung. The Perception in Art

2017

Kunst
Haus
Space01

Space01
→108)

'The exhibition space at the Kunsthaus is not necessarily easy to work with, because, when you put sculptures in it, the room does not give you coordinates. (...) It is (...) hard to define and find the beginning and the end of the room. So I tried to add something to it that dominates through light on the one hand, and form on the other, to create a kind of counterpoint.' This is how the work *Weltraumschwitzer*, a monstrously big sweater for **Space01** of about 40 metres in length and 4 metres in height, became a cosy piece of clothing for the personified exhibition space.

In reference to Sol LeWitt's *Wall*, Wurm highlighted a previous exhibition by disassembling LeWitt's work into its individual elements and with great satirical force created a fusion of artwork, sweater and partition.

Erwin Wurm. Football-sized lump of clay on light blue car roof

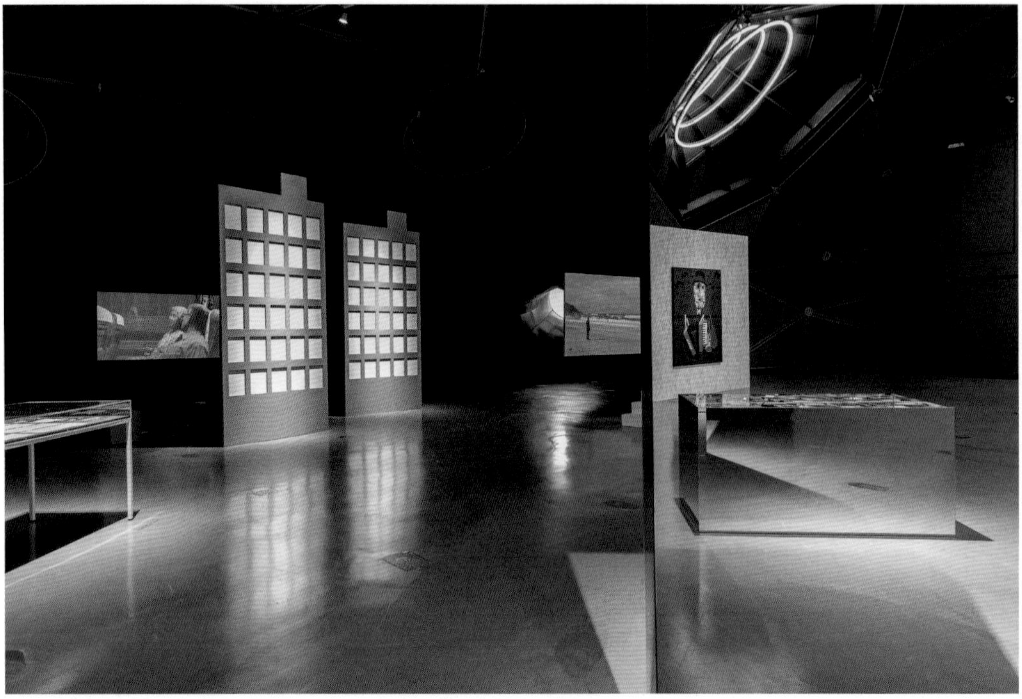

Kunsthaus
→ 019)
Space01
→ 138)

The exhibition **Jun Yang. The Artist, the Work and the Exhibition** challenged assumptions about the artist as subject, the work, and solo exhibitions. The solo exhibition was transformed into a group exhibition, the identity of the artist was doubled (by extending the invitation to another artist named Jun Yang) and even the concept of the 'work' underwent a metamorphosis in the exhibition: Paintings, photographs, drawings, poster, film – the usually clearly identifiable and clearly distinguishable medium – became more and more facetted and dispersed along the two levels of exhibition space.

While at the beginning of the exhibition, art was displayed in classic style on a white background, the distinction between artwork and support slowly dissolved – wall and pedestal themselves became art – while the genre boundaries between art, design and architecture (graphics, exhibition display) were eroded. Finally, one reached an area in **Space01** that bordered on the surreal, combining mirrors, real and artificial shadows, as well as natural and artificial light.

Jun Yang. The Artist, the Work, and the Exhibition

Needle
→146)

China Welcomes You ... Desires, Struggles, New Identities.
Installation by Ai Weiwei

2005/06

Kunst
Haus
Space01

Space02 → 092)

For **M City**, a group exhibition on the development of urban spaces, and specifically the modern, mid-sized European city (such as Graz), the exhibition design was based on the conviction that architects and town planners were not alone in exploring transformation processes or working out new restructuring strategies. Above all it was artists, photographers and videographers who immediately became conscious of changes and focused their work on these developments.

Architekturbüro ReD (Marta Malé-Alemany / Jose Pedro Sousa) took up the **Nozzles** and visually turned them inside out. Each of these funnel-shaped lots housed six commissioned works in video format and provided the necessary darkness for the screening of these city portraits in the otherwise open **Space01**.

M City. European Cityscapes

2002

Nozzle
model

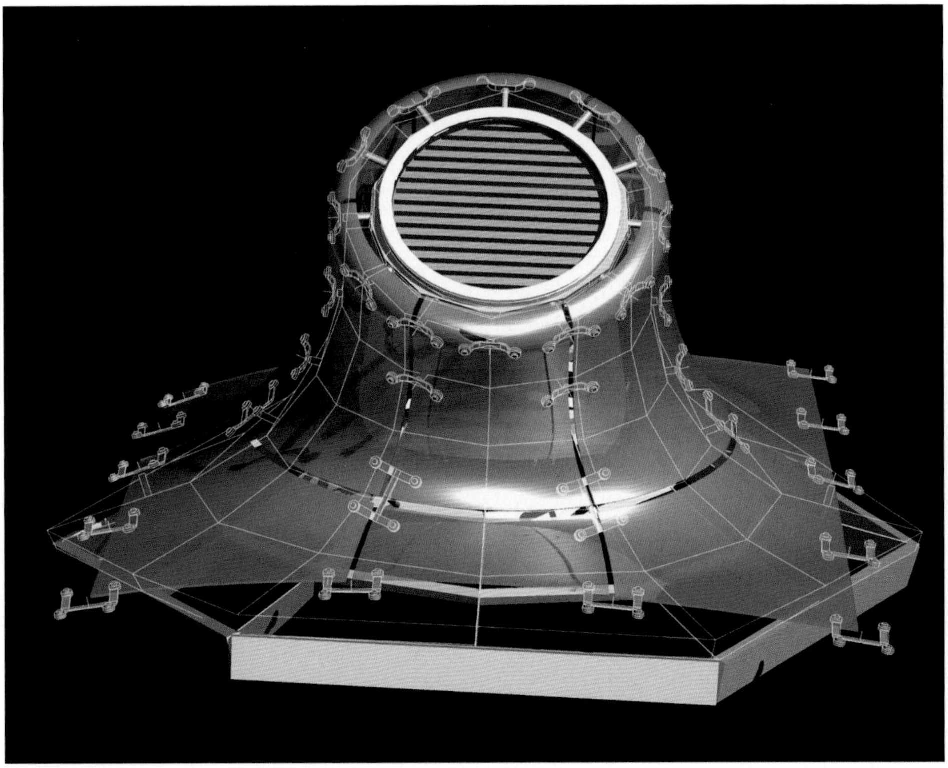

↗ p. 45
↗ p. 47
↗ p. 49
↗ p. 75
↗ p. 237

3D detail of a **Nozzle**. Computer drawing from the implementation plan, Gernot Stangl

2010

Kunst
Haus
Space01

BLESS N°41. Retroperspective Home

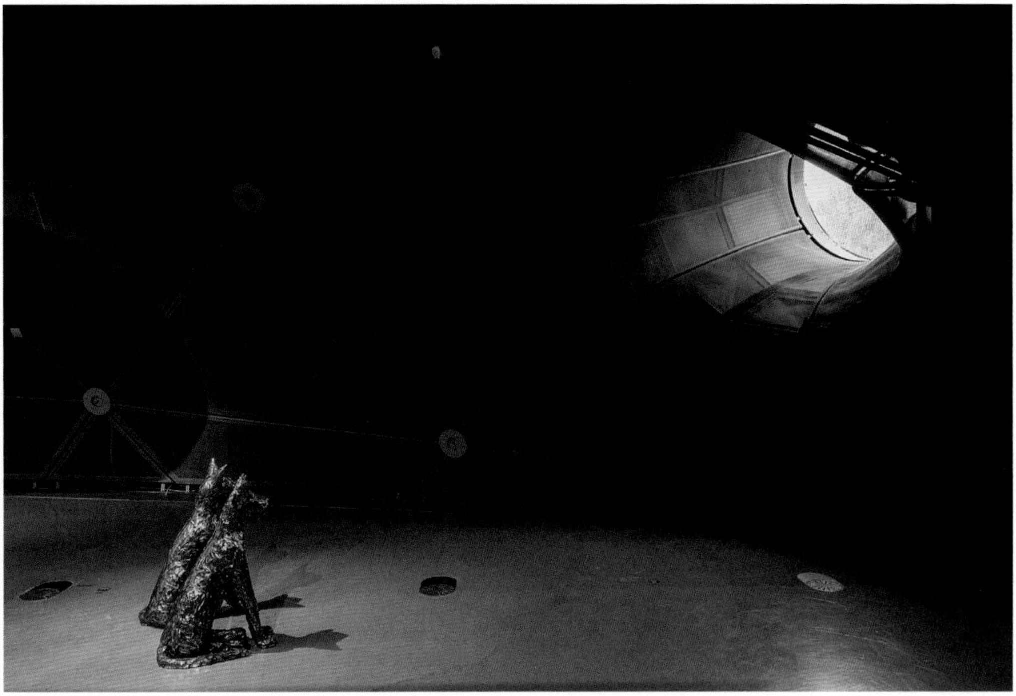

Space02
→104
Space01
→133

Herbert Brandl. TOMORROW

2020

(**Haus**
(Space01
(usage

reference
→122)

'Looking out through the **Nozzle** the visitor has an extraordinary view of the Graz Schloßberg, which creates a subtle dialogue between the modern Kunsthaus and the historic clock tower, the city's landmark. This architectural ingenuity highlights the wealth of cultural diversity to be found in our Styrian capital, where modern and historical ambiences merge in a wonderful way.'

Christopher Drexler, Minister for culture, Europe, sports and human resources, Government of Styria

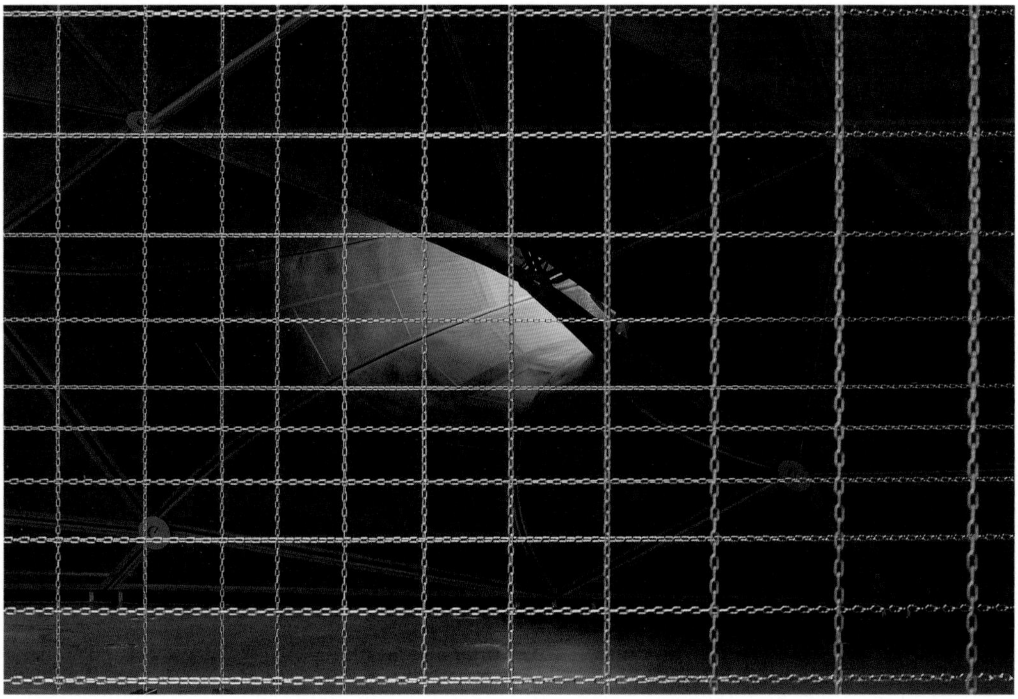

Two or Three or Something. Maria Lassnig, Liz Larner

2013

Kunst
Haus
Space01

In her solo exhibition **In the Flesh**, sculptor Berlinde De Bruyckere used fragmented bodies to trigger physical emotions, which were further intensified by a monumental architectural addition: A huge screen-like wall produced a feeling of tightness, even in **Space01**, which is over 8 metres high. In this way, De Bruyckere transformed the room into a kind of tomb in which hermaphrodite forms recalled the finiteness of ones own existence.

Berlinde De Bruyckere. In the Flesh

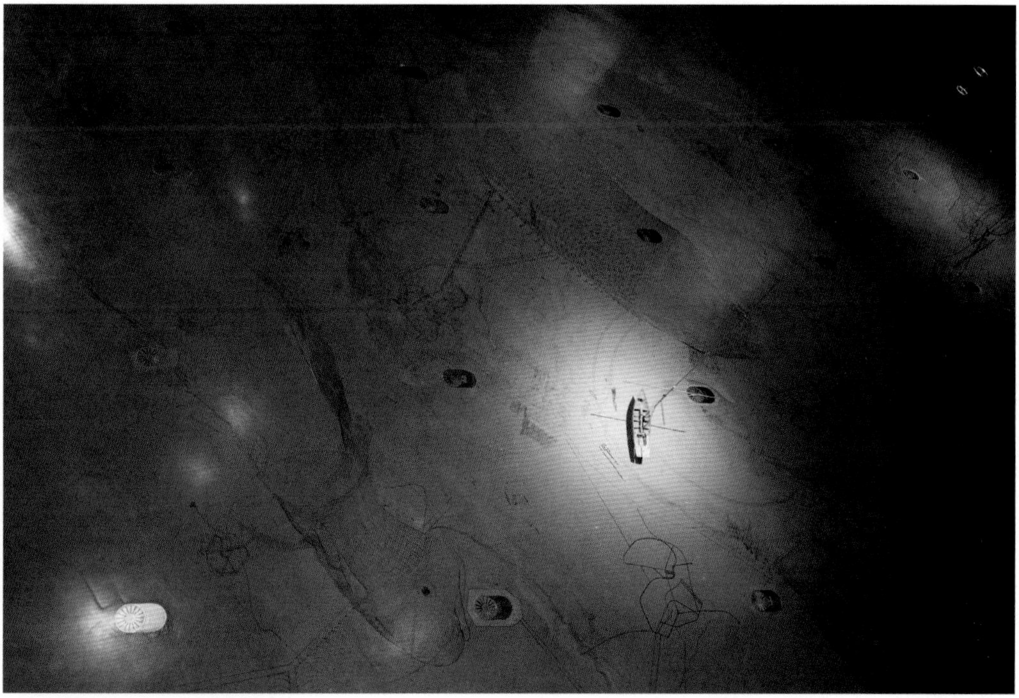

Constantin Luser's solo exhibition in **Space01** was a drawn, three-dimensional system of thoughts and ideas with a playful and interactive character. In his wall-to-wall floor drawing, Luser merged his delicate yet impactful stroke with the existing architecture. With Edding pens – often several at once – the artist created a subjective cartography which combined motifs from a natural or surreal world with a network of relationships, information and thoughts.

Constantin Luser. Music Tames the Beast

Diana Thater tested the media suitability of **Space01** with **gorillagorillagorilla**, a study of human and animal behaviour. The installation consisted of four video projectors, nine video-wall monitors, five DVD players and Lee filters and functioned like a visual machine. The existing architecture was integrated, with the upper level as the stage for Thater's work.

Diana Thater. gorillagorillagorilla

BIX
→ 028)

For Bill Fontana's solo exhibition **Primal Energies** in **Space01**, a live installation was created specifically for the site, exploring the acoustic and visual aesthetics of renewable energies. In the form of a large sound sculpture, the sound artist created an ever-changing installation which immersed visitors in the acoustic and visual structures of water, geothermal, solar, and wind energies.

Bill Fontana. Primal Energies

2019

Kunst
Haus
Space01

Space02
→091)
BIX
→207)
usage
→180)

Connected. Peter Kogler with ...

Kunst Haus Space01

Painter Katharina Grosse's poetic installation transformed the space into a three-dimensional painting. In her exhibition **'Who, I? Whom, You?'**, the artist moulded a bunched and wavy paint base made of soft foam to the organic form of the exhibition space. The material folded in soft waves into the architecture of **Space01**.

Grosse had sprayed this foundation with vibrant colours in a dynamic painting process, creating an abstract artistic landscape of flowing bands of colour. Visitors could walk around the mountains of foam, but not walk on it (as originally planned) for safety reasons. Nevertheless, a feeling of moving amid an un-mounted canvas manifested itself through the tunnels, nooks and caves that resulted from the placement of the foam and its bases.

Katharina Grosse 'Who, I? Whom, You?'

Kunst Haus Space01

The artist Pedro Cabrita Reis, whose works include architecture, sculpture and painting, interpreted **Space01** as a landscape garden. 'The installation **True Gardens #6 (Graz)** marks another bold and radical attempt to conquer and at the same time tame the rebellious and subversive **Space01** at the Kunsthaus Graz,' wrote curator Adam Budak in the text accompanying the solo show.

The artwork consisted of 88 individual elements, each of which had a similar basic structure: a box-like construction made from Doka wood and three to four commercially available fluorescent tubes, which were covered with a large glass panel. Each box also contained one to two slightly smaller glass panels painted in various colours. In this way, and because of its strict horizontal orientation, the work resembled a collage of panel paintings. The positioning of these individual elements created a labyrinth of light and glass, which rested on wooden beams and spread over the open, curved surface of **Space01** following a certain order.

Pedro Cabrita Reis. True Gardens #6 (Graz)

design
→ 034)

'As a society we are constantly changing. At the Kunsthaus this change is reflected in its biomorphic forms, reminiscent of organic structures. These also open up further perspectives for me when I'm looking at works of art, allowing me to take a differentiated approach.'

Christine Benischke, visitor

Space02
→ 104)
Nozzle
→ 122)

Herbert Brandl. TOMORROW

The central idea for this exhibition stemmed from the book *Tram 83* by the writer Fiston Mwanza Mujila, who hails from Lubumbashi and lives in Graz. In it he describes an imaginary location based on the social realities of Congolese cities, but which could actually be located anywhere in the world. The exhibition, which was divided into six sections – 'bar,' 'street,' 'home,' 'spirituality,' and 'exploitation' –, reflected this by blurring the line between real and imaginary spaces.

The individual sections, structured as a narrative, were not strictly separated – rather, they connected and condensed at various intervals through various motifs and themes, much like the exhibition architecture. A timeline spanned two floors and established a structure through its position in the centre of the room, providing information on the most important historical events while also putting the exhibits into context. An almost overwhelming density was created through the accumulation of various materials and visual levels, emulating the density and tension of a large Congolese city.

Congo Stars

Corporate. Xu Zhen (Produced by MadeIn Company)

Romuald Hazoumè. Beninese Solidarity with Endangered Westerners

2019

Kunst
Haus
Space01

Space02
→ 094)

ARTS ↔ CRAFTS. Between Tradition, Discourse and Technologies

2019

Kunst
Haus
Space01

Kunsthaus
→ 019)
Space01
→ 117)

Jun Yang. The Artist, the Work and the Exhibition

Based on the work of Michelangelo Pistoletto, founder of the art laboratory 'Cittadellarte' in the Italian town of Biella, this exhibition embarked on an investigation into the conditions and aspirations of a model of participatory civic society. The exhibition display was designed according to appropriately democratic principles: In a collaborative process, the collective constructLab built a *KunstStadt*, a city of art, whose wooden architecture was the structural framework and base for projects created by participating artists, as well as event space. During the exhibition, visitors could take part in workshops or experience the KunstStadt as communal space by using existing urban functions such as the market hall or the cinema, by taking a walk in the city park or meeting others at the main square. The individual architectural elements (such as a wooden carousel, a functioning kitchen or a huge table) were in turn 'auctioned off' to local initiatives – the best concept for a project with participatory use would win the item.

Cittadellarte. Sharing Transformation

Haus
Space01
usage

"'At its highest point, **Space01** is 8.5 metres above the floor" is a phrase I have uttered countless times over the last 15 years. The Kunsthaus is a building like a Swiss army knife, a building that can do everything. An igloo, a building like a blank canvas.'

Christof Elpons, art education

Drawing by a pupil from BG/BRG Carneri, produced during the construction phase of the Kunsthaus

The friendly alien effect. Types of architectural usage

Sophia Walk

2015

Kunst
Haus
Graz
Needle
roof terrace

↗ p. 41
↗ p. 223

Sarah Bildstein. Der Bien

The friendly alien effect
Types of architectural usage

'"You only see what you already know and understand," Goethe once allegedly said, and we adopt this sentence and make it our own,'[1] observes the Austrian author Teresa Präauer in her long essay 'Tier werden.' When it comes to the medium of the metaphor, we also fall back on what we know. When a metaphor is used, a description is removed from its original context of meaning and applied to another situation. According to the Greek origin of the word, a metaphor (metaphorá [meta: above, phérein: to carry) is nothing more than a transference. And something we understand, i.e. something that has already undergone a cognitive process elsewhere, is more easily transferred. When speaking in metaphors, we rely on familiar descriptions that are transformed into images in another area. A process of visualisation takes place during this transference. Thus metaphors serve as attributions that are borrowed from another discipline. This technique plays a particularly significant role in the description of architecture.[2] Along with the drawing, the model and photography, language is an important tool used in the representation of architecture. In *The Flashing Weapons. The Power of Form*, the Austrian philosopher Robert Pfaller writes '[...] that the metaphor often has a productive function – it not only figuratively describes something that could just as easily have been named in a simpler way, but the transfer is used at the precise point where 'the actual word is missing'.'[3] Many buildings that evoke associations do so because of their iconic effect,[4] i.e. because their architecture has a certain visual quality: *The Pregnant Oyster* (Kongresshalle Berlin, Hugh Stubbins, 1957), *der Mäusebunker* (*Mouse Bunker*) (animal testing labs at the FU Berlin, Magdalena and Gerd Hänska, 1981), *the Big Pencil* (Messeturm Frankfurt am Main, Murphy/Jahn (Helmut Jahn), 1991), *The Gherkin* (high-rise office building in London, Norman Foster and Ken Shuttleworth, 2004), *The Bird's Nest* (National Stadium Peking, Herzog & de Meuron, 2008), *The Shard* (high-rise office and residential building in London, Renzo Piano, 2012) – to name just a few examples. 'When we use a metaphor, we bring two different ideas into a mutually active context. [...] There is a similarity between the actual word and the transferred one. [...] Words are a little like reflections, and refer directly to concrete things.'[5] Since it was completed, and even before, all kinds of reference images have been ascribed to the Kunsthaus Graz. The perception and description of the Kunsthaus are full of metaphors. Whether you are in Graz and approach the Kunsthaus in a physical sense, or see it in photographs – wherever you are, you can hardly avoid applying references in an attempt to understand and describe it. These concepts are borrowed primarily from the field of biology, and especially zoology. They range from the *dragon's skin*[6] to the *whale*[7], the *giant jellyfish*[8], the *cow's heart*[9], the *belly of a suckling sow*[10], the *hedgehog under the lawnmower*[11], the *pale blue skin with kangaroo pouches*[12], the *artful warthog* to the *Return of the proboscideans*[13]. Or it is metaphorical on multiple levels with *the imaginary octopus*[14], being transferred and then transferred back again. There is talk of the *anatomic model of a heart*[15] or – somewhat more domesticated and more architectural – the *pet with warts*[16]. It was even explicitly contended that Cook and

↗ p. 45
↗ p. 47
↗ p. 75

→ friendly alien 203)

→ friendly alien 152)

2017

Kunst
Haus
Needle

usage
→149)

Dizziness as the moment of losing stability and control, as well as a trigger and occasion for critical thinking and creativity, was the focus of a group exhibition that resulted from an artistic-curatorial research project by the artist duo Anderwald + Grond. For the project, the **Needle** was robbed of its usual function as viewing platform: The artist Ann Veronica Janssens filled the elongated room with dense artificial fog to create a feeling of complete disorientation.

Dizziness. Navigating the Unknown.
Installation by Ann Veronica Janssens

Fournier had *built an animal rather than a museum* in Graz.[17] The image of the *blue cloud*[18] is used, or the *air mattress*[19] and the *flowing paste*[20] that *streams out of the Biedermeier collage of the red brick roofs*[21]. 'It comes across, deliberately, as an improbable mixture of various species, an unclassifiable hybrid, a biomorphic presence that is both strange (it does not seek to make reference to any animal in particular but appears to be a creature to which evolution might have accidentally given birth, perhaps on another planet), and at the same time familiar in that it has the charm of a friendly mixed-breed stray dog, definitely highly questionable in terms of pedigree,'[22] remarked Colin Fournier on the animal metaphors that were circulating, some of them invented by the press and architecture critics, others by himself and Peter Cook as the design architects (spacelab) of the Kunsthaus, which opened its doors in 2003. Even in their project description, Cook and Fournier used metaphorical expressions to explain their design for the Kunsthaus: they described the main body of the structure as the **Bubble**, the **Pin** represents the connection between the levels via the travelator, **Nozzles** is the name given to the overhead light openings, the **Needle** is the glass bar that runs sideways above the second exhibition level parallel to the river Mur, and the façade that encloses the two exhibition levels is the **Skin**.

→ design 033)
→ Nozzle 120)
→ design 076)

In her essay *Skins in Architecture. On Sensitive Shells and Interfaces*, the cultural scientist Susanne Hauser writes that the term **Skin**[23] has experienced a new approach to the drawing of boundaries in material, formal and disciplinary terms. She states that a shift has been observed in the last two decades from the transparency and permanence of the skin in the modern age, towards translucency and changeability.[24] Building envelopes are now provided with characteristics that are or should be dynamic and appeal to other senses.[25]

As in the **Skin** of the Kunsthaus Graz, the description *skin* points towards a dissolution of the elements that constitute architecture, such as walls, floor, roof. Transitions dissolve. The **Skin** of the Kunsthaus is not only a structure that depicts all of this, but also one that covers everything. To describe it as a surface would be as misguided as seeing the human skin as a surface, as the skin fulfils far more functional tasks – as a human organ on the one hand, and as the shell of the building on the other. The metaphor of the skin expresses the physicality of architecture, along with the processes of change that characterise both the human and the architectural body.

Cook and Fournier originally intended the Kunsthaus **Skin** to be alive, mobile and active, with the ability to react to its surroundings. This mobility concept could only be realised in the form of the **BIX** façade.[26]

→ design 007) 171) 176)
→ BIX 208)

Familiar strangers

Metaphors are used to transport properties, which, in their turn, become comprehensible through being transmitted in this way. So the process of alienation leads to familiarisation. The architectural historian, Charles Jencks, was one of the first to write about the importance of architectural metaphors. 'The more unaccustomed a modern building seems (to people), the more they will compare it in a metaphorical way

2015

(**Haus**
(Needle

↗ p. 239

Needle, view to the north

with things they are familiar with. [...] At the end of the 1950s, for example, the first prefabricated concrete grids were described as "cheese graters", "beehives", "chain link fences".'[27] For Jencks, the reason for this is 'that the forms of the architecture are not familiar and suggest associations with other visual objects.'[28]

The best-known metaphor that exists in relation to the Kunsthaus Graz, featuring alienation and familiarity at the same time, is certainly that of the **friendly alien**. The term originates from Colin Fournier himself. In the beginning, the residents of Graz and visitors to the city perceived the building as more of an alien. However, over time, they realised that its unfamiliarity was of a friendly nature, and as such they accepted it. Most people value its presence in the city today. This process of viewing an object as a living being, or bestowing the character traits of living things on architecture, is related to the fact that people use metaphors to create an emotional connection. It gives them the opportunity to classify something different (alien) as intimate (friendly). An animation in the sense of an attribution of life becomes apparent here, a topic that Irene Albers and Anselm Franke dealt with in their exhibition *Animismus* as the 'borderline between life and non-life'.[29] In *Architektur und Metapher – Zur Bedeutung metaphorischen Sprechens in Architektur und Architekturvermittlung*, Tassilo Eichberger writes the following: 'The great ancient rhetorician Quintilianus, for example, picks up on the specific aspect of transfer and describes the transfer of the animate to the inanimate as "animation".'[30] It is as though the speaker wishes to bring the building to life through linguistic references, filling it with verbal life in order to understand its architecture and make it understandable for others. Therein lies the essence of the metaphor. In the special case of the metaphorical approach surrounding the Kunsthaus Graz, it is used to examine and classify the friendliness of the alien. An incarnation takes place in the form of metaphorical speech, breaking down boundaries and crossing thresholds.

On the one hand we use metaphors because we ourselves want to understand something, and on the other to help others to understand it. So in metaphors, we place what we observe in a new location. We observe the Kunsthaus and locate it in the animal world in order to assess its character. In this way, the unfamiliar, i.e. the foreign structure that doesn't appear to belong in its environment, becomes familiar – because we have described it in terms of something we know. This does not mean that it is only possible to understand something alien by means of the metaphor. But it can be seen as a linguistic path that creates a connection between metaphoric speech and this strange, amorphous structure. For example, such metaphors hardly existed for historicist buildings, whose frame of reference is now clear.[31] The fact that so many choose this linguistic path may be related to the dissolution of stylistic orientations in the course of the 20th and 21st centuries,[32] or because iconicity in itself is perceived as a new style. The assignment of names in the form of metaphors usually implies an element of invalidation.[33] Metaphors are not only used to make something unknown into something familiar, but also to demean it, ridicule it, take away its power.[34] 'Typical metaphors that [...] have been used to demonise modern architecture are the "cardboard box", "shoebox", "egg carton", "filing cabinet", or "squared paper".'[35]

2016

(**Kunst**
(**Haus**
(Needle
(roof terrace

staircase
→184)
↗p. 41

Aldo Giannotti. The Museum as a Gym

Something that is different can therefore make discourse possible and keep architectural events open to discourse. '"What interests me is architecture in the form of monstrosities, these objects that are simply catapulted into the city, having come from somewhere else [...]" Baudrillard is fascinated by what he describes as the 'monstrous architectural object', i.e. an object that is completely inconsistent with its surroundings, standing out like an apparition from outer space, a unique singularity like the Centre Pompidou when it landed in Paris,'[36] said Colin Fournier in a lecture on the French philosopher and media theorist Jean Baudrillard. Eichberger recognises a certain unpredictability in Baudrillard, which for Fournier also exists in relation to the Kunsthaus Graz and the experience of its architecture, remarking that 'he [Baudrillard] also follows on from the concept of the event, in which he sees something like the uncontrollable remains of a building's independent existence.'[37] The moment a building is emotionalised, experienced, people begin to use it. They use it in the sense that they speak about it, so that it becomes part of a discourse. This also works the other way around; when a building is used, it begins to be emotionalised.

→ design 081)

The Museum as a place of self and as a place of non-self

Making architecture come to life through the use of linguistic expressions also infers a reference to the self. The person who is speaking establishes a relationship with this self. The process of creating intimacy by means of rhetoric turns the building into a being that can be more easily related to. Initially this happens on the level of personal perception, before something larger and more complete can be abstracted from the use of metaphor. In other cases, it perhaps stops at the level of 'myself'. The process of expressing things in words reminds us of our own movements, since the lowest common denominator lies in movement, in the ability to move our self around in the world. But it also lies in the confrontation between the self and the 'other', architecture as 'a space that allows us to confront the "Other", to tell stories untold, and to imagine new ones altogether.'[38]

Alongside language, other forms of use include movement within the building and immediate usage. Whereas movement and direct usage happen without distance, language is reflexive – sometimes in connection with direct use, sometimes without this connection. 'Visiting the Kunsthaus is characterised by the experience of "walking in and out", of open and enclosed spaces, the contrast between dark and light, the perception of the three-dimensional body of the Kunsthaus and the experience of one's own body in relation to it.'[39] The museum is a place of the self, but it is also always a place of the non-self. As a visitor, we are challenged to leave this self and perceive ourselves through the eyes of the other. In the museum we experience the other, something we are not. The self is called into question when a process of correlation between this self and the other takes place – in the exhibition. By surrendering our own body in a space that is created by architecture and becomes material through (art) objects, this process of you, of me and of everything outside becomes visible.

→ usage 043) 066)

2007

Kunst
Haus
Needle

Space01
→118)
↗p. 49

China Welcomes You ... Desires, Struggles, New Identities.
Installation by Yangjiang Group

In places where language can be a means of reflection, the use of spaces generally takes place without distance, in an absolutely direct way. However, there is also an element of indirectness in the use of buildings, which here in the case of the Kunsthaus Graz is experimentally divided into *reflected* (artistic/curatorial) and *unreflected* (everyday) use. Everyday use, such as cleaning, security or building services, is carried out in an unreflected way, because it has become a matter of course in daily life. Artists, curators, mediators, reflect on their use of the building, because for (more or less) each new exhibition they have to reconsider how it is used. Additional categories might include a use in which something special is expected (e.g. by visitors) and strategic uses that can be attributed to politics or marketing. Of course, the assignment of user groups to the various categories and the transitions between them are fluid.

As part of the research undertaken for this book, an *exhibition registrar*, two *visitors*, a member of the *visitor management team*, the *café manager*, a *facility manager*, an *in-house technician*, two *infopoint staff members*, two *(art) mediators*, two *artists*, two *curators*, a *building manager*, two members of the *cleaning staff*, a *conservator*, the *shop operator*, the *Minister for Culture* and the *City Councillor for Culture*, an *event manager*, two members of the *workshop staff* and one member of the *supervisory and security staff* were asked to name a structural element that would exemplify their use of the Kunsthaus. On the one hand, the details they named, related to the specific type of use, are representative of their individual use. On the other, they demonstrate the variety of forms of use that come together at the Kunsthaus.[40] The survey developed in a dynamic way. The answers were diverse, although they overlapped in many places. In the survey, and resulting from it, the Kunsthaus was broken down into component parts, so to speak.[41] Through the answers of the interviewees, the Kunsthaus can be understood and reassembled as a sum of these parts. Distinctive architectural features such as the **Skin**, the **Needle** and the **Nozzles** emerged as clear intersection points.

→ usage
202) 079) 132)
058) 024) 075)
096) 065) 066)
140) 178) 105)
180) 109) 181)
072) 074) 090)
016) 070) 123)
149) 201) 185)
110) 043)

→ foyer
064)

→ usage
123) 149) 180)

The extent to which the metaphor becomes constructively relevant is revealed through these people's (individual and collective) use of the Kunsthaus. It becomes clear that the way they use the Kunsthaus building brings it to life even more than name attributions – how the in-house technician deals with the sprinkler system, how the artist approaches the walls (**Skin**) or the exhibition registrar handles the heavy door when receiving deliveries, to name just a few examples. The users who approach the Kunsthaus in an unreflected, direct way are especially qualified to make statements on how the building sweats, gets cold, breathes or behaves like a living being, even if only in a metaphorical sense.

→ Space01
127) 129)

→ usage
075) 202)

If the use of language is indirect, in that metaphors are employed,[42] the way in which people use it directly reveals that the Kunsthaus is an organism, a machine in the spirit of Deleuze.[43] This machine can be understood through the way it works, and it always needs the human operator in order to function. To put it another way: the function of the Kunsthaus becomes visible only through the user. Under this premise, the actual secret of the metaphorical description of a building lies in the building itself, and less in attributions from the outside.

2017

Kunst
Haus
Needle

↗ p. 49
↗ p. 239

For the UNIQUA Family Day, which took part in the frame of the exhibition **Graz Architecture**, artist Gerald Hartwig and architect Clemens Luser drew a continuation of the city views from the Needle and encouraged the public to add their very own designs for Graz to a city map.

The Kunsthaus is clearly used by the people who work there in the areas of administration, security, exhibition installation, exhibition organisation, facility management, in-house technology, logistics, cleaning, restoration, event management, mediation, at the **infopoint**, in the museum **shop** and in the **café**. If these areas are considered explicit, in the sense that the work in these areas is carried out directly on the object itself and on a regular, daily basis, the use of the building by curators, visitors, politicians and artists becomes implicitly visible. Within the city and beyond national borders, the Kunsthaus Graz is also used by all of these people from all of these areas as a representative figurehead of the Styrian capital. These areas together are important for the understanding of the direct and indirect use of the Kunsthaus. The representativeness that lies in the usage of the building can be attributed to all of these groups, not to the same extent, but on an equal level. Because they all share personal histories with this building.

→ usage
065) 066) 070) 024)

Representativeness through use / use through representativeness

How do representativeness and usage relate to one other? Does representativeness emerge from usage or does usage only become apparent through representativeness? When something is representative, it also means that it is in use. However, representativeness is also used to enhance the value of something. So something is representative because it becomes important through being used. There is an indirect and a direct representative use. Politicians, for example, use the Kunsthaus indirectly for representative (and strategic) purposes. Marketing employees as well as cleaning staff can use it in both respects. They work on the Kunsthaus directly, advertising or cleaning it. But they also use the Kunsthaus representatively by speaking to others about it. What does it mean in terms of use and reception, from both an unreflected and a reflected point of view, if an exhibition building like the Kunsthaus has walls that are not walls at all, but **Skin**? If you have to deal with an actual bubble when it comes to exhibition design, using this architecture for its specific purpose of exhibiting? If there is not only one entrance, but several? If there is only one surface? What does the platform concept mean for an individual's use of the building? What is the difference between gliding into a museum on a **Travelator** and using a moving walkway in an airport or an escalator in a department store? In a practical and technical sense, the **Travelator** is a hybrid between a moving walkway, which allows you to glide forwards, and the escalator, which transports you upwards. This becomes clear in the dramatic effect of the **Travelator**, which is unique in this form: the visitor glides from the **ground floor**, where the urban environment is clearly visible, into the darkness of the museum space. If you take the escalator in a department store, you are already likely to be inside the building, moving upwards with no view of the surrounding urban space. And most moving walkways do not move upwards.

→ Space01
119) 129)

→ Travelator
080)

→ usage
079)

And yet – apart from these purely structural aspects: are they not both concerned with travelling to other worlds, cultures, places, and with consumption or an apologetic

2017

(**Kunst**
(**Haus**
(Needle

foyer
→ 050)
→ 051)
→ 060)
↗ p. 49
↗ p. 239

Haegue Yang's **VIP's Union** was the first time that the entire building was used for one exhibition. The artist asked 'very important persons' from the city and its surroundings to loan a table or chair to the exhibition. The mixed form of the furniture (varied in style, material, colour and shape) stemming from different sources mirrored the social landscape. During the first phase of the exhibition, the furniture was distributed throughout the building and could be used by visitors (with a few exceptions).

Yang purposely steered the domestic, almost intimate atmosphere on a collision course with the institutional requirements for safety standards and everyday use.

Haegue Yang. VIP's Union – Phase I

statement like: *I'm just looking around?* In the aspect of representativeness, there is a differentiation between various types of use. All user groups – i.e. all kinds of use – be they indirect (representativeness) or direct (related to the object itself) – are connected through the use of language.

The first blob that behaves like one

A 'blob' like the Kunsthaus building really seems to inspire people to speak in images. As though the prerequisite for a linguistic image of this kind were a piece of architecture whose structure was described as biomorphous, fluid, and which gained recognition in the context of blob architecture. A blob is something that gets caught up in the element of onomatopoeia involved both in its appearance and in the way people speak about it. 'I like the cactus. I like the idea of cactus as architecture. Marvellous! The Cactus. Nasty, spiky, funny, blobby [...],'[44] says Peter Cook, and this statement also serves to express the barbed hook of this architecture. *Blob*[45] not only stands – also in a metaphorical sense – for the linguistic expression of a sound, for example the sound of a bottle being uncorked or the dripping of viscous emulsion – it can also be ascribed to the flow (of architecture), i.e. it is metaphorically transferrable.

Today, Colin Fournier describes the Kunsthaus as a dinosaur. Not because of its shape, but because of the digital design possibilities available at the time it was created: 'This project in a sense is a dinosaur in terms of the contemporary culture of digital design. It is a project that was at a turning point between two cultures.'[46] This shift from analogue to digital design tools took place at the dawn of the millennium, at the time when the Kunsthaus came into being and the age of so-called 'Blobism' began.[47]

It is true that Peter Cook sees the parallels between the architecture of the Kunsthaus and the work of the Archigram collective, which he co-founded in 1960, as too simple, too obvious, too short-sighted.[48] However, its similarity to ***Walking City*** (1964) by Ron Herron, who also belonged to Archigram, is difficult to deny.[49] → reference 156)

Even though a number of other blobs exist,[50] in the days when the Kunsthaus opened, Tom Dyckhoff pointed out in the *Times*: 'The Kunsthaus is the first blob to start behaving like one.'[51] In Dyckhoff's view, the behaviour of the Kunsthaus, in contrast to other blob buildings, goes beyond the pure iconography of the construction. The Kunsthaus is a utopian structure that has become reality. It emerged from the imaginary buildings created by Archigram, constructions that can walk or be carried on your back; they merely provide a platform with infrastructure that can be plugged into with the right equipment. Reveries that can be read, felt in the Kunsthaus, were at the same time fantasies, bound to fail as built reality. 'Why can't architecture be friendly, not functionalist? Why can't it fulfill us, delight us, respond to us, as if it were a creature?' asks Tom Dyckhoff. And the Kunsthaus replies in the way it behaves, fulfilling these characteristics, which go beyond mere visuality: '"We wanted it to look cuddly and friendly," Fournier says, "like a bouncy dog. It wants you to play with it." They wanted, he adds, "something alive about the building".'[52] → reference 030) → design 033)

Needle
→143)

'From the **Needle** you can get very close to the surface of the external skin. The **Needle** is a bright, friendly area that makes you feel like lingering and reflecting on what you've seen after an exhibition, and the view it offers of Graz is powerful and impressive.'

Günter Riegler, City Councillor for culture, science and finance

So how does the Kunsthaus behave? Towards itself? Towards others? Is it actually able to behave at all? Or are these behaviour patterns mere attributions, i.e. metaphors? What Dyckhoff suggests here is a humanisation of architecture. He addresses ways of bringing architecture to life by swathing it in linguistic images, to make it understandable to oneself and to the people with whom one speaks about it. In the first instance, this behaviour implies the way in which the building is used.

→ friendly alien 203)

'The architecture is both an empty, flexible shell in which curators/shop managers can invent a fantasy for each exhibition and the framework for the experience, a network of snakes and ladders, cat and mouse, thrills and spills,'[53] states Dyckhoff. This humanisation also includes the experience of architecture, a process of relating to it, getting involved with it, even being open to the unexpected: 'The "friendly alien" swallows everything with its **Travelator**. It is like a giant Hoover, like the belly of the whale, evoking the distant memory and unconscious desire that we have, since childhood, of being swallowed by the dragon, the subtle pleasure we experience when licked by the family cat's sandpaper tongue. It is the black hole of the whale's stomach, where one can find all sorts of things: old boots, lost treasures, bewildered fish, Jonah himself: that's what a museum has to be, a place that plays on our desire to find ourselves in the company of surprising and unexpected things, bizarre confrontations, things that sometimes are not yet quite fully digested.'[54]

→ design 081)

While being exposed to its influence, moving through the building – in the sense of using it – we also encounter the 'other'. The other that challenges us to take a stance. Seeing objects in a museum means seeing them in a fluid state, while we are walking, in relation to other objects next to them, beneath them, in front of them, behind them. Stopping, walking, stopping, walking, lingering, walking back. Seeing things several times. Seeing them anew. Objects are rarely completely separate from one another. You go from one to the next, permanently moving in an intermediate space, in several intermediate spaces, in which the connections within an exhibition and the way in which the building is used become apparent as a whole. '[...] the durational performance of the museum becomes an unfolding inquiry into life itself, catalysed by something perhaps as simple as a cup of tea.'[55] The intermediate space in the museum is just as self-evident and unconscious; it is more than just a transition zone between one object and the next. This intermediate space is, as it were, a relational space, a place where things are placed in relation to one another. This intermediate space is not only where art, objects, exhibits are seen, but also where other 'seers' can be observed. How do they look at what is being exhibited? What do they see? How long do they look at what I am seeing? Do they see what I can see? Do I overlook what they can see? Or do they just interpret it in a different way?

Exhibiting means showing something in the context of understanding

The role of architecture, the extent to which it affects how the building is used, and thus the architectural experience, only becomes apparent when you have curated,

2017

Haus
forecourt

forecourt
→ 036)

Forecourt, design by Topotek1

set up, mediated, visited several exhibitions in the same building. Which, in the case of the Kunsthaus, are completely different from one another. For Cook and Fournier, elements of the unknown, the unexpected, the unpredictable, play an important role in the architectural experience. This also applies to creating exhibitions because, particularly at the Kunsthaus, each exhibition is newly negotiated with the architecture. Fournier described the Kunsthaus as a building characterised by adventure and surprises. In this context, he speaks of a kind of surprising curiosity: 'The nice thing about the Kunsthaus is that each time a new curator comes to do an installation, he or she reinvents the space. And so for me, coming up into the Kunsthaus is always a surprise. It's always: what has been done with the space?'[56] Exhibiting at the Kunsthaus Graz means dealing with the space. Having to deal with the space.[57] Being able to. As an artist and as a curator, in the setting up, in the mediation and in the reception of the exhibition. In this space, exhibitions have to be thought of in a vertical as well as in a horizontal sense. Dealing with the horizontality and verticality of the exhibition architecture begins at an earlier stage at the Kunsthaus. It starts at the point where, in other buildings, the rooms are more specifically defined, for example through white walls, which at least provide verticality.

→ Space02 088)

→ Space01 093)

The space of the Kunsthaus calls for a different kind of behaviour, which works according to a different kind of logic. The walls must be thought of in a new way, the way people move through the museum must be reconsidered, new lighting conditions created. The architecture of a museum or exhibition building can, as in the case of the Kunsthaus Graz, become a condition that governs which artists are willing to show their work against this specific architectural background.

If exhibiting means showing something in a context of understanding, architecture always exhibits itself – it is always exhibited. The context of understanding not only incorporates the architectural environment, but also the context of (urban) space, society, politics, community, time. It is practically impossible to view and understand architecture without taking its special context into account. It is also impossible to understand a museum without considering the multiple ways in which it is used. However, this aspect is still given too little consideration when it comes to the design and planning of museum buildings. In the museum as a place of display and reference, types of display are influenced by the specific architecture. Display possibilities are influenced by the architecture and its details. These are used to negotiate the questions of what the special features of a space consist of and how exhibitions affect this space.[58]

→ design 011)

Architecture as an image projected into the world

Several features of the Kunsthaus Graz show how the relationship between a building and its surroundings can be defined through its interior: for example, the glazed **ground floor**, which is open to the city, or the **Nozzle** on the upper exhibition level (**Space01**), which points towards the clock tower. This is the only one of the **Nozzles** that also functions as a window with a view. The Graz landmark on the Schloßberg thus

→ foyer 058)
→ Space01 122)

reference
→ 041)

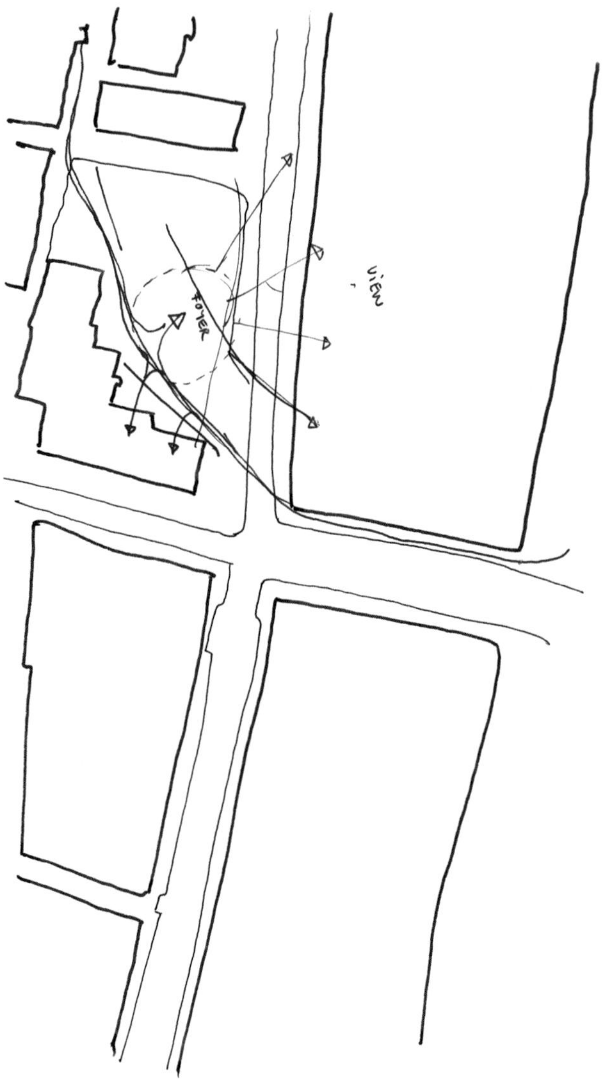

Pathways / open **ground floor**.
Sketch from the competition, Niels Jonkhans

becomes an exhibition object, even though it is situated outside the museum. And the **Nozzle** becomes a picture frame, which brings this object into the museum. The 'nozzle frame' literally draws the clock tower into the museum building, evoking a certain form of user behaviour – the visitor takes out a camera and captures the 'image'. The **Needle** provides further views of the city from the building, making a significant contribution towards anchoring the museum building within the city.

→ Needle 142) 144)

In museum buildings that are expressive in appearance, moving far away from the white cube, what is shown and the way in which it is shown is also circulated around the world.

The architecture helps to determine the possibilities of showing. The representational image a museum projects into the world is primarily that of its architecture. This image stands for permanence, whereas the contents of the museum represent change. Of course, exhibitions circulate around the world in the form of photographs, documented in interior shots. However, it is primarily photographs of the exterior, the architecture, that reveal where the photographer actually was. The photographs that are taken, sent and shared are often similar. 'There are thousands of similar motifs of the Kunsthaus on the Internet. One of the motifs that returns every year, like Christmas, is the Kunsthaus with its roof covered in snow – presumably because it looks so cute. As soon as the first snow arrives, there are hundreds of photographs of the Kunsthaus in the snow. Each photographer thinks that he or she has taken the most unique picture. Unfortunately they are all rather similar, not to say interchangeable.'[59]

The architecture makes a significant contribution to the image of Graz and its Kunsthaus, an image that is projected into the world. The building is a constituent part of this image. In the case of the Kunsthaus, and this is probably true of most other buildings, variations in the use of architecture do not only arise when one is physically present. On the one hand, they result from people talking about the Kunsthaus – linguistic use – and on the other, through the distribution of images.

→ friendly alien 203)

We can use architecture through language, i.e. indirectly, and we can use it directly through our actions within buildings. What connects the language component to carrying out activities in architecture is a kind of familiarity that emerges, and this shows itself in many ways: in emotional relationships with the building (both in a positive and in a critical sense). These connections are established through use itself, both in a reflected and in an unreflected way. Metaphors make language into a form of use, while actions within buildings create an architectural use. Linguistic use is also a connecting element between the use of the Kunsthaus itself and the reception of its architecture. Each of these allows us to approach the building and feel closer to it, which I describe as the *friendly alien effect*. We enter into a relationship with this building. '[...] like a human personality, a building can become more and more intriguing as we delve inside and get to know it.'[60] Perhaps we have not yet completely understood it, and we may not yet be in a position to classify it in terms of time and space, within this cityscape that has developed through history. We may never even be able to do so definitively, but we see it in the knowledge that it is part of the architectural narrative of this city, which will continue to develop. We will also be required to permanently renegotiate the connection between the use of language and the use of architecture.

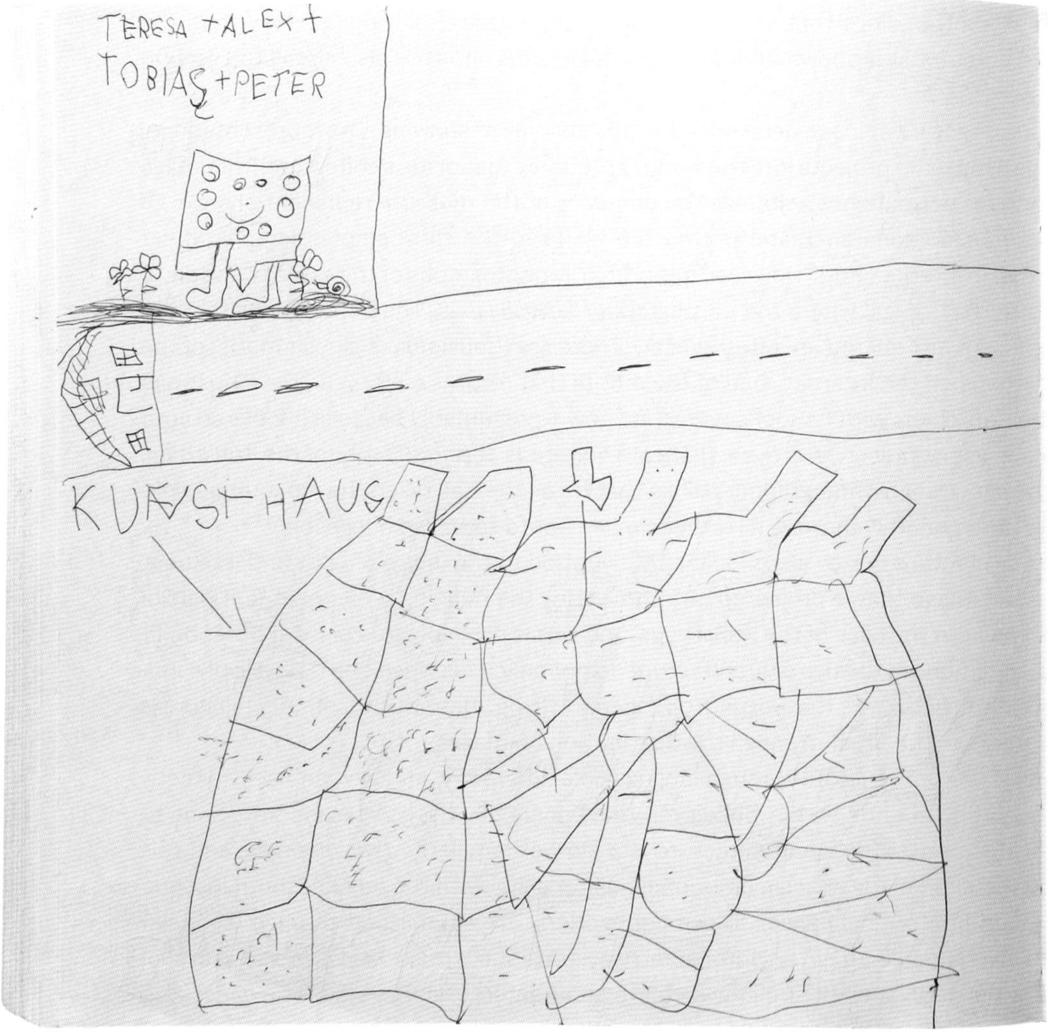

Extract from the visitors' book

1 Teresa Präauer, *Tier werden*, Göttingen 2018, p. 32.

2 'In relation to space, the metaphor is not just a rhetorical device, but a basic scheme of human experience and appropriation of the world.' (Tilo Felgenhauer, 'Metapher', in: Stephan Günzel (ed.), *Lexikon der Raumphilosophie*, Darmstadt 2012, p. 256).

3 Robert Pfaller, *Die blitzenden Waffen. Über die Macht der Form*, Frankfurt am Main 2020, p. 19. Quote within the quote: Klaus-Peter Lange, *Theoretiker des literarischen Manierismus: Tesauros und Pellegrinis Lehre von der 'Acutezza' oder von der Macht der Sprache*, Munich 1968, p. 94.

4 On the iconicity of museum architecture see the contribution by Pablo von Frankenberg in this volume. p. 99.

5 Sonja Hnilica, *Metaphern für die Stadt. Zur Bedeutung von Denkmodellen in der Architekturtheorie*. Bielefeld 2012, p. 15.

6 Helmut Bast, Klipp, October 2003.

7 Ulrich Weinzierl, Die Welt, 06.10.2003.

8 art 12/2003.

9 Rainer Metzger, Tages-Anzeiger, 04.11.2003.

10 Günter Eichberger, Kleine Zeitung, 28.10.2003.

11 Kieler Nachrichten, 24.09.2003.

12 Walter Titz, Kleine Zeitung, 09.04.2000.

13 Erna Lackner, Frankfurter Allgemeine Zeitung, 10.10.2003.

14 Helmut Schödel, Süddeutsche Zeitung, 29.10.2003.

15 Loc. cit.

16 Martin Behr, Salzburger Nachrichten, 26.09.2003.

17 Benedikt Loderer, 'Die Rache der Panzerechse', Süddeutsche Zeitung, 22.09.2003.

18 Thomas Trenkler, Der Standard, 14.04.2000.

19 Denise Leising, Der Standard, 28.11.2000.

20 Johann Reidemeister, Süddeutsche Zeitung, 15.10.2001.

21 Paul Kreiner, Der Tagesspiegel, 30.09.2003.

22 Dieter Bogner, Kunsthaus Graz AG (ed.), *A Friendly Alien. Kunsthaus Graz, Peter Cook, Colin Fournier Architects*. Ostfildern 2004, p. 114.

23 According to Susanne Hauser, the term *skin* is more commonly used as a metaphor in the English-speaking world than the term *Haut* in German-speaking regions.

24 Cf. Andri Gerber, Brent Patterson (eds.), *Metaphors in Architecture and Urbanism. An Introduction*. Bielefeld 2013, p. 115.

25 'Dealing with skins means dealing with multiple diffusion. Subjects, individuals and closed bodies are beyond the self-evident preconditions of a discussion of boundaries that involve skin. Speaking about skin brings other senses – especially touch, but also taste and smell – and their disruptive powers into play.' Loc. cit. p. 109.

26 See the index on the **BIX façade** with the accompanying texts by Elisabeth Schlögl in this volume, p. 323.

27 Charles Jencks, *Die Sprache der postmodernen Architektur*. Stuttgart 1988, p. 40.

28 Loc. cit. p. 43.

29 Exhibition in the spring of 2012 at the Haus der Kulturen der Welt in Berlin. The accompanying book (eds. Irene Albers, Anselm Franke), *Animismus. Revisionen der Moderne* was published after the exhibition. Zurich 2015. Quote from: www.hkw.de/de/programm/projekte/2012/animismus/start_animismus.php (01.08.2020).

30 Tassilo Eichberger, *Architektur und Metapher – Zur Bedeutung metaphorischen Sprechens in Architektur und Architekturvermittlung*. Munich 2010, p. 6.

31 However, the same fate can befall historicist buildings that are out of the ordinary, for example the Altare della Patria in Rome (1885–1927), which Romans refer to as 'macchina da scrivere' (typewriter).

32 One of the earliest examples is the Secession building in Vienna (Joseph Maria Olbrich, 1898), which can be described as the first modern building in Vienna and one of the first modern buildings in Europe. Due to its unusual appearance, it has been called 'Krauthäuptel' (head of lettuce), 'Grave of the Mahdi' and many other names by the press and the inhabitants of the city.

33 '[...] in the distinction made by Cicero in his *De optimo genere oratorum* (46 B.C.), metaphors would not only have to *delectare*, to delight, but also to *movere*, that is to impress, and *docere*, that is to teach. But the negative connotation of rhetoric and metaphors remained [...]' Gerber, Patterson (eds), *Metaphors in Architecure and Urbanism*, loc. cit., p. 15.

34 Abstract, avant-garde art, which is thus difficult to understand, has always been encountered in this manner by cultural philistines (for example, Marcel Duchamp's Nude Descending a Staircase was described as an 'explosion in a brick factory'). Even Le Corbusier, who at that time (1907/08) was still named Jeanneret and had not yet converted to Modernism, called the Church of St. Leopold am Steinhof and the Post Office Savings Bank by Otto Wagner 'une cuisine hollandaise ou un WC modèle' (because of all the ceramic cladding). [For this and also references 31 and 32 I would like to thank Anselm Wagner, along with Pablo von Frankenberg for comments regarding contents on this topic in general.]

35 Charles Jencks, *Die Sprache der postmodernen Architektur*, loc. cit. p. 40.

36 Colin Fournier, 'Jean Baudrillard und radikale Architektur', in: Peter Gente, Barbara Könches and Peter Weibel (eds.), *Philosophie und Kunst – Jean Baudrillard. Eine Hommage zu seinem 75. Geburtstag*. Berlin 2005, p. 283.

37 Tassilo Eichberger, *Architektur und Metapher*, loc. cit., p. 14.

38 Christopher Kennedy, 'the museum is a theater of time', in: Kate Clark, Christopher Kennedy, Pablo von Frankenberg (eds.), *Museum Futures. A Speculative Investigation of Museums Past, Present & Future*, 2011.

39 Svenia Schneider, *Blob-Architektur für das 21. Jahrhundert – Neues Paradigma oder Relaunch einer ehrwürdigen Tradition?*. Marburg 2014, p. 65.

40 'As Caulfield noted, the museum stays the same, it's the people who are changed. How museums

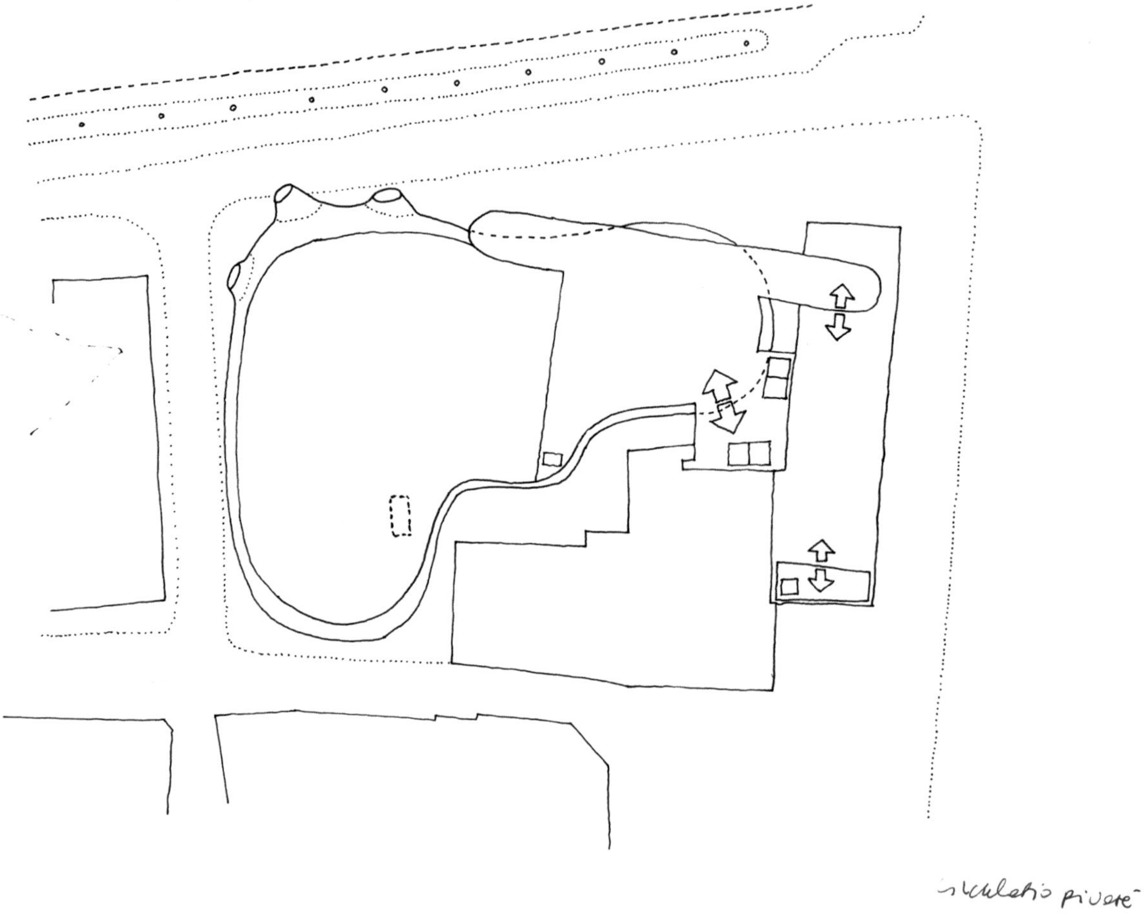

Escape routes. Sketch from the preliminary design, Anja Jonkhans change people is the most important question and the greatest goal in museum design.' (from: 'A Place of Focus and Concentration: Terry Riley on Good Museums', in: Clark, Kennedy, von Frankenberg (eds.), *Museum Futures*, loc. cit.

41 The picture series by Martin Grabner in this volume shows the places in the Kunsthaus the interviewees named as individual parts.

42 'The metaphor is not a class of words but rather a particular usage of words.' (Gernot Böhme, 'Metaphors in Architecture – a Metaphor?', in: Gerber, Patterson (ed.), *Metaphors in Architecture and Urbanism*, loc. cit., p. 48.

43 'We do not start out from the metaphorical use of the word machine, but from an (unclear) hypothesis concerning its origins: the manner in which random elements are made to be machines through *recursion* and *communication*.' (Gilles Deleuze, Félix Guattari, *Anti-Ödipus*. Frankfurt am Main 1977, p. 498.)

44 Schneider, *Blob-Architektur*, loc. cit., p. 104 f. (quoted from: Peter Cook, *Six Conversations* (= Architectural Monographs, vol. 28), 1993, p. 24).

45 In this context, blob also stands for *Binary Large Object*. The main researchers of blob architecture are Greg Lynn, Karl Chu, Kees Osterhuis, Mario Carpo.

46 Colin Fournier during his lecture entitled 'Not quite digital' in the autumn of 2019 at the TU Graz during the conference *Digital Practice*, transcript Sophia Walk.

47 Domes, vaults and shell structures have belonged to the history of architecture and building for centuries. In the second half of the 20th century, for example, the Mexican architect Félix Candela Outeriño or the German civil engineer Ulrich Müther (along with Heinz Isler from Switzerland, Eduardo Torroja from Spain, Pier Luigi Nervi from Italy) realised pioneering concrete shell structures. The acquisition of new digital media and design techniques, such as CAD programs, did not immediately enable the emergence of an extended approach to form and design, especially the use of new building materials, but it did facilitate it. What distinguishes blobs from other organic architecture is the multiple curvature of the entire structure and the 'fluidity' of the lines and forms.

48 'Archigram was involved in the possibility of disappearing architecture, replaceable architecture, whereas this [the Kunsthaus] is made of modern materials to some extent. It's less inherently replaceable. It is more in a tradition of a building that sits in the particular place and is particular to that place.' (Peter Cook in the film *The Sky is Glass (test/excerpt)* by Isa Rosenberger, 2017, 04:53–05:15).

49 On this and other projects related to the Kunsthaus, see the contribution by Anselm Wagner in this volume. ↗ p. 259

50 Other blobs already existed: the Selfridges department store in Birmingham by Future Systems (completed around the same time as the Kunsthaus, in 2003), the Poppodium Mezz in Breda (NL, 2002) by Erick van Egeraat, the conference room of the DZ Bank in Berlin (2001) by Frank O. Gehry, the restaurant 'Le Georges' in the Centre Pompidou (Renzo Piano and Richard Rogers, 1977) in Paris (2000) by Jakob & McFarlane. This selection is based on the research by Svenia Schneider mentioned in notes 39 and 44.

51 Tom Dyckhoff, 'The Blob Has Come To Earth', in: The Times, 16.09.2003.

52 Loc. cit. (In this article it is not confirmed exactly who is meant by 'they'. The context suggests that 'they' refers to the organisers of the competition, i.e. the City of Graz.)

53 Loc. cit.

54 Colin Fournier, project author, spacelab Cook/Fournier, London, in: Bogner, Kunsthaus Graz AG (ed.), *A Friendly Alien*, loc. cit., p. 116.

55 Christopher Kennedy, 'the museum is a theater of time', in: Clark, Kennedy, v. Frankenberg (eds.), Museum Futures, loc. cit.

56 Colin Fournier in the film *The Sky is Glass (test/excerpt)* by Isa Rosenberger, 2017, 01:57–02:15.

57 On the question of chance and curse in dealing with museum buildings and the role played by architecture as a background to this, see the conversation between Barbara Steiner, Pablo v. Frankenberg and Sophia Walk in this volume, ↗ p. 135

58 See the exhibition index with accompanying texts by Katia Huemer in this volume.

59 Barbara Steiner in a conversation with Pablo von Frankenberg and Sophia Walk in September 2019.

60 Dyckhoff, 'The Blob Has Come To Earth', loc. cit.

My sincere thanks go to Arnold Stickler → 072) from the logistics department of Universalmuseum Joanneum for his willingness to travel with me to the press archive in St. Radegund and his patience while I looked through hundreds of newspaper articles there from the time of the Kunsthaus opening.

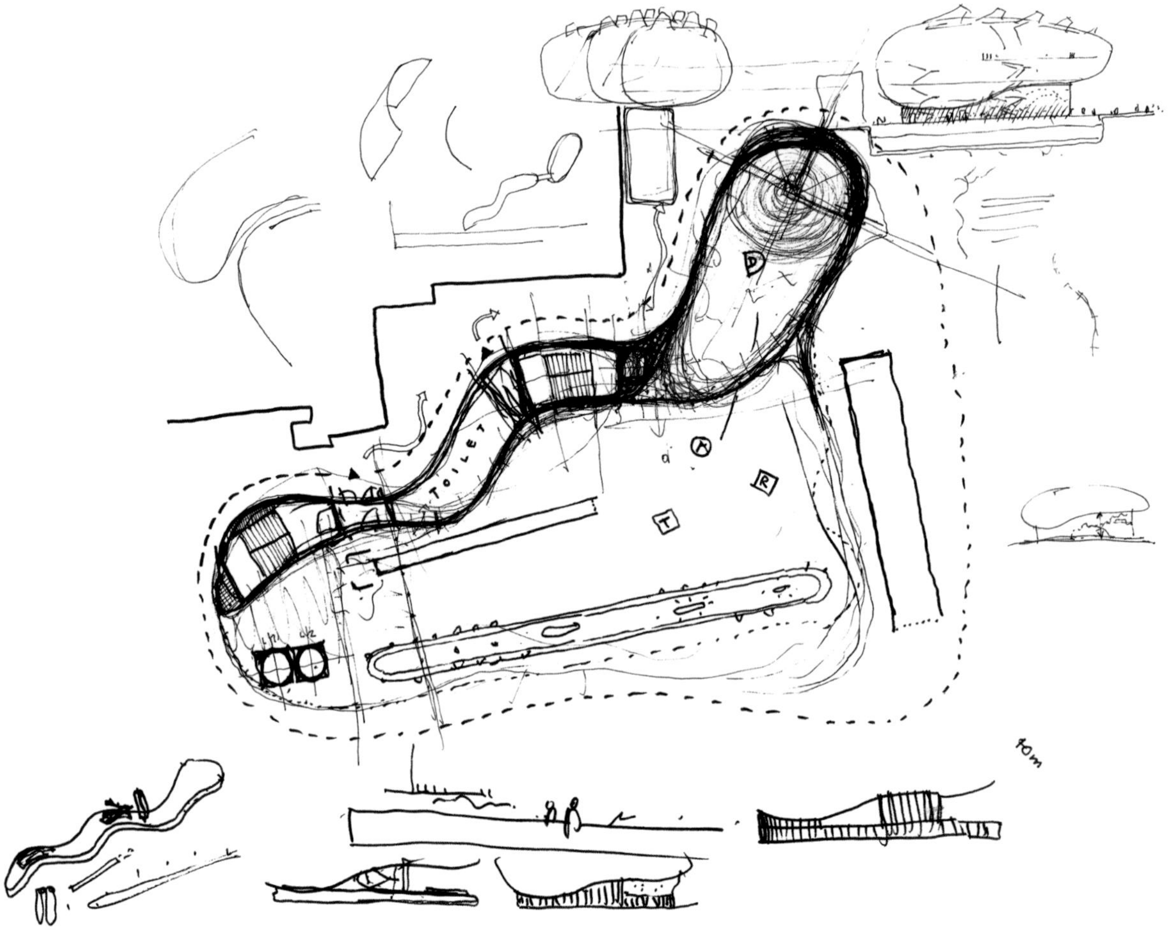

Ground floor. Sketch of floor plan, preliminary design phase, Niels Jonkhans

2017

(**Favoriten**

Arthur Zalewski, selection from the series **Favoriten** as part of the exhibitions **Graz Architecture** and **Up into the Unknown**.
Motifs: Kunsthaus Graz, Botanical Garden Zurich

Favoriten
→ 039)

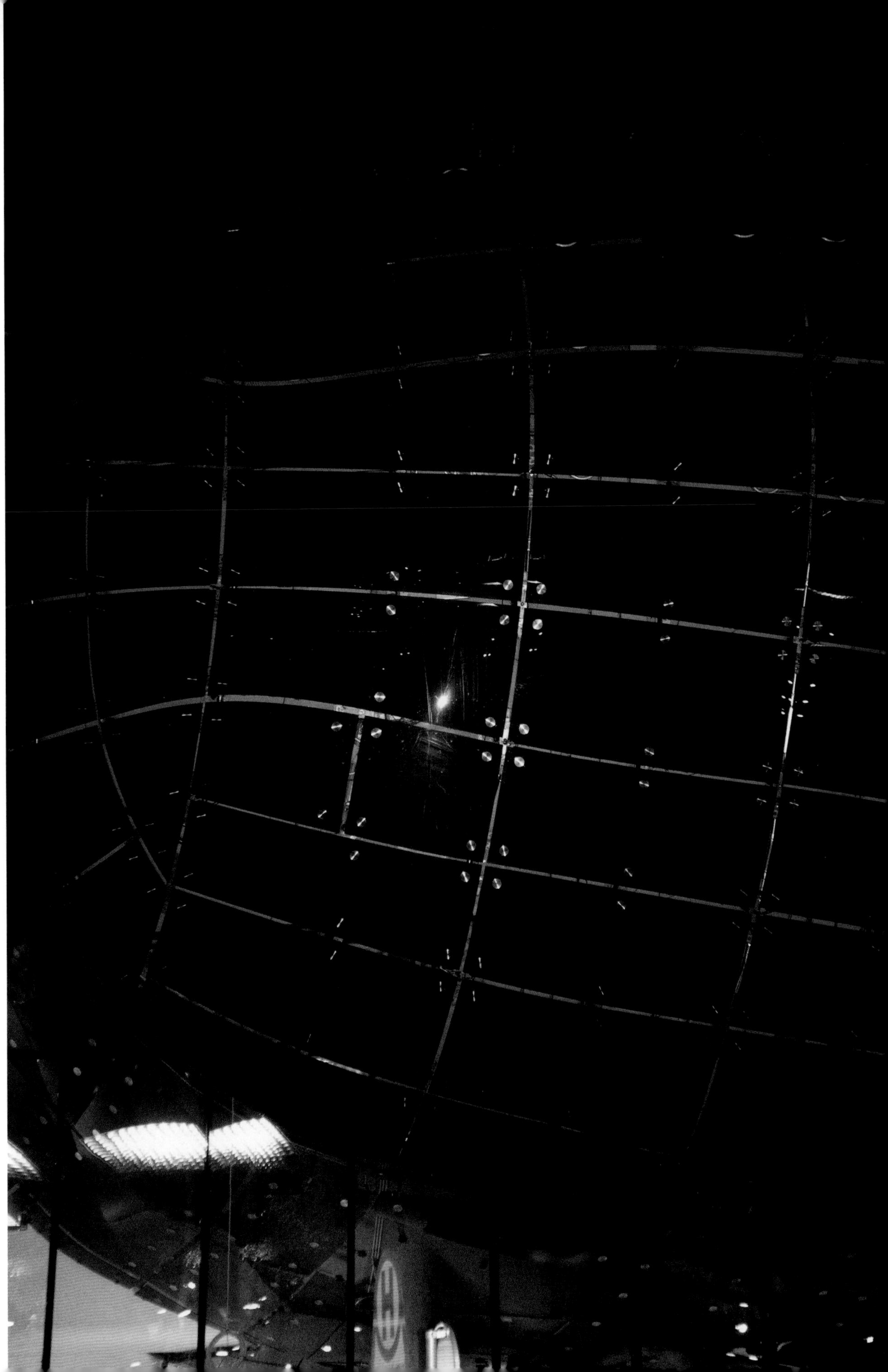

KLÖCHER
Universalmuseum
WOLF
Gösser
Zwiebel-Suppe
Gebackene Leber
Heidensterz salat
7,90
Fußgänger
gänger

NEUROTH

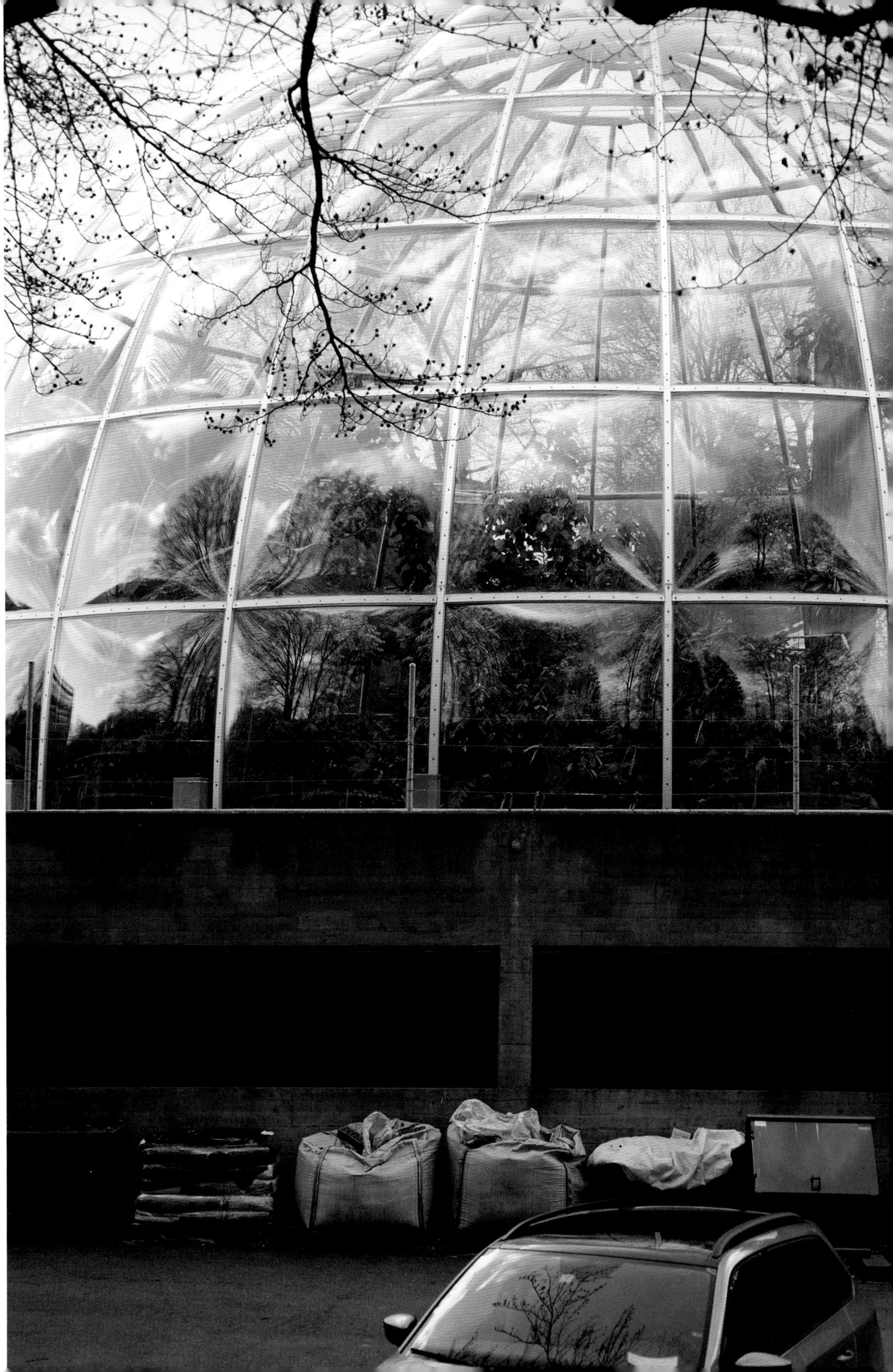

1964

(**reference**

↗ p. 233
↗ p. 261
↗ p. 265

(fig. 1) Ron Herron, A Walking City

A familiar alien. The Kunsthaus Graz, Archigram and the 'Graz School' 1962–2003

Anselm Wagner

1 Hans Hollein, 1963/64. Flugzeugträgerstadt. Transformation und Transposition

2 Raumstation (mit freundlicher Genehmigung des Life Magazine nach einem Gemälde von Robert McCall)

3 Die Walking City (von Ron Herron und Bryan Harvey) ist eben in New York hereinspaziert. Guten Tag.

Hans Hollein

ZUKUNFT

DER

ARCHITEKTUR

Architektur ist der Wille des Menschen, seine Umwelt selbst zu bestimmen. Städte entstehen, der dreidimensionale Ausdruck seines Verhaltens. Heute muß der Mensch von der ganzen Erde Besitz ergreifen. Sie wird vollkommen vom Menschen geschaffener Raum. Die ganze Erde wird eine unendliche kontinuierliche Stadt, ein einziges Gebäude. In gewisser Hinsicht wird dies eine neue vom Menschen geschaffene Natur. Bauwerke werden die Erde überziehen, in, auf und mit denen wir leben werden, wo und wie wir es wollen. Das freie Land wird weder mit Ansiedlungen überstreut noch eine beziehungslose Barriere zwischen isolierten Ansiedlungen, sondern ein integraler Teil dieser menschengemachten Umwelt.

Die Städte der Vergangenheit waren bestimmt durch Notwendigkeiten anderer Art. Sie waren bestimmt von Handelsrouten oder strategischen Positionen, von machtpolitischen und religiösen Voraussetzungen. Ihr prominentester räumlich-plastischer Ausdruck waren Mauern und Türme — Verteidigung und Kult. Die heutige Stadt, die heutige Umwelt ist in viel weitergehender Weise Ausdruck aller Verhaltensweisen und Beziehungen des Menschen, seiner Errungenschaften, seiner Emotionen und Leidenschaften. Die heutige Stadt ist weniger Mauer und Turm als eine ungeheure Maschine der Kommunikation, Manifestation der Eroberung und Beherrschung des Raumes und der Verbindung der ganzen Menschheit. Sie ist dynamisch, nicht statisch. Ihre Symbole sind anders, ihr plastischer Ausdruck wird bestimmt durch die Elemente dieser Kommunikation, durch Zeichen der räumlichen Ordnung und Organisation, durch die dreidimensionalen Manifestationen ihrer Versorgung. Die Pyramiden waren einfach in ihrer Bestimmung und aus einem Material. Die Stadt, die Architektur von heute ist im Aufbau komplex, eine Vielfalt von Voraussetzungen und Materialien. In ihrer Verwirklichung hat sie die fast unbegrenzten Möglichkeiten einer perfekten Technologie und Wissenschaft zur Verfügung. Städte — ein menschliches Ereignis — sind heute eine menschliche Notwendigkeit. Heute heißt Städte bauen Politik machen.

5 Jakov Tschernikov, 1930. Stadt

4 Hans Hollein, 1958. Schräge Gebäude

9

(fig. 2) From: Bau. Schrift für Architektur und Städtebau 20, issue 1, 8

A familiar alien
The Kunsthaus Graz, Archigram and the 'Graz School' 1962–2003

'A friendly alien' was the name Colin Fournier gave to the gift he designed with Peter Cook for Graz, which was European Capital of Culture at the time.[1] 'The building is quite obviously different from any other building in the city,' said Fournier in an attempt to explain his catchy nickname. 'It is a piece of architecture that makes a clear statement, quite provocatively revealing itself as something that is not from here. [...] It was our intention to create a building that brings something unknown to the city.'[2] Contemporaries immediately noticed that the 'friendly alien' bore a certain formal resemblance to the beetle-like ocean liners of Ron Herron's *Walking City*, published in *Archigram*[3] in 1964[4]. The only difference was that the utopia that had become reality had not docked on the Hudson River, but on the banks of the River Mur. Otherwise, it seemed, the Kunsthaus was as alien to its Baroque surroundings as the *Walking City* was to Manhattan's skyscrapers.

fig. 1 → reference 156)

In the following I would like to provide evidence to show that, even before it landed in the year when Graz was European Capital of Culture in 2003, the 'alien' had a number of acquaintances or even relatives in town, i.e. it was really not something completely new and unfamiliar. My intention here is not to qualify or even cast doubt on the innovative power of the Kunsthaus architecture. Rather, the aim is to show that Cook and Fournier's design had a previous liaison with the Graz architectural scene that went back 40 years. The appearance of the 'alien' bears witness to this, and it is not least what allowed it to become successfully established on the banks of the Mur. It is certainly no coincidence that the most important building to have sprung forth from the ideological soil of Archigram should today stand in Graz.

'Those weird damned Austrians'

The Kunsthaus was quite clearly 'not from here', first and foremost because of its British origins. Up until then, people in Graz had not been used to this kind of thing. Apart from the Wienerbergergründe residential development, built by the Swedish office of Ralph Erskine (and his colleague Hubert Rieß from Graz) in 1987, the Kunsthaus was the first building since the Baroque era to be built by a foreign architectural firm in Graz, alongside Vito Acconci's Murinsel, which was built at the same time.[5] Since then, very few international projects have been added: the *MUMUTH* by UNStudio (2008), the roof structure of the department store Kastner & Öhler by Nieto Sobejano Arquitectos (2010) and the *Argos* Serviced Apartments by Zaha Hadid (2020) are the most well-known of a small handful of new buildings in the Styrian capital that were not designed by Austrian architects.[6] This apparent provincialism does not stand in the way of the international charisma that Graz has enjoyed as an architectural city since the 1970s. On the one hand, a strong autochthonous scene is almost always at the heart of an

IDEA

INTERNATIONAL DIALOGUE
OF EXPERIMENTAL ARCHITECTURE

Vom 9. bis 11. Juni fand in Folkestone, England, ein internationales Symposium für experimentelle Architektur statt, das von der Archigramgruppe (London) veranstaltet wurde, welches eine Anzahl von Personen – und Projekte in einer parallel geführten Ausstellung – zu diesem Thema vorstellte. Es sprachen unter anderen: Peter Cook, Claude Parent, Cedric Price, Yona Friedman, Arthur Quarmby, Josef Weber und Hans Hollein. Bei vollgepacktem Auditorium kam es zu hitzigen Debatten über die Ausführungen. Es ist bemerkenswert, daß solche Bestrebungen in England für so interessant befunden werden, daß der Wohnbauminister Lord Kennet (Wayland Young) diese Tagung eröffnete und an den Vorträgen teilnahm. Reyner Banham gab das Schlußreferat. In einem Teil seiner Ausführungen stellte er die Frage, ob für viele der Aufgaben, mit denen heute das „enclosure business" konfrontiert ist, die Antwort noch Architektur ist. Vielleicht sei es besser, an Stelle einer schützenden Umhüllung gegen die Witterung den Leuten eine Injektion gegen Schnupfen zu geben.

H. H.

1 Superman Reyner Banham
2 Idea-man Yona Friedman
3 Ausstellung

This is the message from London: Skirts are going up.

1

3, 2

55

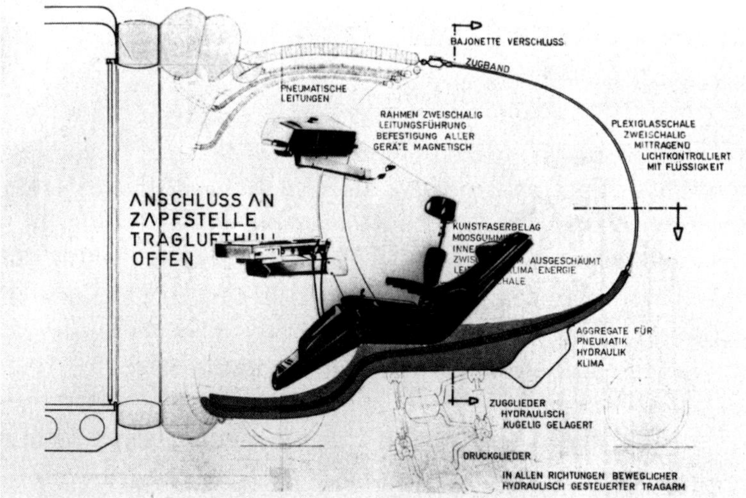

(fig. 3) From: Bau. Schrift für Architektur und Städtebau 21, issue 3, 55
(fig. 4) Konrad Frey, Agglomeration of devices
for satisfying requirements

architecturally interesting metropolis – we only have to think of Porto, Barcelona or Helsinki. On the other, although almost all of the members of the 'Graz School' studied here at the University of Technology (TU), most of them moved abroad after graduating. If they returned, they were able to contribute their international experience to the local building industry. For example Raimund Abraham, Friedrich St. Florian, Heidulf Gerngross, Bernhard Hafner, Bernd Capra, Horst Hönig, Manfred Kovatsch and Helmut Richter went to the USA, Konrad Frey and Herbert Missoni to England, Helmut Croce, Johannes Wegan, Helmut Rieder and Manfred Wolff-Plottegg to France, Dietrich Ecker, Ingo Klug and Werner Nussmüller to Holland, Hubert Rieß to Sweden, Nikolaus Schuster to Czechoslovakia, Günther Domenig, Heinz Wondra and Klaus Kada to Germany and Wolfgang Kapfhammer to Switzerland.[7] 'There is a constant stream of young and exciting Austrians circulating through Europe to England and to America and always they have a curious, edgy contribution to make to the more current questions of architecture,' Peter Cook observed admiringly as early as 1970.[8] Eilfried Huth, Michael Szyszkowitz, Karla Kowalski, Klaus Kada, Manfred Kovatsch and Hubert Rieß later became professors at renowned universities in Germany, Helmut Richter in France and Friedrich St. Florian, Raimund Abraham and Bernhard Hafner in the USA. In this respect, building activity in Graz in the late 20th century benefitted from a great deal of international expertise, even though it was almost exclusively in the hands of local offices.

In the above-mentioned publication *Experimental Architecture* from 1970, which is concerned with a historical and international self-contextualisation of Archigram, Peter Cook dedicates a chapter to the 'Austrian Phenomenon'. 'In the last ten years there have probably been more interesting young architects coming out of Austria than of any other country,'[9] is the introductory sentence that has been quoted in this country many times since then.[10] Cook was most impressed with Hans Hollein, who was without doubt the leading figure of the generation of young architects at the time, followed by Walter Pichler and Haus-Rucker-Co, whose *Audiovisueller Helm* or *Ballon für zwei* appeared in *Archigram* No. 8 as early as 1968.[11] Cook also briefly mentions the TU Graz graduates Raimund Abraham, Friedrich St. Florian, Günther Domenig and Eilfried Huth, showing the utopian megastructures and the cybernetic light spaces created by Abraham and Florian.[12]

Cook added a touch of informality to his chapter on Austria in *Archigram* No. 9, which was also published in 1970. The words 'those weird damned austrians ... they're great' appear in bold letters, winding around a Coop Himmelb(l)au collage. It was suggested that while other Europeans would theorise, the Austrians, who were far more cynical and at the same time more formalistic, would get straight to the point: '[...] the Austrians needle the problem. They are inventive and articulate.'[13] Although he never mentioned the three protagonists by name, Cook largely identified the 'Graz group' as Bernhard Hafner, the brains of the 'first Graz School',[14] who was teaching in Los Angeles and working on cybernetic urban planning models,[15] and Helmut Richter and Heidulf Gerngross, who were studying information theory or economic science at the UCLA: 'Even the Graz group (who are mostly transplanted to the University of California at Los Angeles) are committed to mathematics and the computer terminal:

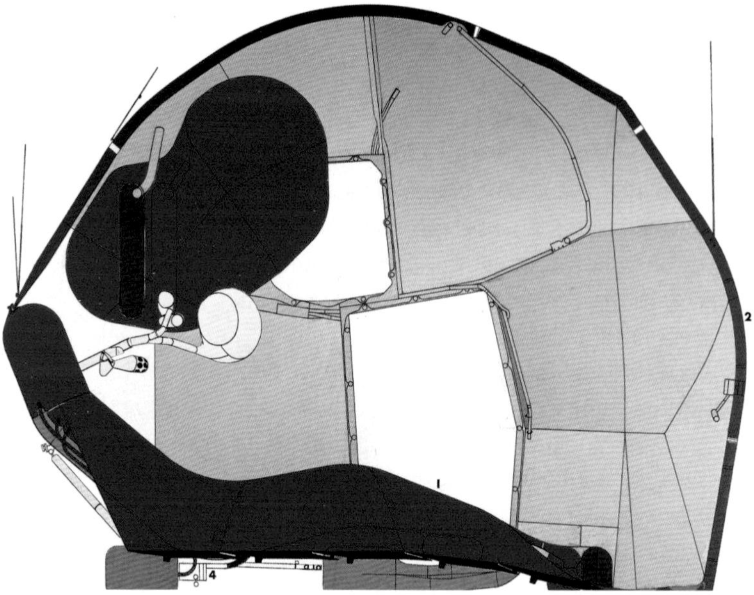

(fig. 5) Michael Webb (Archigram), Cushicle
(fig. 6) Konrad Frey, Cowicle/Kuhwickel

yet they attack this scene with a similar archness: which compares strangely with the pragmatic view that most Anglo-Saxons have of computerised analysis.'[16] Acknowledging the fact that architects spent countless days and nights writing their own computer programs in order to outflank urban planners with comparatively abstract diagrams, Cook must have found such cunning and 'archness' both fascinating and alienating.

Airlift of utopias

Archigram was also held in high esteem by the Austrians. Hans Hollein's attention was drawn to Archigram by Philip Johnson in 1964, after one of his works had been reproduced in a magazine[17] (apparently without Hollein's knowledge). At the beginning of 1965, in the first issue of the magazine Bau, which he edited together with Sokratis Dimitriou, Günther Feuerstein and Gustav Peichl, Hollein presented a reproduction of Ron Herron's ***Walking City***[18] to illustrate his theories on the city of the future.[19] In June of the following year, Hollein took part in the 'International Dialogue of Experimental Architecture', organised by Archigram in Folkestone/Kent. Cook was one of the speakers at this event, at which the ***Walking City*** was used as a backdrop.[20] *Bau* again printed a report on Archigram[21] in 1968, and in 1969 Cook was able to use material from the two special issues 'Neue Konzeptionen aus Wien' (which was not actually published until the summer of 1970 and also contained many projects by Abraham and Florian)[22] and 'Neue Konzeptionen aus Graz'[23] for his 'Austrian Phenomenon'. In the editorial of the Graz issue, Hollein indirectly referred to a book that Cook was writing at that time, and even appeared to be familiar with its contents: 'The Viennese (or Austrian) phenomenon is being talked about all over the world, and work and publications about it are planned in places including USA and England.'[24] Although they did not know one another, he saw Archigram as a group that 'works along similar lines' to the experimental architects of Austria, until it was joyfully acknowledged 'that similar tendencies were being observed in several places, and this was confirmation of the efforts that had been vehemently rejected or ridiculed by the "experts".'[25] As a result: 'Contacts were initiated, information was exchanged and publications on the subject were created.'[26]
From the middle of the 1960s, the Austria/England axis existed as an airlift of utopian ideas, images and buildings, allowing visions of mobile, flexible architecture based on airships and spacecrafts to soar back and forth, temporarily docking onto megastructures or moving around as a permanent satellite. In 1965, in reference to the ***Walking City***, Hans Hollein made the prediction 'we will have mobile cities,'[27] which echoed back a year later from Peter Cook: 'Mobile villages can be used everywhere [...]'[28]
The consistently structuralist contributions in the Graz issue of *Bau*, overseen by Bernhard Hafner as a guest editor from Los Angeles, are almost exclusively the work of students – impressive evidence of the high creative and intellectual standards found in the architectural drawing rooms of the Graz University of Technology. Many of the contributions are not only parallel phenomena, but sometimes real tributes to Archigram. When it is open, Konrad Frey's ***Agglomeration von Apparaten zur Bedürfnisbefriedigung***,[29] which belongs to the project *Auflösung des Hauses*, is confusingly similar

fig. 2 → reference 157)

fig. 3 → reference 158)

fig. 4 → reference 159)

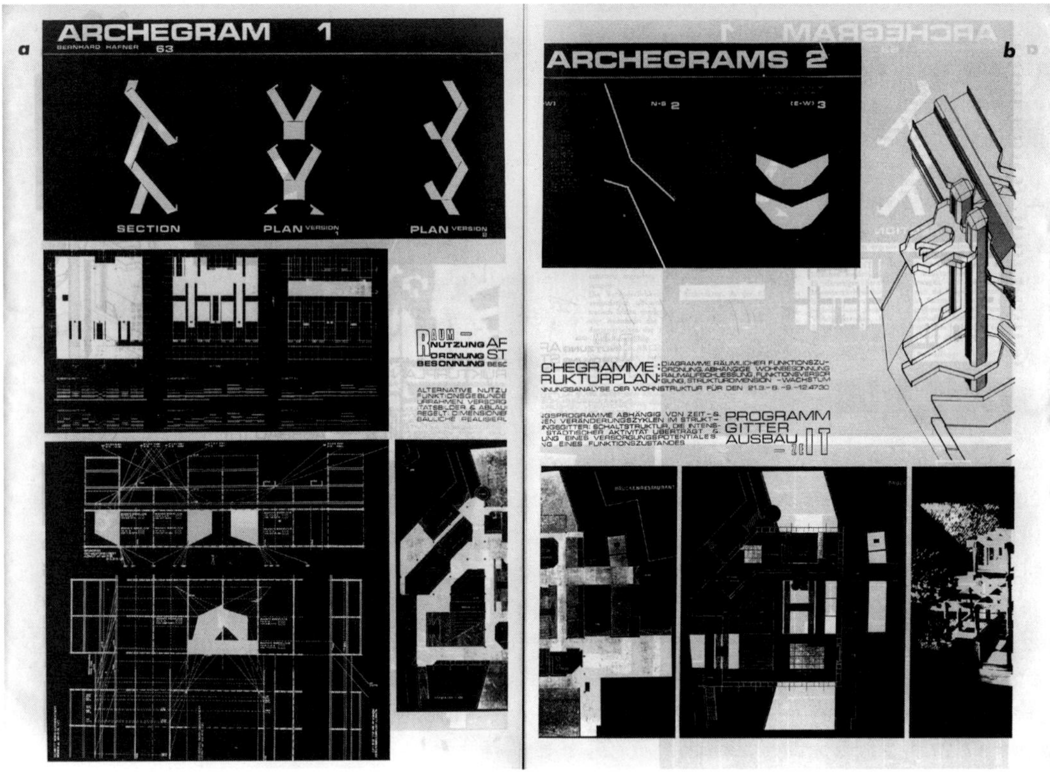

(fig. 7a) Bernhard Hafner: Archegram 1 + 2
(fig. 7b) Peter Cook and Konrad Frey at Archigram symposium, Kunsthalle Wien, April 1994

to Michael Webb's portable living cell, the ***Cushicle***. (Of course, Webb's cover is inflatable, whereas Frey's consists of a fixed plexiglass shell.)[30] A year later, Frey transferred the principle of portable living accommodation to cows, allowing Webb's ***Cushicle*** to mutate to ***Cowicle***.[31] Hafner's ***Archegrams, Diagramme räumlicher Funktionszuordnung***, which were created as early as 1962 at the design studio of the Graz urban planning professor Hubert Hoffmann, differ from the neologism *Archigram* only in that they refer to diagrams rather than telegrams.[32] Hafner chose this title in a deliberate allusion to his London colleagues (whose drawings he saw more as diagrams than as construction plans in the conventional sense). This meant that he took notice of Cook & Co two years before Hollein, at a time when no international medium had made any mention of *Archigram*.[33] In 1968 they met in person when Hafner was teaching at the University of California in Los Angeles together with Warren Chalk, who held a guest professorship there, and Cook, Ron Herron and Dennis Crompton joined them.[34] Cook's impression of Hafner's 'archness' probably stems from this encounter.

fig. 5 → reference 160)
fig. 6 → reference 161)
fig. 7 a → reference 162)

Konrad Frey, who was already the most congenial recipient of Archigram as a student in Graz – the *Archigram* slogan 'economy of means' [35] would later become his credo – developed to become the most important figure in the transfer of Austro-British architecture after Hollein and Hafner. After completing his diploma, he went to London in 1968 to work for Arup Associates. In 1970, he became self-employed along with Florian Beigel, opening the office Building, Planning & Resources (BPR), which operated in London until 1975.[36] Frey, who also taught at the Kingston Polytechnic, became acquainted with Cook and his colleagues through the Architectural Association, as well as Cedric Price, who was admired by both Frey and Cook. He also met Peter Blundell Jones, who later became an architecture critic.[37] Blundell Jones studied at the AA from 1966–72 and made the 'Graz School' internationally known from 1988 onwards, publishing numerous articles in the *Architectural Review*[38] and the book *Dialogues in Time*[39].

fig. 7 b → reference 162)

The project ***Sundome***, which BPR submitted for patenting in 1971 with Anthony Hunt Associates, is a shell structure made of double-curved plexiglass panels, which anticipates the Kunsthaus shell in both technical and formal terms. Behind the bulbous form of coupled (half) spheres were examples of the pneumatic exhibition halls that were so popular in the 1960s. The most famous of these, Victor Lundy's *AEC Pavilion* (1960), was published in *Archigram* No. 6. As was often the case, the Graz contribution consisted of a technical-constructive specification of British pipe dreams.

fig. 8 → reference 163)
fig. 9 → reference 164)

Frey's diploma thesis, a structuralist new construction of the ***Protestant Parish Centre*** at Kaiser-Josef Square in Graz with an underground car park and ramps, was intellectually related to Michael Webb's Master's thesis ***Sin Centre*** from 1962, which featured an equally structuralist leisure centre for London's Leicester Square with a multi-storey car park, ramps, moving walkways and stairs, and a curved plastic skin.[40] This design also belongs in the long line of the ancestors of the Kunsthaus in Graz, along with the ***House for the year 1990*** (1967) by *Archigram*. All of these designs refer to their founding father ***Fun Palace*** by Cedric Price. Frey planned the church interior as an elevated square hall, to which he gave the name ***Environmental Jukebox***. Its 'multiactive

fig. 10 → reference 165)
fig. 11 → reference 166)
fig. 12 → reference 167)

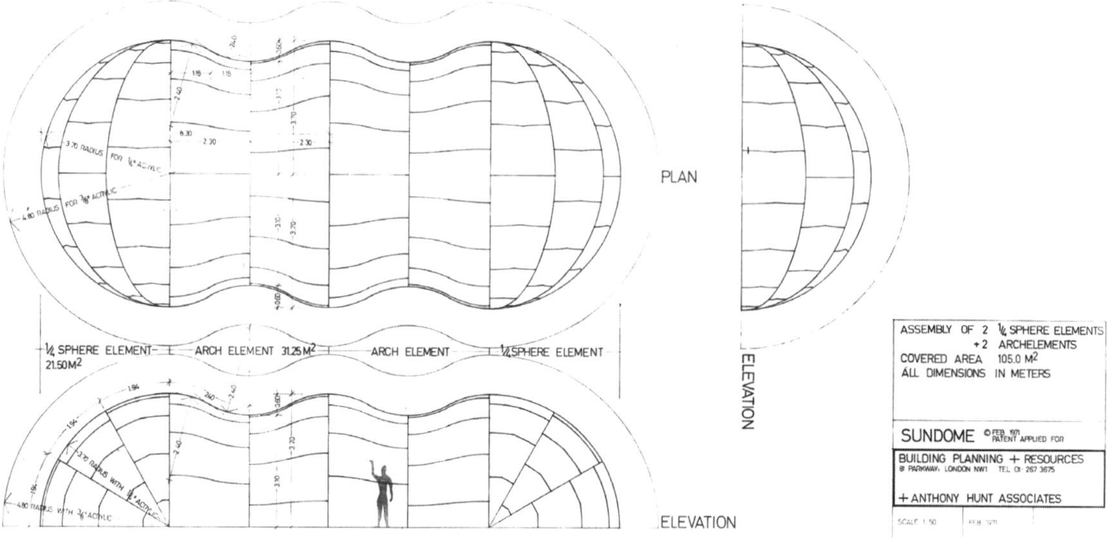

(fig. 8) Building, Planning & Resources and Anthony Hunt Associates, Sundome – shell structures for halls, intersection, floor plan and elevation external skin' was to encourage the creativity of members of the community by creating audio-visual illusions of the images, sounds and smells they designed, in a similar way to the walls of Archigram's future house. Its users – whose emancipation in the architectural discourse of the time was an important democratic-political concern – could also programme these walls with 'images, colours and scents'.[41]

In Cook's and Fournier's description of their competition design for the Kunsthaus, which fused the belief in progress that reigned in the 1960s with the digital euphoria of the 1990s, this external multimedia skin was expanded to become an organic-flexible technological wonder: '*Two different kinds of Media Cells are proposed along or within the skin: Individual multimedia stations that might include flatscreen LCD displays or VR goggles, along the folds of the western part of the skin. Larger Media cells provided along the skin at various locations along the north and east facades. The display hardware is implanted within the skin surface [...]. The Media Cells can also be unplugged from the skin surface and relocated elsewhere within the exhibition area. [...] The skin is a laminated fabric incorporating a mesh of tensile threads and compression ribs enabling it to span the width of the roof without intermediate structural supports. [...] Fluids, fiber-optic cables and other infrastructure elements are channelled through the fabric by means of laminated bladders. It is also proposed to use the structural carbon threads of the laminate as network cabling connections to node point load and light sensors that can in turn control smart fabric panels and flexible solar cells. The lamination technique is also used to insert within the skin discrete elements such as audio-visual display-screens, loudspeakers, lighting elements and projection equipment. The performance specifications of the skin vary continuously along its surface, from the properties of a rigid, opaque surface to those of a flexible, transparent membrane.*' [42] As we know, due to a lack of financial and technological means, hardly any of these ideas were realised. The opaque to transparent Skin was replaced by a cladding made of double-curved plexiglass sheets over a reinforced concrete core (which proved difficult enough in its implementation) and the multimedia element was reduced to one **BIX** (big pixel) façade consisting of 946 simple white fluorescent lamps ('simply bathroom fittings', as Cook would later somewhat coquettishly write).[43] What remained was the external form, the fossil of a utopian bubble from the 1960s with science fiction from the 1990s – whereby, as we shall see in a moment, the Kunsthaus was moving even closer to its existing local relatives. However, it must be admitted that the emancipatory idea from 1968 was not, as is often the case, immediately replaced by a neoliberal logic of marketing. The concept of retaining a low threshold on the **ground floor**, both literally and metaphorically, was still pursued, at least in the first few years. It was also opened up to media art, which attracted a mainly younger audience.

→ competition 219)

→ BIX 205)

→ Medienkunstlabor 014)

Return to earth

20 years after *Experimental Architecture*, Cook published a successor: in *New Spirit in Architecture*, which Cook edited in cooperation with Rosie Llewelyn-Jones, the focus of the 'Austrian Phenomenon' had shifted somewhat from Vienna to Graz. Out of the

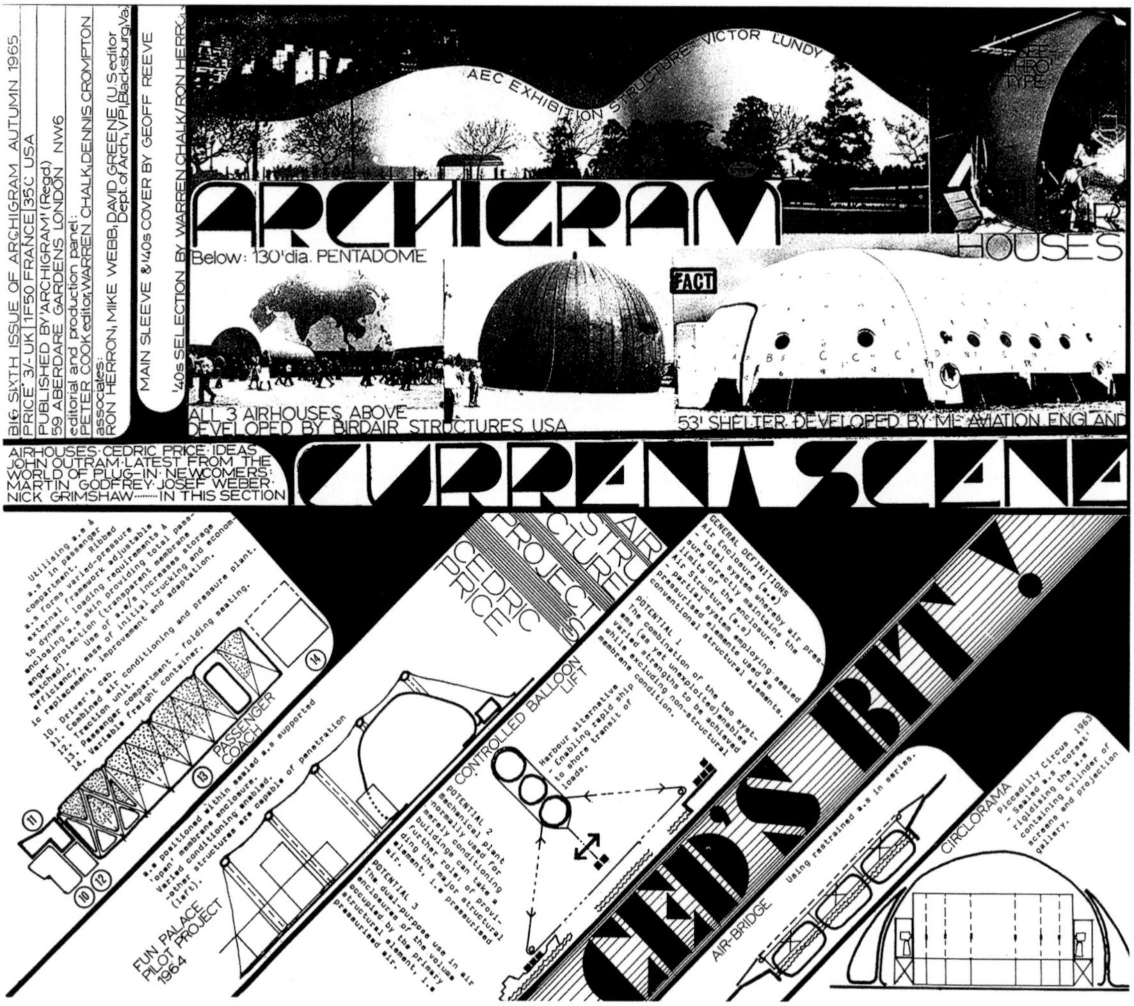

(fig. 9) Victor Lundy, AEC Pavilion in: Archigram No. 6 – 'Current Scene' and 'Cel's Bit,' 1965

40 architectural offices from Europe, Israel, Japan, Australia and the USA mentioned in the catalogue section, three were from Vienna (Coop Himmelb(l)au, Haus-Rucker-Co and Christoph Langhof, although the offices of the latter two were located in Düsseldorf and Berlin) and three from Graz: Günther Domenig, Szyszkowitz + Kowalski and Volker Giencke.[44] Hollein, who had remained too postmodern for Cook's liking, was only attributed a historical role in the introduction. Being considered 'too formal', he no longer appeared in the catalogue. The sculptor Walter Pichler, on the other hand, advanced to become the new founding father not only of Austrian but of international experimental architecture, providing inspiration on a worldwide scale.[45] It was now no longer the mobile and ephemeral charm of inflatable space capsules that attracted Cook in Pichler's work, but the archaic and physical quality of 'earthbound chambers'.[46] The postmodern ending of utopias and their replacement through the individual myths of art did not go unnoticed by Cook. The same applied to the 'Graz School's' development away from megastructural technological utopias to the radical/individual gesture,[47] which was especially typical of Szyszkowitz + Kowalski and Günther Domenig. Cook now identified the latter as a 'key figure' of the 'Graz School', describing him as 'implicitly anarchic' and expressionistic as well as 'dynamic and inventive'.[48] Domenig was responsible for the 1970s building that must be described as the closest local relative of the Kunsthaus, and which Cook in 2016 quoted as being 'certainly an inspiration' for the 'friendly alien': the multipurpose hall at the *Franciscan Sisters' boarding school* in Graz-Eggenberg. The building was commissioned and conceived in 1973, when the partnership between Domenig and Eilfried Huth still existed, and completed in 1977 by Domenig (and his associate Volker Giencke). At that time, anybody else would have responded to the flexibility required for this building with a neutral shell, as light as possible, which could easily be modified. Domenig, on the other hand, built a cave out of sprayed concrete, a technique which, in Austria, had formerly only been used in tunnel construction. In a similar way to the Kunsthaus, the choice of material was not entirely voluntary, as the building authorities had rejected the original plans for a wooden construction due to the risk of fire.[49] The multipurpose hall bears no relation to the structuralist designs from the first 'Graz School'; rather, Cook's central motif was the connection between archaic corporeality and earthiness discovered by Cook in Pichler's work. The building, which crouches down towards the inner courtyard, seems to have grown organically out of the ground like a rock, and at the same time it has something animalistic about it. Peter Blundell Jones sees it as 'A kind of crouching creature';[50] 'is it crawling out of the courtyard walls [...]?' asks Christian Hunziker,[51] and Friedrich Achleitner observes a 'double effect of cave and shell as the sedimentation of life processes.'[52] Domenig himself attributed the shape of the fossilised reptilian body to a gesture that was not only individual, but collective, since the craftsmen had discovered 'room for creative development' and 'work had become fun again.'[53]

fig. 13 → reference 168)

Irrespective of that, Domenig's change in direction towards the earthly and archaic was also taking place on the other side of the English Channel. At the same time as Domenig began planning for the multipurpose hall, Cook was working on his '*Lump*'

fig. 14 → reference 169)

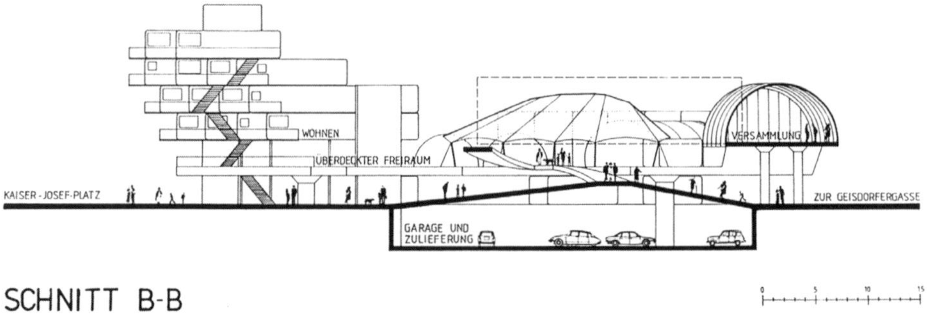

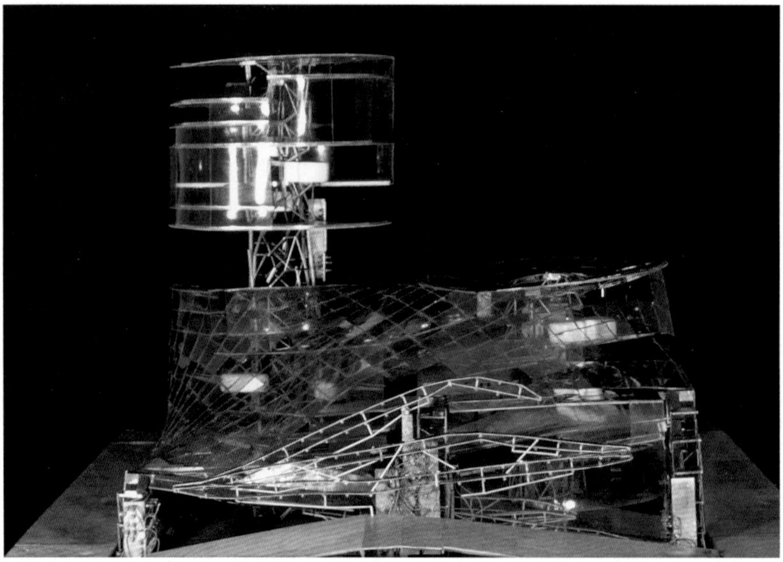

(fig. 10) Konrad Frey, refurbishment of church block,
Kaiser-Josef-Platz, Graz
(fig. 11) Michael Webb, Interments Palace, Leicester Square, London
(The Sin Centre), model photograph

images, overgrown hills with tongues protruding from them and cave-like entrances; these were also designed as smooth domed rooms, the shells of which were thinned out to form a translucent membrane. This change from the space capsule to the cave may seem surprising, but it is still in line with the monadic existence proclaimed in *Archigram*'s slogan 'Everybody is a satellite'.[54] Only now it appeared in a natural *low-tech* or even better *no-tech* version, in response to the rediscovery of 'Spaceship Earth' after the oil shock and the Club of Rome's report *The Limits to Growth*.[55] 'It was years later,' writes Cook in 2016, 'that I realised that [...] Günther Domenig [...], who had grown up among the Alpine foothills of Klagenfurt, had made drawings that were similarly inspired.'[56] Colin Fournier also relates the organic qualities of caves and mountains to the Kunsthaus design in 2003, drawing attention to its similarity with the oscillation between cave and reptile in the Eggenberg multipurpose hall: 'The genealogy of the project's biomorphic form lies in its designers' [Cook and Fournier] long standing fascination with the animal presence of architecture and in the checkered history of the competition for the Kunsthaus, which was originally intended to inhabit a large cavity within the Schloßberg, the hill standing in the centre of the city. The parti adopted by the authors at the time was to line this rocky cavity with an organically shaped membrane filling its complex and rough internal contours and to allow this membrane to protrude out of the mountain and into the city, like the tail or tongue of a dragon. When the location of the museum was changed to its current site along the Mur, the dragon skin found its way across the river, flowed into the irregular geometric boundary of the new site and wrapped itself around the two elevated decks of the museum, forming an environmental enclosure that resembles neither roofs nor walls nor floors but a seamless morphing of the three.'[57] Four years lay between this 'dragon's tongue' or 'skin' and the original vision of a multimedia tech membrane, but the leap of argumentation was well within the range of Cook's oeuvre so far. The fossilisation of the membrane shifted the Kunsthaus closer to Domenig's multipurpose hall, whose roof lights, lined up like a vertebral column, were 'certainly an inspiration' for the '**Nozzles**' of the Kunsthaus.

→ design 106)

→ Kunsthaus 172)

When Domenig became a professor of building typology at the TU Graz in 1980, he invited Cedric Price and Peter Cook to hold guest lectures. 'From this point onward,' writes Cook in 2016, looking back, 'Graz sprouted a continuous series of strange, inventive, often original buildings that were disproportionally vibrant for a small city, so it became one of my regular targets for crocodiles of London or Frankfurt students that I brought to Austria.'[58] Among these 'strange, inventive buildings,' Cook particularly highlighted Giencke's greenhouses at the ***Botanical Garden***, which consist of parabolic cylinders with double-walled plexiglass panels that seem to sink halfway into the ground. Cook and Llewelyn-Jones see it as 'the product of a major air disaster' with broken fuselage and wings as well as 'some winged insect in serious trouble.[59] These associations, which may seem rather far-fetched, are not arrived at by chance. They connect a prototypical symbol of modernity – the aeroplane – with the animalistic, thus following Archigram's path from the space capsule to the dragon and confronting both with the irony of their failure. This cancels out the utopia in deconstruction in a dialectic manner – both preserved and invalid at the same time.

fig. 15
→ reference 170)

(fig. 12) Konrad Frey, refurbishment of church block,
Kaiser-Josef-Platz, Graz
(fig. 13) Günther Domenig / Eilfried Huth,
Multipurpose hall at the Schulschwestern in Graz-Eggenberg,
(view with the zinc sheet cladding fitted in 1989)

When Peter Cook and Colin Fournier took part in the competition for the Kunsthaus in 1999/2000, together with 101 other architectural offices from Austria, Germany, Switzerland, Italy, Holland, England, the USA and Japan, the jury was firmly in the hands of members of the 'Graz School'. On the architectural side, these were the Graz architects Volker Giencke (who was elected chairman) and Klaus Gartler, the TU Graz graduates Kjetil Thorsen (Oslo) and Dietmar Feichtinger (Paris) and, as the only 'non-Graz member' (and the only woman), Odile Decq from Paris. This group was joined by the art mediators Wolfgang Lorenz, Dieter Bogner, Kasper König and Harald Szeemann.[60] Following two days of discussions, a unanimous decision was made to award the 'friendly alien' first prize and, 'because of the excellent quality'[61] of the project, no second and third prizes were awarded. Looking back at the competition entries today, it must be acknowledged that the jury did not, as is so often the case, opt for a feasible compromise, but took the risk of selecting the strongest and boldest project. We could also say that the members of the 'Graz School' chose as their winner the design that 'appears to be quite out of this world',[62] but which at the same time had been deeply familiar to them for a long time.

↗ competition p. 349)

(fig. 14) Peter Cook, Vegetated Lump/Smooth Lump

1 Cf. Cook, Fournier, 'Skin und Pin. Wettbewerb', in: Renate Ilsinger/Haus der Architektur (ed.), *Kunsthaus Graz. Dokumentation des Wettbewerbs*, Graz 2003, pp. 20–37, here 20; 'Friendly Alien gelandet – Über das neue Kunsthaus in Graz'. Heinz Schütz in conversation with Peter Cook and Colin Fournier, in: Kunstforum International 169 (March–April 2004), pp. 391–394, here 391.

2 Loc. cit.

3 The architecture fanzine *Archigram* was first published in 1961 by Peter Cook, David Greene and Michael (Mike) Webb in London. In 1962 Ron Herron, Dennis Crompton and Warren Chalk joined the editorial team. From 1963 onwards, the six young architects worked together on joint design projects and exhibitions, naming themselves Archigram. The 10th and last edition of *Archigram* (No. 9 ½) was published in 1974; in the same year the office of Archigram Architects closed. Cf. http://archigram.westminster.ac.uk/about.php?pg=archi (23.07.2020). In secondary literature, the fact that they went under the same name often resulted in the contents of the journal *Archigram* being mistaken for the work of the Archigram group of architects. This meant that the many articles on other architects (e.g. architects from Austria) that appeared in Archigram were misappropriated. A negative example in *this respect is A Guide to Archigram 1961–74/Ein Archigram-Programm 1961–74*, exhibition catalogue, Kunsthalle Wien, London 1994, the most important reference publication on Archigram/Archigram to date.

4 Cf. *Archigram* 5 (1964), 17, online: http://archigram.westminster.ac.uk/magazine.php?id=100 (21.07.2020).

5 The comparison falls a little short, of course, because the Renaissance and Baroque master builders from northern Italy and Graubünden who worked in Graz did not run businesses in their home towns, but were more like guest or migrant workers who sometimes settled permanently in Graz.

6 Cf. overview: Anselm Wagner, Sophia Walk (eds.), *Architekturführer Graz*, Berlin 2019.

7 Cf. the biographical information in: Peter Blundell Jones, *Dialogues in Time. New Graz Architecture*, Graz 1998, pp. 355–63; Bernhard Hafner, 'Editorial', in: *Bau. Schrift für Architektur und Städtebau* 24 (1969), issue. 4/5, p. 26.

8 Cook, Peter: *Experimental Architecture*, London 1970, p. 76.

9 Cook 1970 (loc. cit.), p. 71.

10 Cf. Porsch, Johannes/Architekturzentrum Wien (ed.): *The Austrian Phenomenon. Architektur Avantgarde* Österreich 1956–1973, Basel 2004, p. 138.

11 Cf. *Archigram* 8 (1968), 14/2, 18/1, online: http://archigram.westminster.ac.uk/magazine.php?id=103&src=mg (21.07.2020).

12 Cf. Cook 1970 (see note. 8), pp. 72, 73, 74, 134–137.

13 Peter Cook, 'archizone 2: Europe', in: *Archigram* 9 (1970), p. 19, online: http://archigram.westminster.ac.uk/magazine.php?id=104&src=mg (21.07.2020).

14 On the distinction between the 'first' and the 'second Graz School' cf. Anselm Wagner, 'Wie die "Grazer Schule" zweimal erfunden worden ist', in: Anselm Wagner, Antje Senarclens de Grancy (eds.), *Was bleibt von der 'Grazer Schule'? Architektur-Utopien seit den 1960ern revisited* (= architektur + analyse vol. 1), Berlin 2012, pp. 55–73.

15 Cf. Bernhard Hafner, 'Rethinking Structures. Die Stadt auf dem Prüfstand des Strukturalismus', in: loc. cit., pp. 238–259.

16 Cook, 'archizone', 1970 (s. note 13).

17 Cf. Hans Hollein, 'A comment from Hans Hollein', in: Peter Cook (ed.), *Archigram*, New York 1999, p. 6. This must refer either to Hollein's *Architektonische Form* in *Archigram* 4 (1964), 14, online: http://archigram.westminster.ac.uk/magazine.php?id=99&src=mg (21.07.2020) or to *Stadtzentrum* in *Archigram* 5 (1964), 9, online: http://archigram.westminster.ac.uk/magazine.php?id=100 (21.07.2020). Walter Pichler's *Stadtstudie* can also be found on the same page of *Archigram* 5. On page 21f., Hollein and Pichler are mentioned as 'contributors'.

18 Cf. Hans Hollein, 'Zukunft der Architektur', in: *Bau. Schrift für Architektur und Städtebau* 20 (1965), issue 1, pp. 8–11, here 8, fig. 3.

19 Loc. cit., p. 11.

20 Cf. Hans Hollein, 'International Dialogue of Experimental Architecture', in: *Bau. Schrift für Architektur und Städtebau* 21 (1966), issue. 3, p. 55.

21 Cf. Hans Hollein, 'Die große Zahl. 14. Triennale die Milano 1968. Internationale Ausstellung für moderne dekorative und angewandte Kunst und moderne Architektur', in: *Bau. Schrift für Architektur und Städtebau* 23 (1968), issue 4, pp. 68–78, here 72.

22 Cf. *Bau. Schrift für Architektur und Städtebau* 24 (1969), issue 2/3, pp. 14, 16–18.

23 Cf. *Bau. Schrift für Architektur und Städtebau* 24 (1969), issue 4/5.

24 Hans Hollein, 'Zu diesem Heft', in: loc. cit., p. 25.

25 Loc. cit.

26 Loc. cit.

27 Hans Hollein, 'Zukunft der Architektur', in: *Bau. Schrift für Architektur und Städtebau* 20 (1965), issue 1, pp. 8–11, here 8; printed in: Porsch, 2004 (s. note 8), pp. 774–775, here 775.

28 Cook, Peter: Blow-Out Village [1966], in: *A Guide to Archigram* 1994 (s. note 3), pp. 190–191, here 190.

29 *Bau. Schrift für Architektur und Städtebau* 24 (1969), issue 4/5, p. 33.

30 Cf. Ingrid Böck, 'Wohnen im Universalwerkzeug', in: *Konrad Frey: Werkkatalog*, KF 006, Auflösung des Hauses, http://konrad-frey.tugraz.at/projekt/aufloesung-des-hauses (21.07.2020). The project is not from 1967, as stated in *Bau*, but from 1966.

31 Cf. *Bau* 1969 (s. note 23), p. 32.

32 Cf. loc. cit., pp. 37. Bernhard Hafner kindly informed me of the development history in an e-mail dated 21.07.2020; cf. also Blundell Jones, 1998 (s. note 7), p. 67, 80, note 15.

33 The first reports are published in 1963 in the Italian journal *Edilizia Moderna* – little known in Austria – and the English

↗ p.79

(fig. 15) Volker Giencke, greenhouses, University of Graz Botanical Garden

Living Arts Magazine; from 1964 onwards in more widely known journals such as *L'Architecture d'aujourd'hui and Architectural Forum*; cf. Cook, 1999 (s. note 17), pp. 142.

34 Cf. Bernhard Hafner in an e-mail to Anselm Wagner dated 21.07.2020.

35 Cf. *Archigram* 6 (1965), 4, online: http://archigram.westminster.ac.uk/magazine.php?id=101&src=mg (21.07.2020).

36 Cf. http://konradfrey.tugraz.at/biografie/ (16.07.2020).

37 Cf. Konrad Frey in a conversation with Anselm Wagner, Graz, 04.06.2020.

38 Cf. Peter Blundell Jones, 'Graz 2020: Raum, Bedeutung und Partizipation', in: Wagner, Senarclens de Grancy, 2012 (s. note 14), pp. 36–54, here 36.

39 Cf. Blundell Jones, 1998 (s. note 7).

40 Cf. Mike Webb, 'Sin Centre', in: Cook, 1999 (s. note 17), pp. 12.

41 Cf. Living, 1990, in: *A Guide to Archigram*, 1994 (see note 3), pp. 197–199, here 199.

42 Cook/Fournier 2003 (see note 1), 26, pp. 32–35.

43 Peter Cook, *Architecture Workbook. Design through motive*, Chichester 2016, p. 180.

44 Cf. Peter Cook, Rosie Llewelyn-Jones, New Spirit in Architecture, New York 1990, pp. 20–23, 36–39, 60–63, 88–91, 100–103, 116–119.

45 Loc. cit., p. 16.

46 Loc. cit.

47 Cf. Peter Weibel, 'Zur steirischen Architekturszene. Zwischen Konzeption, Formalismus und Pragmatik', in: Alexandra Foitl, Christa Steinle (eds.): *Styrian Window. Ein Handbuch zur Gegenwartskunst der Steiermark*, Graz 1996, pp. 108–114, here pp. 108; Anselm Wagner, 'Wie die 'Grazer Schule' zweimal erfunden worden ist', in: Wagner, Senarclens de Grancy, 2012 (see note 14), pp. 55–73, here pp. 64.

48 Cook, Llewelyn-Jones, 1990 (see note 44), p. 17.

49 Cf. Günther Domenig, *Werkbuch*, Salzburg/Vienna 1991, p. 70. In 1989, the concrete skin had to be covered in zinc sheeting for building physical reasons.

50 Blundell Jones, 1998 (s. note 7), p. 57.

51 Christian Hunziker, 'Hängt es oder steht es denn wohl?' in: *Steirische Berichte* 15 (1982), issue. 1, pp. 21–22, quoted in Gudrun Pleyer, *Günther Domenig. Bauten und Projekte*, Diss. University of Graz 1987, p. 149.

52 *Friedrich Achleitner, Österreichische Architektur im 20. Jahrhundert. Ein Führer in drei Bänden. Vol. II. Kärnten, Steiermark, Burgenland.* Salzburg/Vienna 1983, p. 366.

53 Günther Domenig, 'Gedanken zur Architektur', in: *Steirische Berichte* 15 (1982), issue 1, p. 23ff., quoted from Pleyer, 1987 (s. note 51), p. 151.

54 *Archigram* 8 (1968), 15/1, online: http://archigram.westminster.ac.uk/magazine.php?id=103&src=mg (21.07.2020).

55 Cf. Dennis Meadows, Donella Meadows, Erich Zahn, Peter Milling, *Die Grenzen des Wachstums. Bericht des Club of Rome zur Lage der Menschheit*, Stuttgart 1972.

56 Cook, 2016 (s. note 43), p. 26.

57 Colin Fournier, 'a friendly alien. Kunsthaus Graz', in: Kristin Feireiss, Hans Jürgen Commerell (eds.), *curves and spikes. Peter Cook/Colin Fournier and Klaus Kada. Kunsthaus und Stadthalle für Graz*, exhibition catalogue, Aedes West Galerie, Berlin 2003, pp. 8–13, here pp. 10.

58 Cook, 2016 (s. note 43), p. 176.

59 Cook, Llewelyn-Jones, 1990 (s. note 44), p. 119.

60 Cf. Ilsinger/Haus der Architektur, 2003 (s. note 1), p. 159. The jury also included – without the right to vote – the journalist Gerfried Sperl and the gallery owner Rudolf Schilcher.

61 Loc. cit., p. 160

62 Volker Giencke, 'Vorwort', in: loc. cit., p. 17.

Skin
→ 171)
→ 176)
→ 180)
↗ p. 77
↗ p. 79

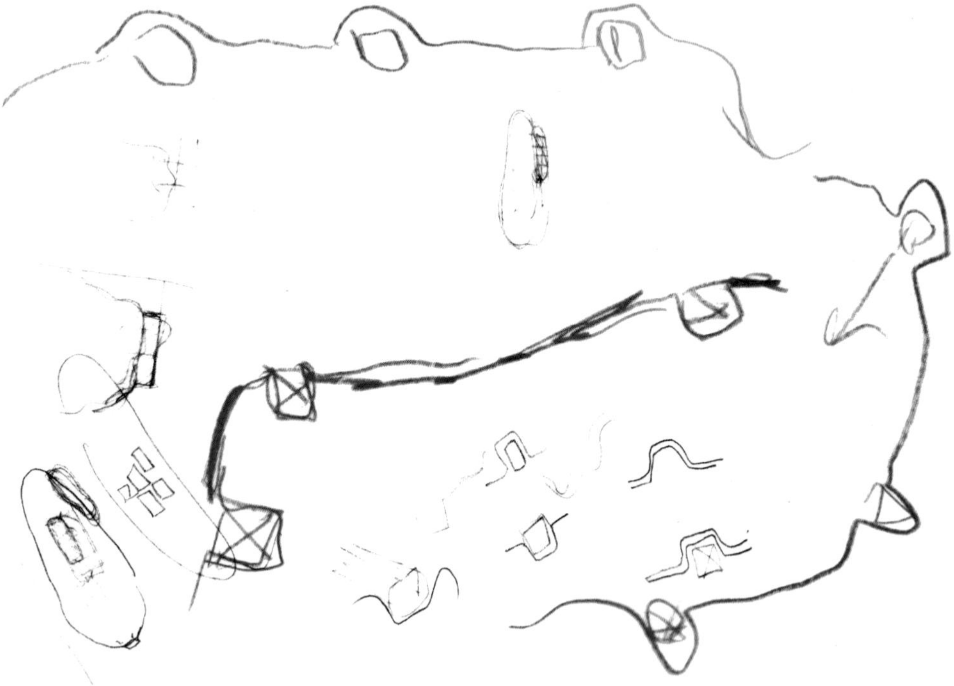

Organic shell with embedded functions. Sketch from the competition, Peter Cook

2004

(Haus
(Bubble

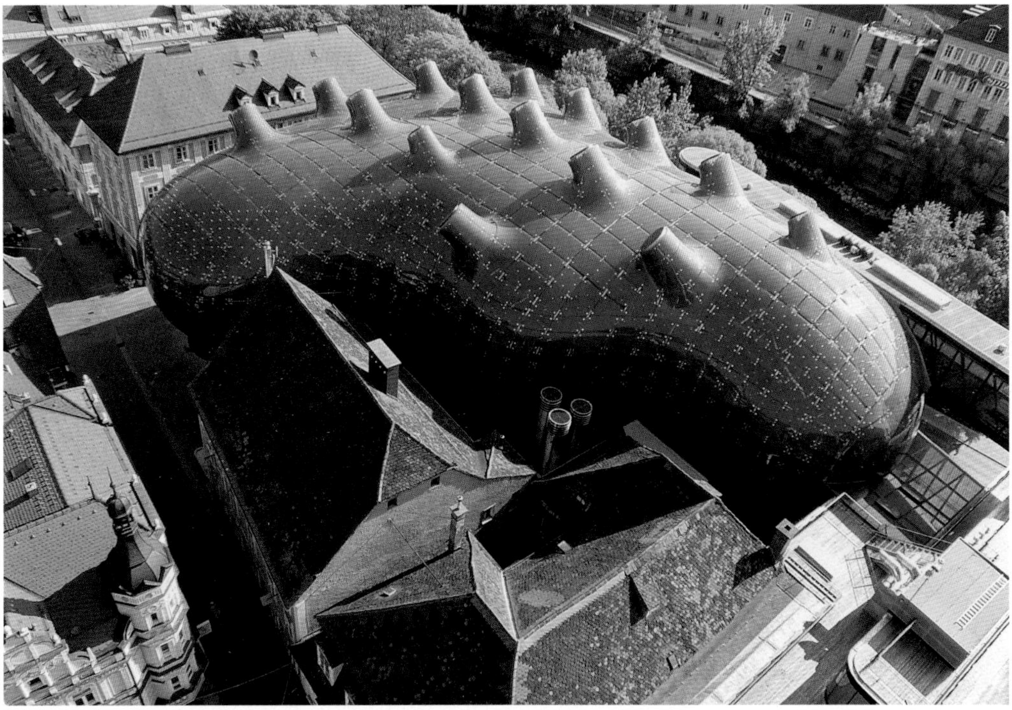

Bubble
→ 173)
→ 174)
Nozzle
→ 141)
design
→ 033)

Photo of Zepp-Cam

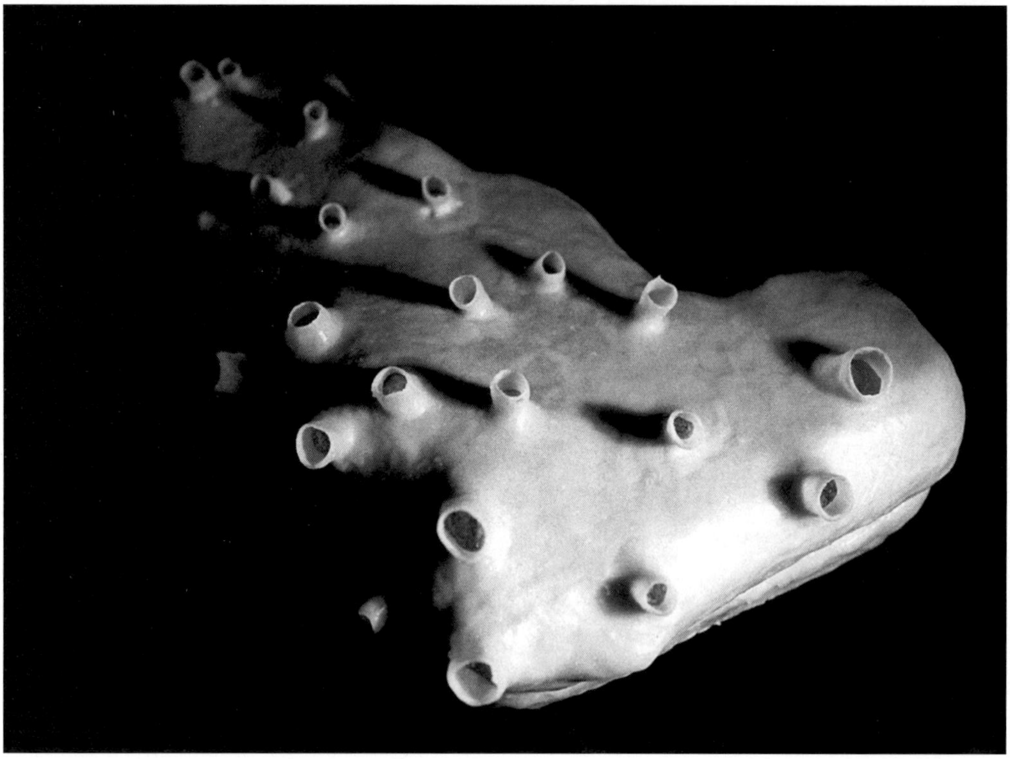

design
→ 176)
↗ p. 49
↗ p. 273

Outer Skin with **Nozzles**. Concept model from the competition, Marcos Cruz

2002

Bubble design

usage
→ 180)
Space01
→ 047)
↗ p. 47

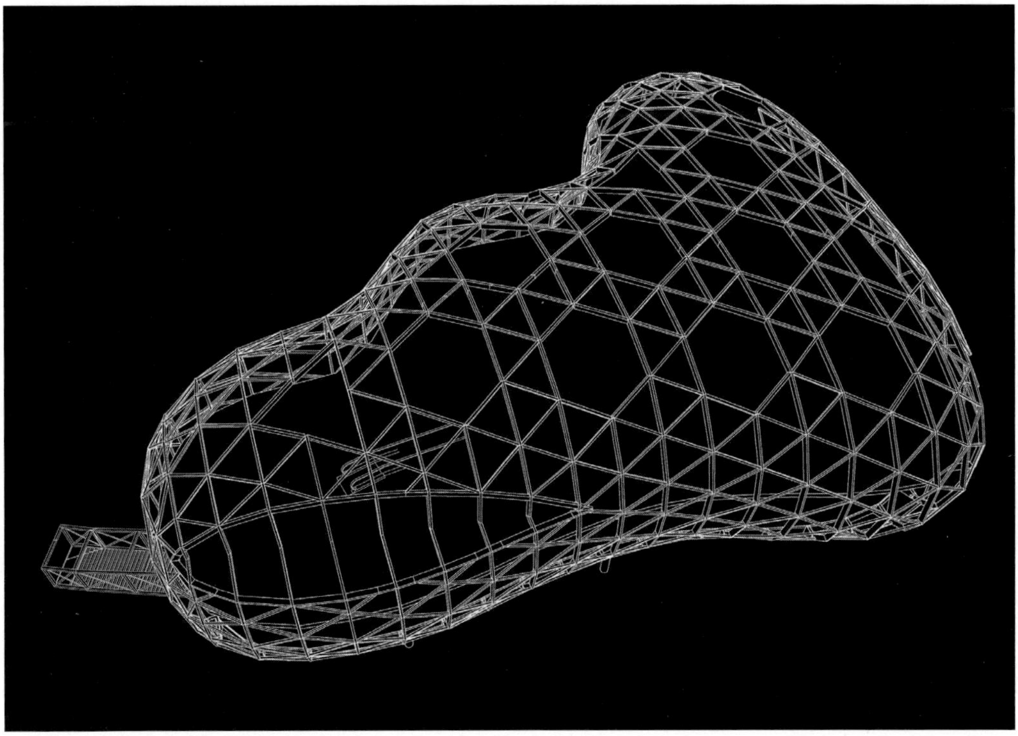

3D drawing of the supporting structure, Gernot Stangl

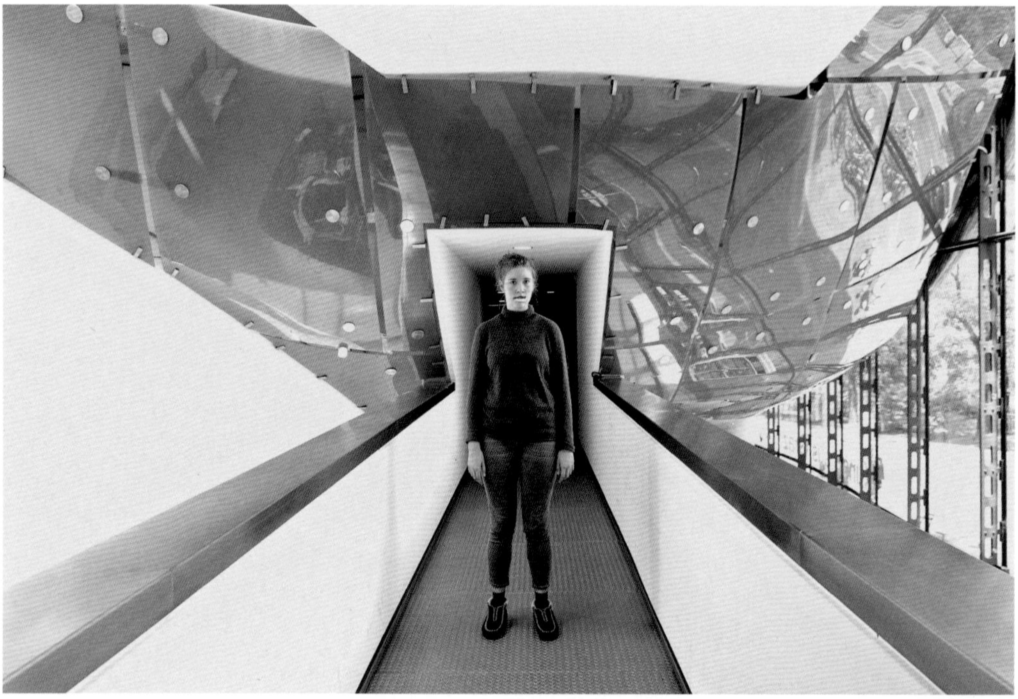

Annou Reiners in ‘I don’t think I am trying to commit suicide’.
Performance Now. Bridge link between Iron House and **Space03**

Space01
→ 047)

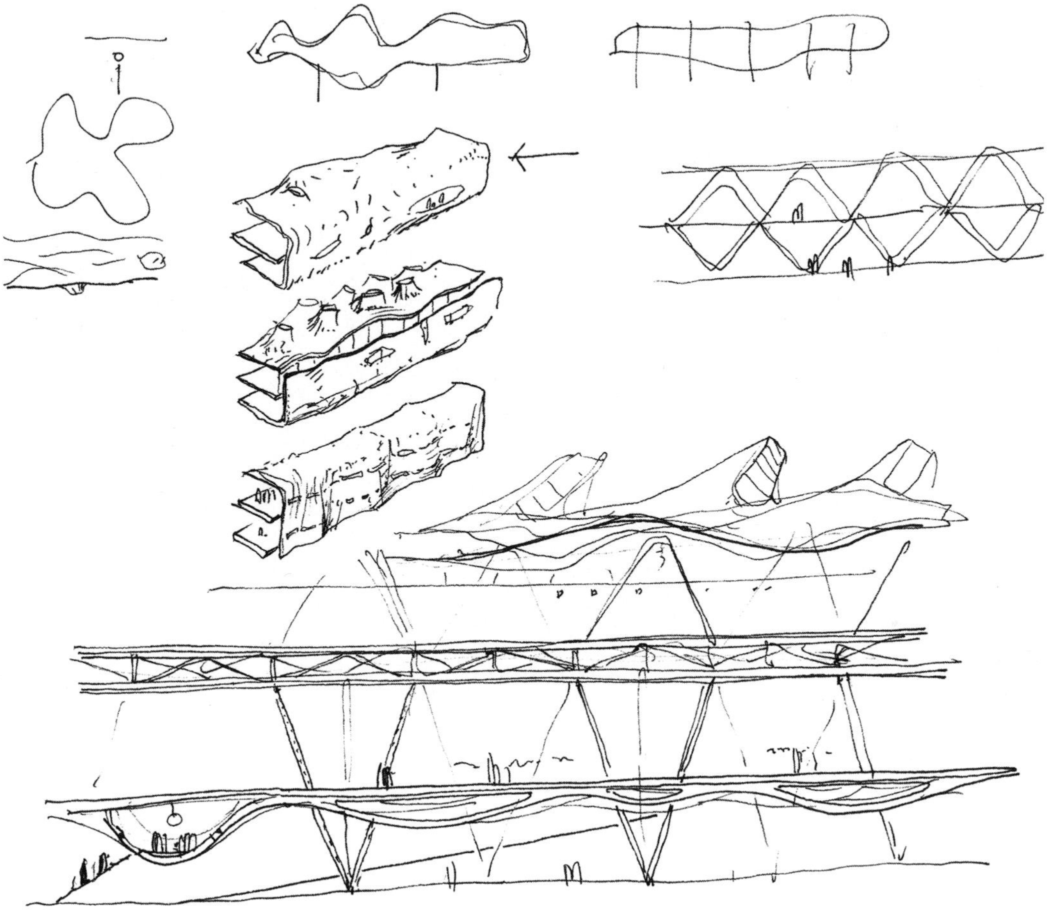

Studies for the organic shell and supporting structures.
Sketches from the competition, Niels Jonkhans

2003

Haus
Space03

↗ p. 49

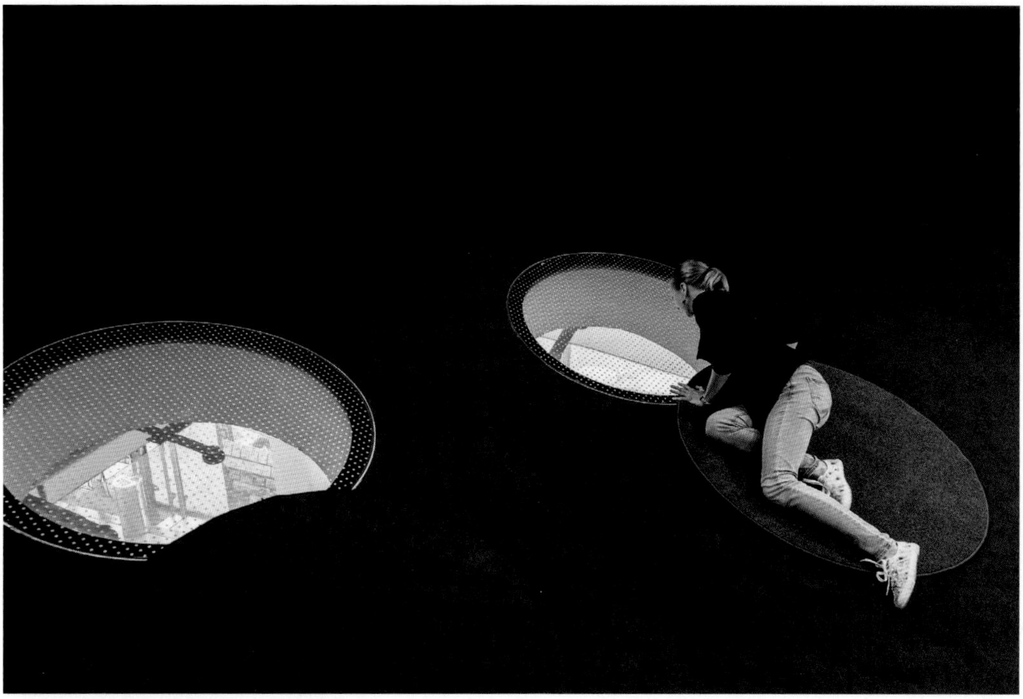

'The windows in **Space03** tell you a lot about the uniqueness of this building. The fact that you can see through the floor is something that piques your curiosity. In effect, these windows allow you to experience up close the shape of the building and its shade of blue, in a kind of microcosm. And the carpets are actually the curtains.'

Antonia Veitschegger, art education

For culture theorist Mieke Bal's video installation **nothing is missing**, **Space03** (lovingly dubbed 'belly' by the architects) was used as exhibition space for the first time. The windowless room in the lower section of the bubble, normally used for children's educational programmes, was the perfect setting to create an intimate living-room atmosphere: Visitors were encouraged to lounge on sofas or chairs while close-ups of women could be seen on surrounding monitors and heard via headphones. The project focused on women who have suffered the loss of relationships through the migration of their own children.

Mieke Bal. nothing is missing

Space01
→ 129)

'My work explores surface perceptions and how surfaces serve as image carriers. The internal membrane of the Kunsthaus, which the architects Cook and Fournier called the **Skin**, is a special projection surface – it reveals the algorithms underlying the architecture, i.e. the way it is constructed. Here, my work overlaps with architecture.'

Peter Kogler, artist

2020

(**Haus**
(staircase
(usage

'In the **staircase** on the top floor, the curvature of the side wall merges with that of the roof and the load-bearing exposed concrete structure becomes clearly visible and actually tangible. In terms of its physicality and form, this is an extremely sensual place – for years I have been observing how our visitors like to stroke and touch it.'

Katrin Bucher Trantow, curator

Looking back. Isa Rosenberger in conversation with Sir Peter Cook, Colin Fournier and Niels Jonkhans. Excerpts from the film The Sky is Glass, 2017

Birke Gorm. Site/Cite. Speaking in Tongues While Splitting One's Own

Looking Back

On the occasion of the exhibition *Up into the Unknown* (Kunsthaus Graz, 2017) the artist Isa Rosenberger was invited to look at the Kunsthaus and its history from today's perspective. For her film *The Sky is Glass*, she had a conversation with Sir Peter Cook, Colin Fournier and Niels Jonkhans, excerpts of which are printed here.

→ Up into the Unknown 037) 107)

PC **Sir Peter Cook**
CF **Colin Fournier**
NJ **Niels Jonkhans**
● **Isa Rosenberger**

● **After a few years, you are now back at the Kunsthaus for the first time. Much has changed since then. What was your first thought?**

PC I think the first thought is, how did we get away with it *(the Kunsthaus)*? And the second thought is, perhaps, would we get away with it today? You know the climate of acceptability of avant-garde architecture has changed.

CF My first thought is perhaps curiosity: each time a new curator comes, he or she totally reinvents the space. I am interested in what happens to the space.

● **What does this building mean to you?**

PC ... in fact, this building was for me personally a trigger of suddenly rescuing me from being a sort of interesting figure in history who has done some books and some teaching and some little tiny things – with Colin suddenly I have done a building that many people talked about and continue to talk about, and that led to building other buildings, and at the age of 80 I am a working architect.

CF It was an amazing opportunity. We would not have been able to do it in London. It just happened that Graz, at that point, as you know, was the Cultural Capital of Europe for 2003. The city was keen to have a new public building, as quickly as possible, in time for the celebration. Therefore, it was made quite easy for us. People always ask us if it was difficult, in a country as conservative as Austria and in a relatively traditional city such as Graz, to propose a radical design, but surprisingly it was not. There were some difficulties, but people wanted this building to happen and the experience turned out to be an extremely satisfying one. The construction was complex, because nobody had done a building of this kind before. Since then, many double-curved buildings have been built, but at the time it was difficult to find a construction company capable of handling a complex geometry. It was really exceptional. It worked out in the end, but it was hard work.

→ design 174)

Big Draw, installation by studio ASYNCHROME, **1st basement**
(under construction)

● **How do you see your relationship with the English group Archigram?**

PC I mean, the relation to Archigram is something which is always made by critics vis-à-vis this building, I have to say I'm a little bit irritated by it, because I think it's a very one-dimensional association and it's an easy association. Certainly you could say Colin and I were involved in Archigram, me particularly, I invented it, and then sort of relative silence, doing this or that, and then the public suddenly takes notice again, and says, 'Ah, wait a minute, Archigram, therefore Kunsthaus is Archigram.' It's a little bit too clear, too easy, because I think Archigram was involved in the possibility of disappearing architecture, replaceable architecture. This *(the Kunsthaus)* is made of modern materials to some extent, it's less inherently replaceable, it's more in the tradition that sits in a particular place, and is particular to this place. I say this, repeatedly, doing a building in another place, we would not repeat the formula as here.

CF Well, there is one Archigram project that is worth mentioning in reference to the Kunsthaus and another project that is not from the Archigram period but that Peter and I did together just before this one: first, the ***Bâtiment Public du Portier*** in Monte Carlo, which was the first competition that Peter and I did together, many years ago. I had just obtained my diploma from the AA school (Peter was at that time director of its Diploma School): the day I got my diploma, Peter asked me if I would join him on a competition for a multi-purpose performance space in Monte Carlo. This project (we won the competition but it was never built) is a very important one in relation to the concept of the Kunsthaus, because what we designed was a building that was completely flexible. It was just an empty platform capable of many transformations, just as the Kunsthaus is, conceptually, an empty platform, a space within which any exhibition can be imagined by the curators. The Monte Carlo building could turn into a skating rink for sporting events, metamorphose into a concert hall for classical music performances or a venue for big conferences, glamourous gala events, etc. it had an incredibly complex programme, and the idea was to offer an open, flexible solution. It was a building that was underground and therefore, unlike this one, and it had no external appearance. Incidentally, it was, in this respect, similar to the underground scheme that Peter and I originally proposed for the Kunsthaus, when the site was in the Schloßberg. In both these projects, the emphasis was on the usage, on the activities, not on the architectural form.

→ reference 031)

● **The second reference is the Schloßberg project?**

CF Yes, our Schloßberg project is another important precedent for the Kunsthaus scheme. The museum, according to the competition brief, had to be buried in the hill. The city intended to connect the air-raid shelters that had been dug in the 'mountain' during World War II, and turn them (which, by the way, they have now done) into one large underground space. In order to make that space useable as a museum, we decided, for our competition project, to line the inner surface of this big cave with a membrane that had to follow the shape of the cavity. The cave had a complex geometry, so the only way to achieve that was to design the membrane as a three-dimensional double-curved surface. At that point, very few people knew

→ reference 077)

2016

Kunst
Haus
staircase

What is the space of the Kunsthaus and how can it be infiltrated? What are the rules in a public institution, and what can we do with them? What barriers exist - architectural, structural and in the minds of people, and how can one overcome them? These questions were the theme of a competition titled 'Open House,' held among a group of selected participants and with the goal to 'infiltrate' the Kunsthaus Graz with artistic tools. One of the two projects chosen was **The Museum as a Gym** by **Aldo Gianotti**, who – with an ironic wink – took a closer look at the behavioural rules and codes of the exhibition space.

Inspired by the idea of an art museum as 'gym for the mind' he created a setting reminiscent of a gym in the exhibition space, using only existing infrastructural features. Through a series of drawings that served as instructions, visitors were encouraged to get to know the Kunsthaus on a physical level. In line with the versatile and open character of the building, the project provided a dynamic, collaborative and participatory encounter with an exhibition space for contemporary art.

Aldo Giannotti. The Museum as a Gym

how to do this, but it was the only solution. We developed a membrane design for this inner Skin. We called our scheme *die Zunge* (*The Tongue*) because at some point the Skin had to stick out of the mountain at street level, partly to bring air into the building but mainly, like the tongue of an anteater, to suck the good citizens of Graz into the museum. And so, some of the key details which you can now see in the Kunsthaus, in particular the concept of its double-curved **Skin** and its **Nozzles**, were actually inherited from that original membrane design. In the Schloßberg project, the Skin had to bring air into the building: we therefore inserted Nozzles into the outer tongue, to suck in the air. That is when the **Nozzles**, at least in the context of the Graz Kunsthaus, first made their appearance.

→ reference 106)

→ Nozzle 122) 123)

PC Something like the naughty nozzle is a direct borrowing of a device that was used in an exhibition in 1963, and in fact invented by Michael Webb. The **Travelator** is something which one has talked about the 'poetry of the diagonal', the notion of gliding up into up the space, I've always wanted to do such a thing, and even now the project we are currently working on is full of ramps, so the business of gliding around diagonally rather than going upstairs, up in a box, in a lift, always appeals me, the notion of almost insidiously moving through three-dimensional space.

→ Travelator 080)

→ usage 079)

I would like to come back to Archigram: The other issue of Archigram, shapes like this, sort of discussed in the 60s, must it all come from the 1960s? Putting on my academic hat I can say, no, we were looking at certain things from the Baroque, we were looking at Expressionism in Germany in the 1920s, we were certainly looking at Poelzig, people like that, we were looking at the tradition of architecture as theatre. In a book that I brought out a year ago, a whole chapter, before I even talk about Graz, I am talking about the notion of architecture as theatre. I am a strong believer that most architecture, which I would describe as boring, it's not because the format is boring, not even the mannerism is boring, but it does not enjoy the notion that event or change of event or progression might occur.

● **Do you see a connection with pop culture?**

CF Pop music, pop art and pop culture in general were so radical in England that they indeed had a considerable impact, and I would agree that they had a background influence on the design of the Kunsthaus, although not explicitly. It was in our DNA not to want this building to be a boring museum, a conventional institution. We were influenced by the pop movement in the sense that art had to be made more accessible. It should not be on a pedestal, behind a classical façade, not an institution that would appear to be a privileged space. It was indeed part of our culture to think in this way. The main point at the time was about exploding all conventions, it was about questioning and changing the institutional archetypes of a city and the museum is one of its major archetypes. We wanted nobody to think of this building as a conventional museum: it had to be playful, it had to be amusing, it had to be something that should be intriguing rather than impressive, and so, in this respect, our project indeed had a very important connection to the culture we came from.
To come back to your previous question concerning the influence of Archigram, we should also listen to what Niels has to say: the Archigram office had closed many

2020

Haus
staircase
usage

'We fulfil the artists' wishes – from artist support through to repairs. As carpenters, painters and electricians, we produce everything needed for the exhibitions that is not delivered, then bring it up and install it. At the Kunsthaus exhibitions can be everywhere, such as a sound installation here in the **staircase**.'

Markus Malisniak, Erich Waisch, workshop and exhibition setup years before the Kunsthaus competition; the Kunsthaus therefore has nothing to do directly with Archigram, it does have to do with the fact that Peter and I were involved in Archigram, particularly Peter, but Niels certainly wasn't: he is from another generation.

NJ So, for me, the project started with a coincidence. I happened to be at a party at the Bartlett School of Architecture, where I'd graduated three years before, and I was working in a big architecture firm in London. At that party I met Peter Cook and Colin Fournier, and some of my student colleagues, and the question came up whether I would like to join a competition team, because the competition in Graz was just being announced - both Colin and Peter knew me, and I happen to speak German, so in a way it's a coincidence.

● **The competition began...**

CF When the competition was submitted, we had to write a description, and I wrote the text for our competition entry. That text contains a statement of all our dreams: since we had only one chance out of a hundred of winning the competition, it was basically an enthusiastic statement of our desires, a statement about what we wanted the building to be. It was agreed between Peter and I that I would write this statement, so I take responsibility for what I wrote. I mention this because Volker Giencke, who was the president of the jury for the competition, said that this description of our dream for the building was a key element in making him understand our ambitions for the project.

↗ competition p. 269

I have not read this text for ten years, or fifteen years: we started the competition in 1999, we won it in 2000, so it's now been seventeen years, but I remember that, at the time, we sat down and thought about all the things we wanted the building to do. For instance, the **Skin**: we really believed that the **Skin** would be an amazing feature, that it would be a solar collector gathering energy, that it would be able to change colour continuously, like the skin of a chameleon, that it would be able to let daylight in as well as screen it off. It was intended to be amazingly responsive and innovative. At that point, such a material did not exist at all, so these were just our dreams, but the writing promised that this is what our building would offer. Indeed, some of our promises have been realised, for instance the **BIX façade**, the electronic façade. But inevitably, in reference to all the ideas described in the competition text, the museum as built achieves only some of the things we initially dreamed it would be able to do: It is able to display information on its **Skin**, but we had wanted it to have more high-resolution images, we had wanted it to really be like a chameleon skin, capable of matching the colour of the sky and of the clouds, to such an extent that it would almost disappear, merging with its background. The **Skin** was intended to be an even more amazingly responsive skin, but at least it achieves what it does!

→ design 171) 176)

→ BIX 210) 212)

→ BIX 206) 215)

NJ Lots of the design development of this project was based on improvisation, answers had to be found while construction of the building was in progress. The questions were clear though: For example the internal **Skin** of the building: The question was how to do it with the extremely low budget – and how to do it fast. As time was really pressing, we thought of lots of materials, also conventional ones, some of which are

2019

Kunst Haus Foyer

foyer
→196)
→197)

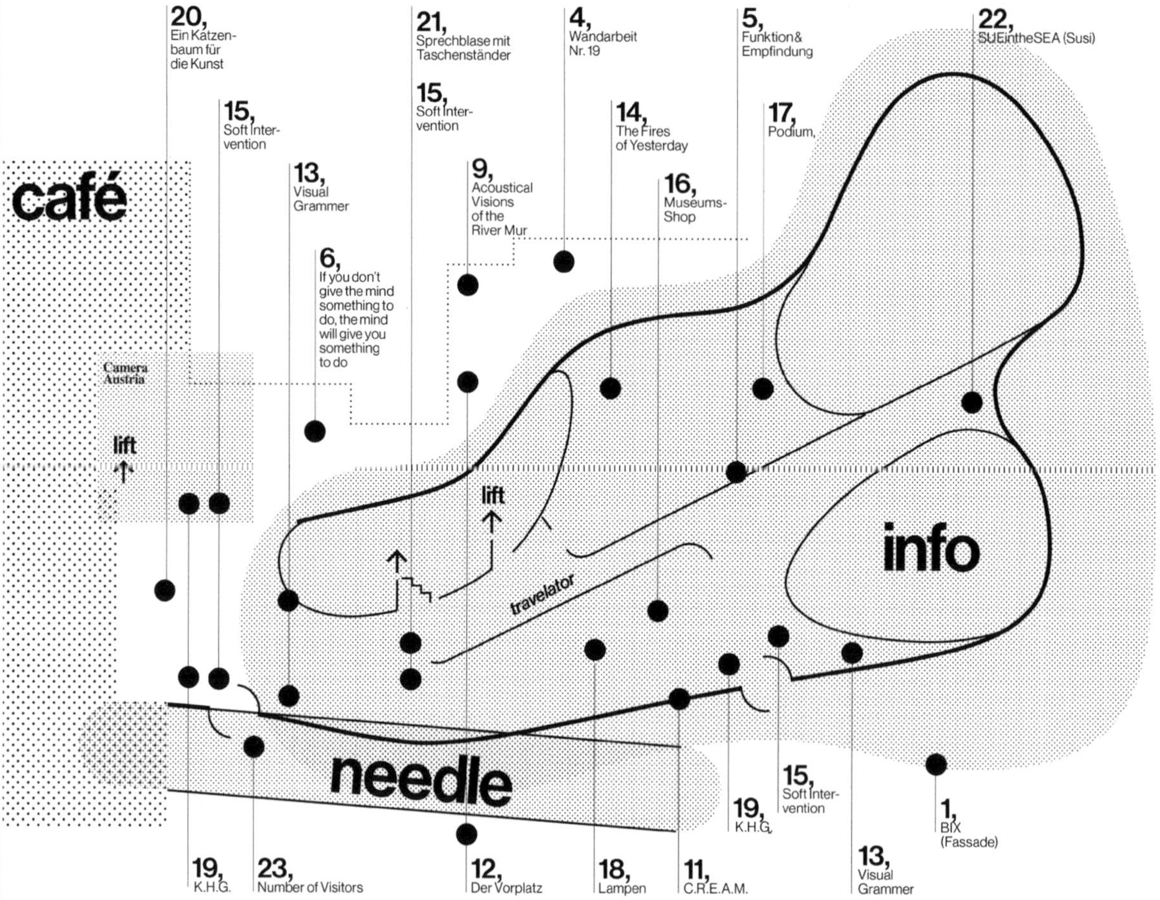

2016–2019

Artists and designers **SUPER-FLEX**, **Topotek 1**, **Anna Lena von Helldorff**, **Hannes und Herta Priesch** and **Oliver Klimpel** were asked to explore the relationship between commercial and non-commercial areas and also to look at and reflect on the functional areas and functions of the Kunsthaus. In doing so the artists and designers not only played a concrete role in furnishing the building, but also examined the routines, standards and requirements of the institution and entered into a (visual) communication with visitors.

The renovation of the **ground floor** and associated changes continued the architects' original intention to anchor the building visibly and permeably in the city by turning the **foyer** into a vibrant meeting space for those interested in art and design.

actually quite banal, so I am not going to mention them. Ultimately, we were really happy that we didn't have to use those. There were basically frantic scenes in the office, and the solution came when we found a little company in eastern Germany that was producing a mesh, that was generally used for sewage systems. It is really a 'bog-standard' material in the literal sense of the word, and it's really cheap: about 10 euros a square metre, if I remember correctly. We had to apply this material to the inner skin of a cultural building, which still is a funny thing in itself. We also had to find a company that could work with it, namely ironmongers that could actually process the material in a proper way, in a way that you can't really see where it's coming from. A fun fact is that the company that sold the mesh never sold the mesh to anybody but sewage companies. So they were really surprised (and amused).

→ Skin 180)

The entire thing was a lucky coincidence in a way – improvisation – and I think improvisation is an appropriate term, because part of the term is *vision*, to envisage something, and to *provide* something, so to take care of something, and it's got the English word of *improving* something, to improve an unforeseen, improbable situation which would have been disastrous otherwise.

CF Very often, improvisation introduces something one had not thought of originally, but actually turns out to be better in the end, leading to a new and unexpected solution. There are many such examples, if you read the description from the competition: for instance, we initially wanted the outer **Skin** to be a completely smooth, continuous surface without gaps, without any cuts; as you know, the **Skin** we now have is not continuous. It would now be possible to achieve this technically and within budget, but in those days, it was impossible. We therefore had to use a large number of individual panels, with a 5 to 10 cm gap between them; so, instead of being a smooth continuous surface, the **Skin** ended up being a fragmented one. That was a rather radical change: the ideal solution could not be done and we had to improvise. But then it led to a result which has got its own aesthetic, and it's an aesthetic that definitely has its qualities. So even if it was certainly an improvisation, it actually led to interesting details that we had not anticipated.

→ Kunsthaus 188)

● **Is that a big disappointment?**

CF No, because, as we have seen, such changes led to positive alternative solutions. Another example is **Space01**, in many ways the most important gallery space in the museum, because it has a double height. The space is not in every respect how we originally wanted it to be: the serpentine lighting, for instance, is something we are not really happy with. We tried to convince the client to give us extra funding so that the inner **Skin**, the metal mesh that you can see inside, could be extended all the way into the **Nozzles**. Now, as one can see, there is only one **Nozzle**, the one facing the Schloßberg, that is fully lined with the inner **Skin**: but all the **Nozzles** were meant to benefit from that inner lining. The inner **Skin** was also meant to be smoother and finer than it is now, but such disappointments are totally insignificant compared to the overall effect.

→ usage 140)
↗ section p. 346
→ Nozzle 122) 123)

2019

Kunst Haus section

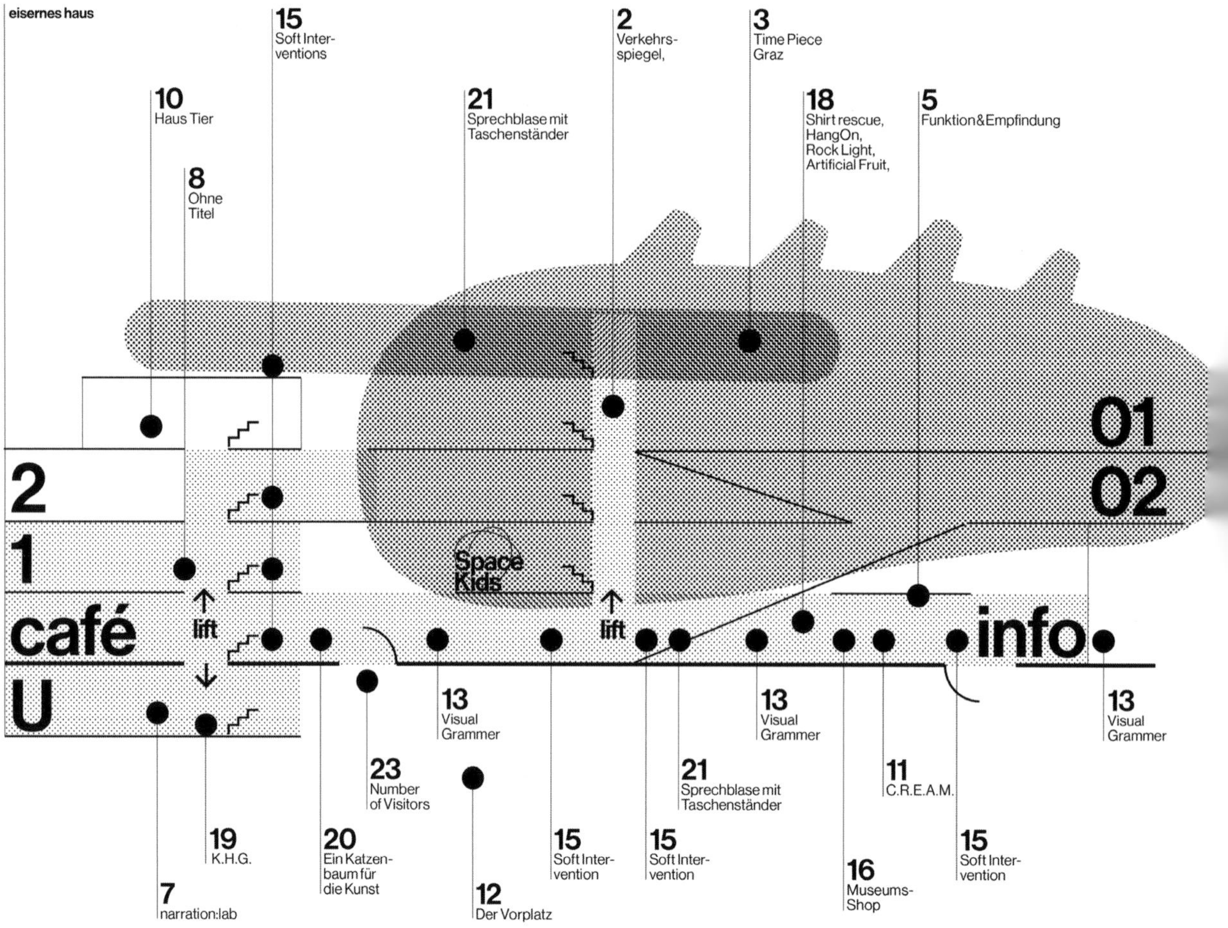

→005) Haustier
→036) forecourt
→042) Visual Grammar
→044) C.R.E.A.M.
→049) Cat-Tree
→057) Visual Grammar
→059) shop
→064) Soft Interventions
→150) forecourt
→190) forecourt
→191) C.R.E.A.M.
→193) Number of Visitors
→196) Visual Grammar

● **In other cases, chance has resulted in effective solutions.**

CF Yes, I have always loved the work of John Cage and his philosophy recognising the importance of chance. One has to honour and welcome chance. It has to be acknowledged as a very important part of one's work as an architect. Some of the things you decide but some of the more interesting things are not decided by you: they just happen. There were, in the design of the Kunsthaus, many decisions or rather 'non-decisions' that happened out of chance, and I think they often turned out to be some of the best decisions. Even the fact that we decided to keep the old historic building, the **Eiserne Haus – Iron House** – which was not our design but which we nevertheless adopted and incorporated in our design, introduced an element of unpredictability, because it had its own set of requirements. We were happy to take them on board. It is always a pleasure when your building is not entirely something that you can decide deliberately and deterministically. One should be willing to let things happen.

→ Iron House 022) 023)

NJ The Kunsthaus is actually blue by coincidence. Mathis Osterhage, the model maker, only had yellow and blue pigments for the resin model that had to be coloured. Yellow obviously was not a good choice, the model's bladder form would just provoke wrong connotations. So we said it had to be the blue pigment, and that's the only reason. There is no other reason than what the model-maker had in his box. Although that coincidence doesn't rule out the fact that blue is really the appropriate colour of the building.

● **From the outset, the building was intended to house temporary exhibitions.**

CF For us, the fact that the museum did not have a permanent collection was a very important and positive point. It was always meant to be an open platform which could be used by different curators, it could change, so we welcomed the fact that we didn't have to design the building around a particular set of art pieces: it could be a neutral platform, it could be something that would always be free to evolve.

NJ You see those stains on the floor? They are a remnant of Sol LeWitt. It was was one of the first exhibitions, an installation called *Wall* by Sol LeWitt – a large undulating brick wall following the circumference of the building. After the exhibition, when the wall was dismantled and all the bricks were gone, you could still see their stains on the floor. Some people said, 'oh, oh my god, this is a case for the insurance company' – but I think this is exactly what the building should have, what it deserves: Friendly ghosts of some really great exhibitions of the past.

→ usage 109)
→ Space01 108)

● **Can you say something about how the Kunsthaus is embedded in its urban context?**

PC When we saw all the projects for the competition, which I think were 103 or whatever number, the really interesting factor was to me, that so many of them made it very complicated. This is actually a very simple building, an odd building, but it is fundamentally very simple, you have a site, you fill up the site, and then you go up into it, basically that's it, and you don't look for anything more, in a sense.

→ design 081)

CF We always felt that the urban significance of the project was as important as its architectural significance, and there is no doubt that it has been received as such and perceived as such. You know, I was actually the one who gave the name to the project,

2015

Kunst
Haus
façade
forecourt

façade
→190)

Big Draw

'friendly alien'. The notion that it looks like something coming from another civilisation, or another age, or another country, or another world, was very important to us. But it was also important that it should be perceived as being friendly, in the sense of being accepted, as being something that is growing out of here, out of its site, making its nest in the city. So, the tension between the familiarity of the building, the ease of access, its popularity, its friendliness, on the one hand, and its alien nature, on the other, was a very important combination of attributes, a very unusual and difficult combination. I think we achieved it, I think it works.

● **Did you have any concerns at the time about contributing to the gentrification of the neighbourhood?**

CF Well, that's a difficult topic, because it is indeed a mixed blessing. Gentrification, inevitably, was one of the triggers and potential dangers behind the commissioning of the Kunsthaus as well as that of most new museums, in cities other than Graz; it was also one of the outcomes of its construction. It is a difficult situation to be in, a very difficult role for architects to be in, because we are in a way complicit in the whole process of land speculation and gentrification that ensues. It is an uncomfortable position for architects, because we want to introduce a positive new element into the city but we also realise that as soon as we do, we create an attraction, which then displaces the people who were there beforehand. So, in fact, the existential battle of an architect is to try to reconcile this conflict and to engage in projects that address social issues fairly, in compensation for some of the damage that we do, I would say, unintentionally.

PC In retrospect: The whole Kunsthaus phenomenon was surprising in that it verified much of the early Archigram work and the good creative chemistry that came from Colin and I working together. In some ways it is a total project: not dependent upon esoteric or over-complex sub-plots. Hence its ability to be constructed relatively consistently with the competition version. In the circles in which Colin and I move, there are too many architects who want to seem clever by making things too obscure. It has been a great 'trigger' for more recent buildings – even spawning a blue infant in England – the drawing studio of the Arts University Bournemouth. Perhaps Graz, after all, is unwittingly a perverse breeding ground for original architecture: if you look around you'll know what I mean.

2018/19

Kunst
Haus
façade
forecourt
entrance

Forecourt; model for visually impaired people and snowy furniture, design by Topotek1

2018–2022
(**Kunst**
(**Haus**
(façade

foyer
→ 044)

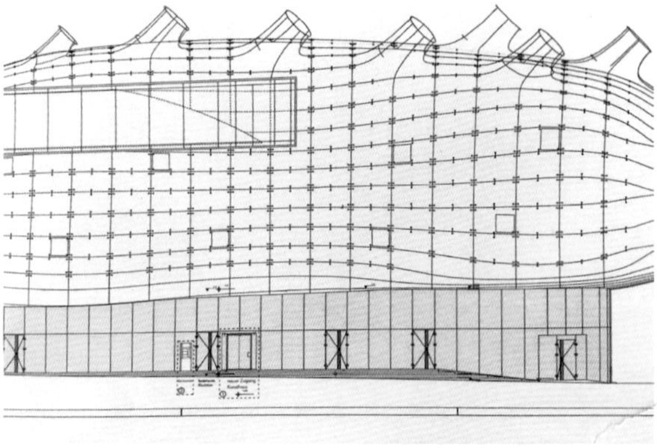

SUPERFLEX, C.R.E.A.M. Cash rules everything around me

foyer
→186)

The artist collective SUPERFLEX has realised their third project at the Kunsthaus Graz within three years. Following on from their cash machine sculpture **C.R.E.A.M.** in 2017 and **Free Shop** in 2018, the installation of **Number of Visitors** (2015) focuses on the economic conditions and 'success criteria' set for cultural institutions. Mounted above the **entrance**, a manual counter displays current visitor numbers to the Kunsthaus for the running year.

SUPERFLEX and Jens Haaning, Number of Visitors

Photo by Christoph Edlinger

Photo by Martina Margarete Berger

2017/18

Haus
foyer
façade

foyer
→057)
→058)
→186)
façade
→042)

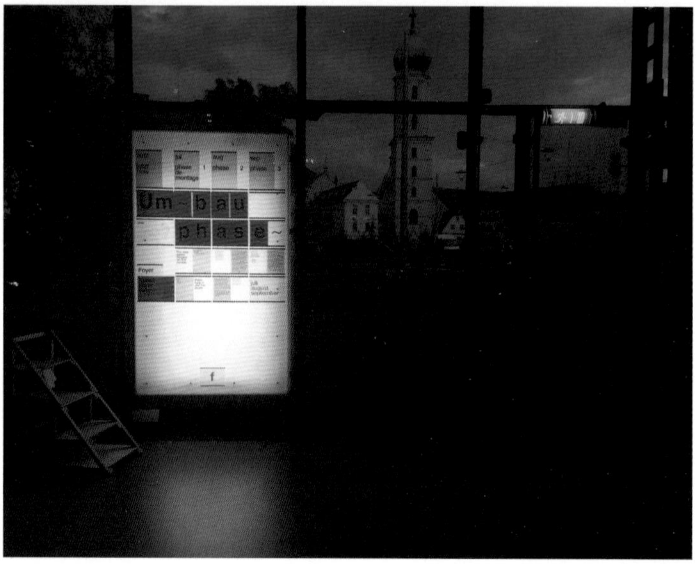

Reconstruction phase in **foyer**, lightbox,
Visual Grammar by Anna Lena von Helldorff

2012

Haus
façade

Photo by Gerhard Moderitz

2019

(**Haus**
(façade

Photo by Gerlinde Becker

Photo by Meinrad Hopfgartner

(**Haus**
(façade
(usage

'The aquarium office, as I call it, serves as the event headquarters. From the large glass front, I have a perfect view of the **delivery zone** and any incoming equipment and catering deliveries. From up here at quieter moments I can also watch the lively bustle of Mariahilfer Straße, and because of the reflection in the windows the passers-by usually don't notice me.'

Magdalena Kermann, event management

usage
→ 072)

'The huge door at the back of the Kunsthaus is incredibly heavy, but has worked reliably for years without creaking or getting stuck. This is the main entrance for exhibits. I actually open the doors for the art and the artists, because part of my job is to ensure that works arrive on time at the museum and are presented correctly.'

Doris Psenicnik, exhibition registrar

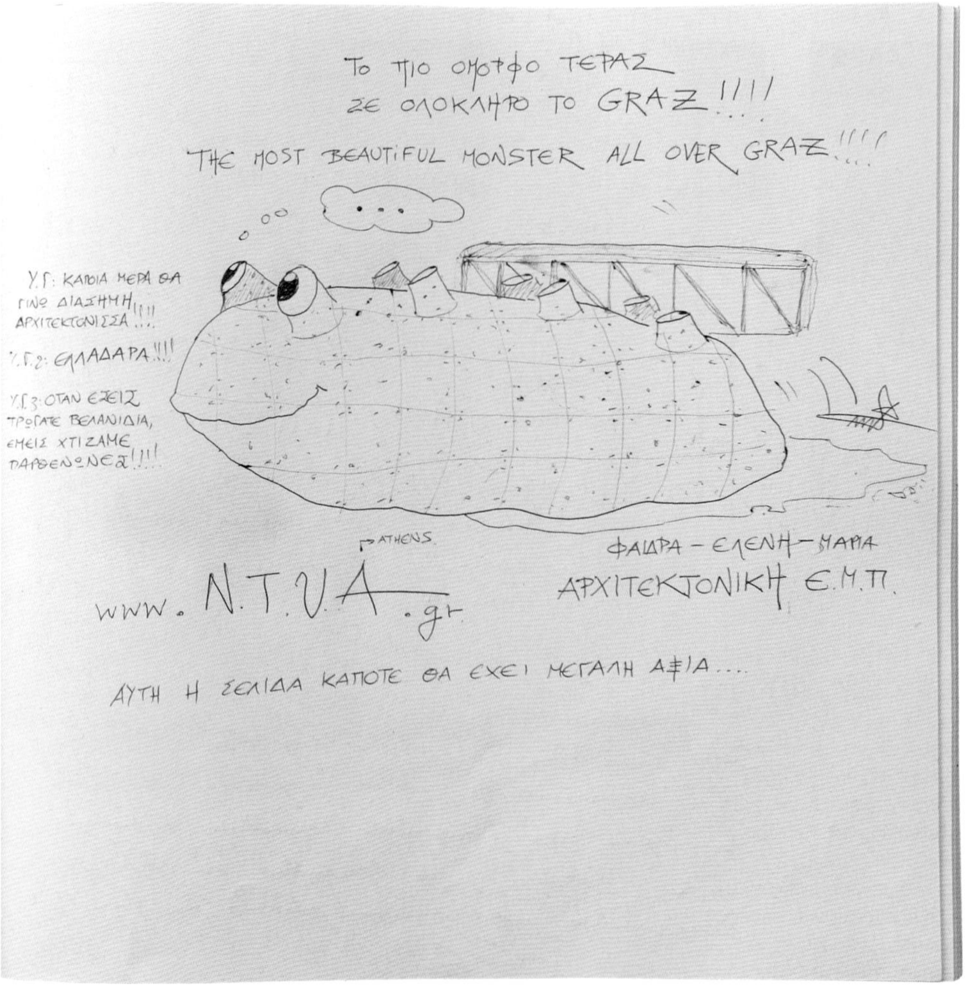

Extract from the visitors' book

usage
→ 075)

Sprinkler system test

2004

Kunst
Haus
Graz
BIX

2004

(**Kunst**
(**Haus**
(**Graz**
(BIX

Lia, int.5_27/G.S.I.L.XXX

2019

Kunst
Haus
Graz
BIX

Space02
→ 091)
Space01
→ 129)
usage
→ 180)

Peter Kogler. BIX [Connected]

BIG + PIXEL = BIX. A selection of BIX light and media façade projects

Elisabeth Schlögl

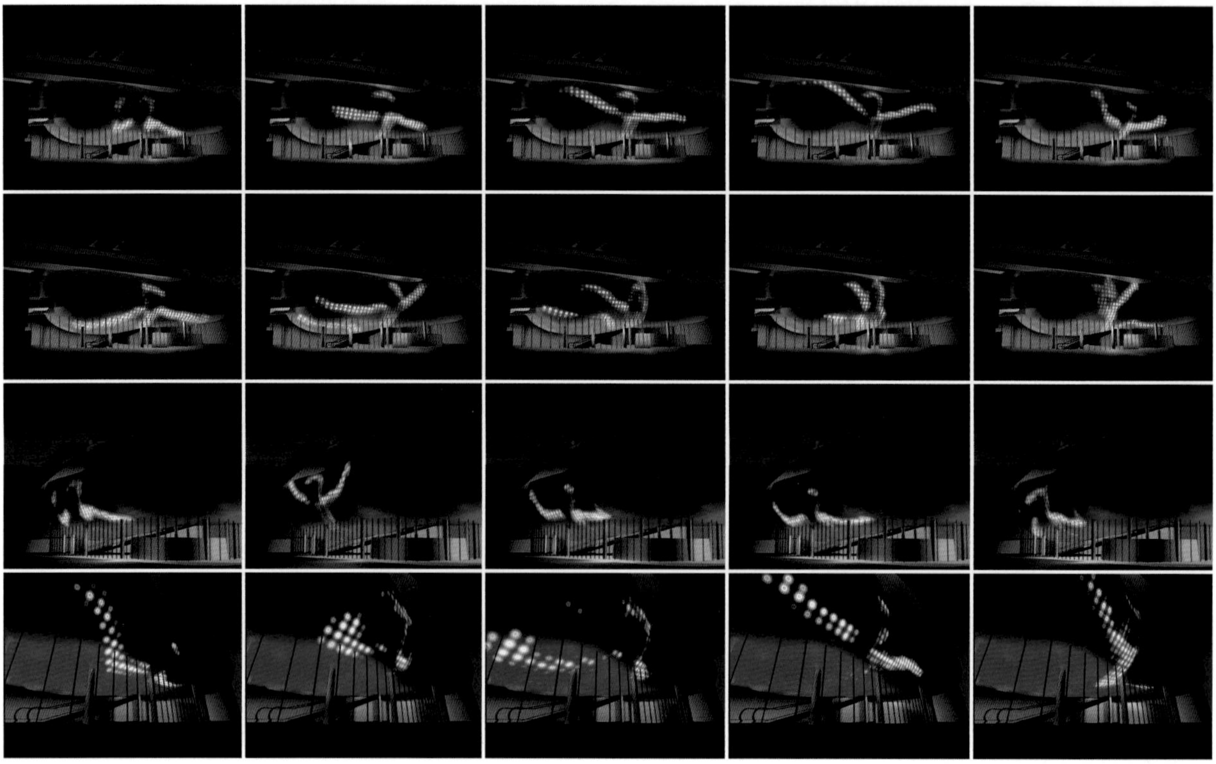

Animation on the simulation software of the **BIX façade** (screenshots), realities:united, planning phase

BIG + PIXEL = BIX

A selection of BIX light and media façade projects.

Compiled by Elisabeth Schlögl,
project coordinator of the BIX light and media façade since 2018

As dusk falls, the 946 fluorescent tubes of the **BIX light and media façade** shape the unique look of the Kunsthaus building. In her text *The potential of the non-perfect*, Barbara Steiner provides some key facts about the **BIX**: she explains that it was created because a transparent outer shell was not feasible in 2003, her understanding of realities:united as a communication tool for curators and artists, and also its (deliberately limiting) technical realisation, intended to inspire creative processes.
This section details a selection of the BIX projects carried out since 2003. Drawn from a total of 23 projects, it is based on their grouping into different 'categories.' The projects chosen each represent a category:

- **The BIX light and media façade**
  as an extension of the exhibition
- **The BIX light and media façade**
  as a medium for a site-specific, self-referential work
- **The BIX light and media façade**
  in the context of performance/music
- **The BIX light and media façade**
  as a medium for interactive projects

These categories demonstrate the (technical) possibilities of (art) projects for the **BIX light and media façade** so far. They serve both to give a structure to the text and to allow the reader an overview of all of the projects (and possibilities) to date. However, it is important to point out here that these categories cannot be neatly separated – there are many BIX projects that fit into several categories. One example of this is *BIX [Connected]* by Peter Kogler (27.06.–20.10.2019), created on the occasion of his exhibition *Connected. Peter Kogler with ...* It can therefore be seen as an extension of the exhibition through to the **BIX light and media façade**, yet at the same time it 'reacted' to the BIX façade in a site-specific way: an animated line structure, also a key feature of his exhibition in **Space01**, made the boundaries of the building dissolve in our perception. In many places, the design of light and media façades has, among other things, sought to change the appearance of architecture that for centuries had been determined by static (prestigious) façades, making it shift and become 'alive'. The animated lines of *BIX [Connected]* conveyed the feeling that the Kunsthaus had been transformed into a 'pulsating' building, again referencing the organic character of its form.

→ BIX 207)
→ Space02 091)
→ Space01 129)

2004

Kunst
Haus
Graz
BIX

Thomas Baumann / Michael Klaar, Plot:Bach

• The BIX light and media façade as an extension of the exhibition

In addition to Peter Kogler's project, we should mention a number of other BIX projects that were created as part of an exhibition for the **BIX light and media façade**, expanding these exhibitions out into urban space.

05.02.2010–01.05.2011

Xavier Veilhan. Pendule

As part of the exhibition *Catch me! Grasping Speed* (06.02.–25.04.2010)

→ BIX 210)

In a digital pendulum movement, several dark circles 'flew' back and forth and from left to right on the fully illuminated **BIX light and media façade**. The animation *Pendule* played on our perception of dimensions and the laws of physics. The slow pace of the pendulum movement offered a contrast to the speed of urban traffic and city life.

28.09.–22.12.2012

Michelangelo Pistoletto. Terzo Paradiso

As part of the exhibition *Cittadellarte. Sharing Transformation* (28.09.2012–20.01.2013)

→ BIX 216)
→ Space01 139)

This animation showed a reconfiguration of the mathematical infinity sign, consisting of three successive circles, blinking and rotating on the façade. The sign stands for a new age proclaimed by the artist – the 'Third Paradise' – in which art and life, artifice and nature, merge together 'infinitely,' with the focus on bringing one's self into a responsible and participatory society.

18.11.–31.12.2014

Daniel Egg. Information Stream

As part of the exhibition of the same name

Daniel Egg's series of photographs was exhibited in the former café *Luise im Kunsthaus* alongside a video on the light and media façade. The works centred on smoke as a medium of (earlier) forms of communication (keywords: smoke signals, intellectual gesture, youthfulness). In a performative self-experiment, Egg filled his lungs with smoke to create a visual alphabet of the spoken German language. Each cloud of smoke visualised a spoken letter. These smoke signals were shown on the light and media façade one after the other, in alphabetical order.

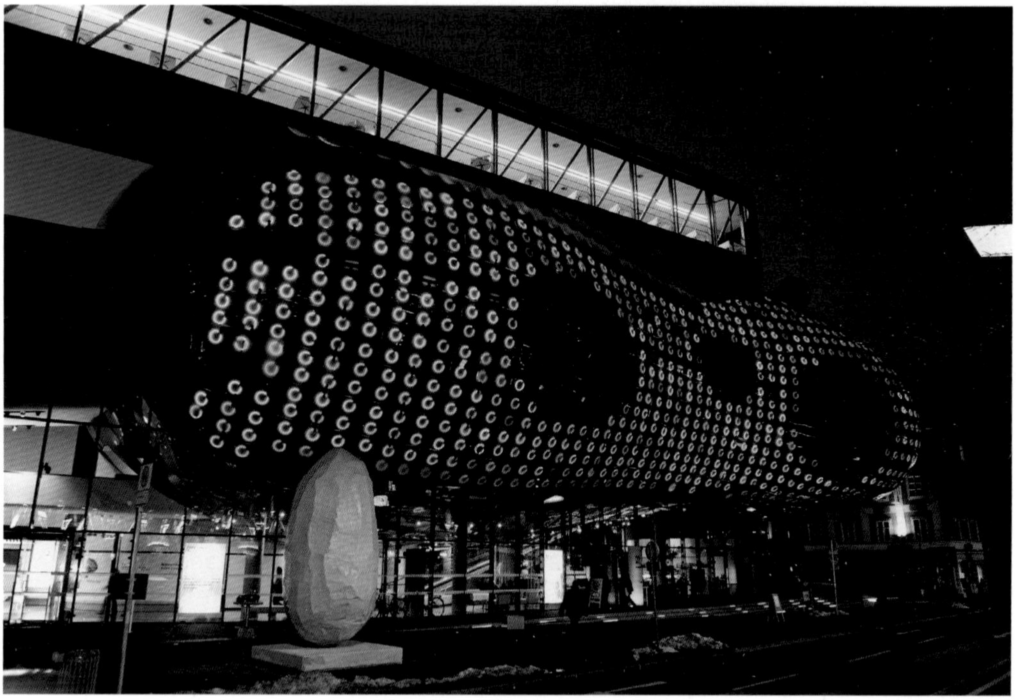

Xavier Veilhan, Pendule
Sculpture: Franz West, En Hod, 2008

11.04.–26.08.2018

Monica Bonvicini. GUILT

On the occasion of the exhibition *Faith Love Hope* (13.4.–26.8.2018) and as part of *Klanglicht. Das Kunstfestival der Bühnen Graz* (28.–30.04.2018) → BIX 211)

The word 'GUILT' flashed up in capital letters on the BIX light and media façade and was also mirrored within the exhibition as an installation. It became a visual statement addressed to no one in particular. As in this piece, Bonvicini's cross-media works often explore power structures and complex social, political and economic relationships. *GUILT* was an inspiring and unsettling position within the ecclesiastical and theological context of this show, which was staged as an art and anniversary exhibition for the 800th anniversary of the Diocese of Graz Seckau.

22.09.2018–27.01.2019

Fiston Mwanza Mujila: Einsamkeit 12

On the occasion of the exhibition *Congo Stars* (22.09.2018–27.01.2019) → Space01 134)

The writer Fiston Mwanza Mujila, who was born in Congo and lives in Graz, was city writer in 2009/2010 and a curator of the group exhibition *Congo Stars*. It showed popular painting from the 1960s to today and contemporary art from the democratic Republic of Congo. His poem Ein*samkeit 12* (Solitude 12), a lyrical examination of the concept of exile, could be read as a scrolling text during the course of the exhibition.

- **The BIX light and media façade as the medium of a site-specific, self-referential work**

The following projects were developed specifically for this location and explore the nature and conditions of the **BIX light and media façade**.

10.06.–24.06.2005

Renée Levi, Kassiber

This video showed Levi's head covered with a stocking, her arms braced. *Kassiber* is a secret message passed between prisoners. With slow, hulking movements, like a captive, Levi attempted to locate her upper body on the building's façade. Personal experience of space is a recurring theme in Renée Levi's work. Kassiber examined the relationship between the human body and the architectural structure, exploring the organic design of the Kunsthaus.

22.09.–02.11.2006

Katarina Löfström, Little Star

As part of the exhibition *Protections. This is not an exhibition* (23.09.–22.10.2006) → BIX 215) → Space02 089)

Monica Bonvicini, GUILT

This animation investigated the West's relationship with Islam and its iconography. It was created after the publication of caricatures of Mohammed in a Danish newspaper, followed by a cartoon dispute. The video showed a character – although never in its entirety – that was frequently used in the Alhambra. The strictly geometrical network of lines moved slowly, creating a contrast to the 'biomorphic' architecture of the Kunsthaus. The technical limitations of the **BIX light and media façade** (no high resolution, rough pixellation of images) proved to be 'a fantastic creative working approach' for the animation, according to Löfström (Katarina Löfström in conversation with Adam Budak and Christine Peters, in: Booklet for the DVD *BIX Projects #04. Little Star. Katarina Löfström*, 2006), since it became impossible to depict a 'whole'.

03.11.2006–07.01.2007

Andres Ramirez Gaviria, modal.patterns

modal.patterns was a project about data visualisation: two sentences (letters and punctuation marks) were used to produce visual animation sequences based on the formal principles of Gestalt perception (similarity, continuity, closeness, unity, size, symmetry). One of the sentences came from Roy Behrens' book *Design in the Visual Arts* (1984): 'A whole is more than the sum of its parts'– a key tenet of Gestalt psychology. Behrens discusses the influence of Gestalt theory on modern art and design. The second sentence was an anagram of the first sentence created by Gaviria: 'a misshape of truth torments.' Central to this project was the question: How do 'new' visual representations of complex data employing new technologies change our processes of perception and organisation? Gaviria interpreted the **BIX light and media façade** as a space for such experiments and asked (also ironically, see anagram) how new technologies can generate new types of communication. The DVD *BIX Projekte#05. modal. patterns. Andres Ramirez Gaviria* (2006) was released to accompany the project.

Last but not least, we should touch on the many collaborative projects that have been carried out with university institutions. Time and again, students from the fields of architecture, information management and visualisation have investigated the conceptual and technological qualities of the **BIX light and media façade**. To illustrate this, two collaborative projects are described here:

24.05.–27.05.2007

Fourth Dimension. A project by students from the Institute
of Information Management at the FH Joanneum
on the occasion of the exhibition *discoverIT* at the Medienkunstlabor Graz

The theme of this project was **BIX** as a medium of communication. Passers-by were 'allowed' to send a personal message as a ticker over the **BIX light and media façade** via an SMS text message. This was a direct, unfiltered communication via the **BIX** with the urban space, which is not usually open to everyone.

2005/06
Kunst
Haus
Graz
BIX

Cerith Wyn Evans, The Sky Is Thin As Paper Here ...

15.12.2009–10.1.2010
With the Institute of Computer Graphics and Knowledge Visualization at Graz University of Technology, students wrote programs with the aim of improving text visualisation on the **BIX**, so that viewers could easily follow the scrolling text from closer by.

- **The BIX light and media façade in the context of performance/music**

Time and again, artists have interpreted the **BIX** as a medium for visualising the process of translating sound into image. The following projects are instances of this.

30.01.–30.03.2004

Thomas Baumann, Michael Klaar, Plot:Bach → BIX 209)

In 2004, visual artist Thomas Baumann was one of the first to use the **BIX façade** as an artistic medium in a performative/musical context. The animation *Plot:Bach* is a visual score. Together with conductor Michael Klaar, he developed a visualisation of Johann Sebastian Bach's *Fugue II* from the *Well-Tempered Clavier*, Part II (1740/42). Inspired by the various exercises in dexterity that a fugue represents for piano students, Baumann 'composed' a sequence of visual translations of the piece based on a square grid. *Plot:Bach* can be seen as one of the very first **BIX** projects to implement a visual 'exercise' on the BIX façade, which other artists could then use as a basis.

09.10.–07.11.2004

Lia, int.5_27/G.S.I.L.XXX → BIX 206)

As part of the exhibition *Movable Parts. Forms of the Kinetic* (9.10.2004–16.1.2005)

Graphics programmer Lia developed a site-specific audiovisual project on the visual basis of her video *int.5_27/G.S.I.L.XXX* (published by Edition Medienturm). An application generated the visualisation for the **BIX light and media façade** – denser and less dense hatchings. This also reacted to an external sound source – a directional radio microphone mounted on the neighbouring bridge over the River Mur. A direct visual feedback from the site-specific sound was produced on the **BIX**.

04.11.2005–23.03.2006

Cerith Wyn Evans, The Sky Is Thin As Paper Here ... → BIX 212)

This project translated Evans' audio installation of the same name (2004, Galerie Buchholz, Berlin) into the **BIX** medium. Together with designer Mathias Gmachl, an animation was created from the translation of sound into image into **BIX**. In the video, breaks, gaps and interpretation became perceptible – 'problems' that accompany every translation process. This became fundamental to the video, where Evans' preoccupation with human perception also played a role.

2017

Kunst
Haus
Graz
BIX

Tristan Schulze, Ghost

In addition to **BIX** projects in the context of performance and music, there have also been a significant number of past collaborative projects with the *Springfestival* – an annual festival for electronic music and art in Graz. The following projects are of interest here:

16.05.–20.05.2007

Francesco Tristano, Kelvin Sholar (with Mox (ninjatune), MOXX. Spring seven

15.06.2018,

Marian Essl, MONOCOLOR: Isomorph

19.06.–26.06.2019

Zalán Szakács with sound:frame, Ornament

- **The BIX light and media façade as a medium for interactive projects**

The **BIX** was originally conceived as a communication tool by its creators, realities:united. Communication is interaction – the Kunsthaus establishes a dialogue with the public, and vice versa. The following projects aimed to encourage dialogue in various different ways.

22.02.–22.03.2005,

realities:united, +43-316/8017 9242

Jan and Tim Edler, the creators of the **BIX light and media façade**, developed one of the first interactive projects together with John Dekron, the author of the **BIX** software. The façade showed the telephone number +43-316/8017 9242: anyone could call the number and so reach an answering machine. The voice of the caller was forwarded as an audio signal to the **BIX** server and influenced how the video appeared visually on the façade. The visibility of this influence was limited. In this way, realities:united explored the prevailing hope for equal participation using new digital technologies. However, the caller could never be sure that they had actually influenced the visual appearance of the video.

02.05.2011

Matthias Esterl, BIX Entertainment System (Pong)

As part of the *Lendwirbel* 2011 and 2012, a street festival in the Graz district of Lend, then student Matthias Esterl (Information Design, FH Joanneum, Graz) programmed the computer game *Pong* for the **BIX**. The façade became a screen and allowed two players to compete against each other from a joystick station in front of the Kunsthaus.

2019

Kunst
Haus
Graz
BIX

Klaus Pröbster, Your name on the Kunsthaus **BIX façade**

28.10.–15.11.2015, daily from 5pm to 2am,

Werde Lichtpate. Lassen Sie die BIX-Fassade sprechen

Collaboration between Energie Graz and Universalmuseum Joanneum

www.museum-joanneum.at/kunsthaus-graz/bix-medienfassade/projekte/events/event/4188/werde-lichtpate

Project sponsor Energie Graz and the Universalmuseum Joanneum invited the public to become a 'godparent' or sponsor to a pixel (a fluorescent ring) on the **BIX** and have 'light messages' scroll across the façade. The project arose from the International Year of Light and Energie Graz's support of the museum. A total of 655 sponsorships were awarded. As the godparent of a fluorescent ring, you could decide whether it was illuminated, flashing, or switched off. 'Light for you,' 'Today there were 10 hours of sunshine for Graz,' and 'Be the light' were among a total of 176 light messages submitted, which were shown over 19 days on the **BIX**.

13.07.–10.12.2017

Ghost. In the Space. A project by Tristan Schulze → BIX 213)

'Art is not made for Architecture,' 'Every Day brings new Intelligence' – phrases that appeared on the **BIX façade** during this project. These originated from *Ghost*, an artificial neural network – AI. The vocabulary (art, architecture, intelligence, etc.) was drawn from Kunsthaus web content. The statements were created with audience participation via a web app. Following interaction between the app and the public, the AI 'learned' how to form sentences and communicate them on the **BIX**. Media artist Tristan Schulze explored how artificial intelligence can be shaped by humans – in line with the view that humans define what technology does/can do. This project was also shown on the media façade of the Ars Electronica Center during the Ars Electronica Festival 2017, whose theme was 'Artificial Intelligence – the Other I'.

28.01.–13.02.2019

Your name on the Kunsthaus BIX façade. A BIX project by Klaus Pröpster → BIX 214)

A collaboration between FH Joanneum, Energie Graz and Kunsthaus Graz

The title reveals the concept behind the project: using a web form, anyone could book a timeslot on the **BIX media façade** and 'announce' their first name there. The timeslots were fully booked within a few days. What the participants didn't know: everyone with the same first name was allocated the same timeslot. The project investigated themes such as the search for identity and self-assurance (the participants shared selfies with their name on the façade via social media) in our increasingly heterogeneous society, and asked questions such as: 'How unique am I really?' In terms of its content the project linked in with the following exhibition, in which Austrian-Chinese artist Jun Yang explored individual and collective identity constructions. Klaus Pröpster, at that time a student at the FH Joanneum, developed the project together with interaction designer Florian Lackner as part of an invited competition for the **BIX**.

Katarina Löfström, Little Star

20.05.–18.06.2019

My favourite flaw. What flaw do you love about yourself?
A project by Katharina Diem

→ BIX 217)

'I love my stutter,' 'I love my very shy breasts' – two of the answers Katharina Diem received when she asked: 'What flaw do you love about yourself?' She gathered a total of 170 answers, which the **BIX** showed alternating with animated body images. *My favourite flaw* allowed the public to participate in the communication of the Kunsthaus and its content via social media. This **BIX** project was part of the performance series *'I don't think I'm trying to commit suicide'* on the themes of body and space, which ran at the same time. Its focus lay on social role models, gender relations and the human body. This wide range of themes were reflected on the **BIX**. Katharina Diem was studying Interaction Design at the FH Joanneum at that time and developed the project as part of her bachelor's thesis on the subject of perfectionism. *My favourite flaw* was awarded the Red Dot Award 2019 in an international design competition for product design, communication design and design concepts.

21.10.–13.11.2019

Picture Hunt. Capture the image on the Kunsthaus façade and share it as an Instastory #picturehunt @kunsthausgraz

Collaboration between HTBLVA Ortweinschule, Energie Graz and the Kunsthaus Graz
Picture Hunt was a photo challenge developed during a six-month collaboration with 5th-year students from the Film and Multimedia Art class. The **BIX** showed a stream of flickering images containing hidden symbols invisible to the naked eye. A camera that acted as a kind of filter was needed to reveal the hidden symbols. It was no coincidence that these motifs linked in with the following exhibition, *ARTS ↔ CRAFTS*. The images included a brush, a colour palette and a hammer, and were symbolic of the relationship between arts and crafts explored in the exhibition. The public was invited to participate in the challenge and to share their images on Instagram with #picturehunt and @kunsthausgraz. Thanks to the participation of many people and their posts on social media, a growing number of images became visible 'for all'.

2019

Kunst
Haus
Graz
BIX

Michelangelo Pistoletto, Terzo Paradiso

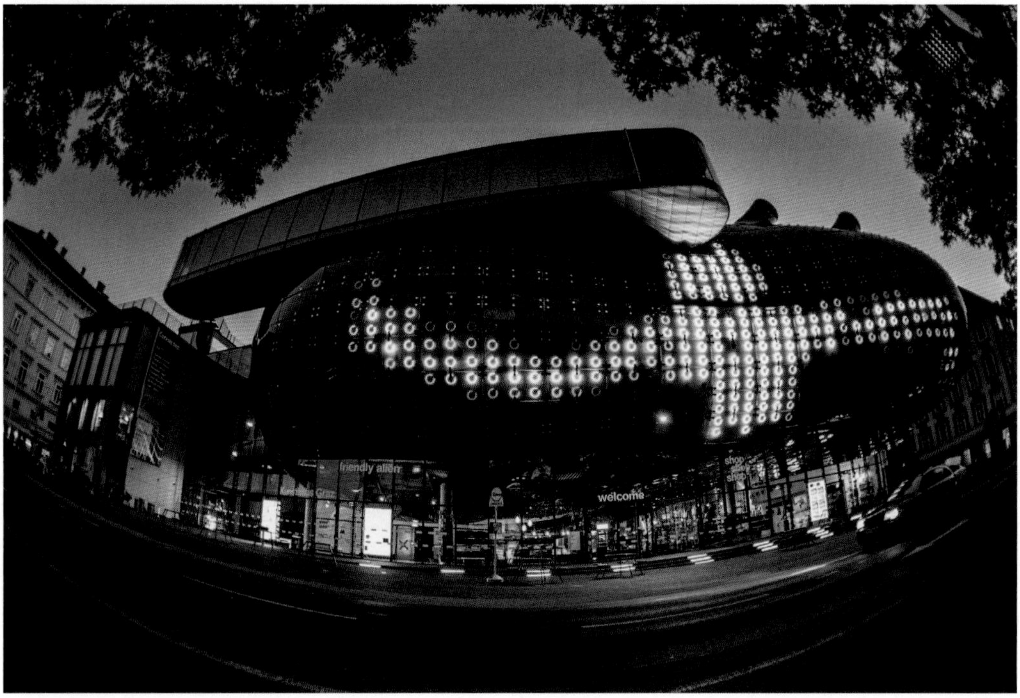

Katharina Diem, Lieblingsmakel

Extract from the visitors' book

Komm Schatz wir gehen auf Urlaub!
Jaa!
Die Erde soll ganz nett sein!
Hallo Erdbewohner!
PUM
PUM
Nein!
Super Kampf Modus!
WROA!
PUM
PUM
PUM
MUSEUM
ENDE

(Appendix)

Kunsthaus plans competition

Exhibitions 2003–2020

A–Z
(Biographies)
(Index)

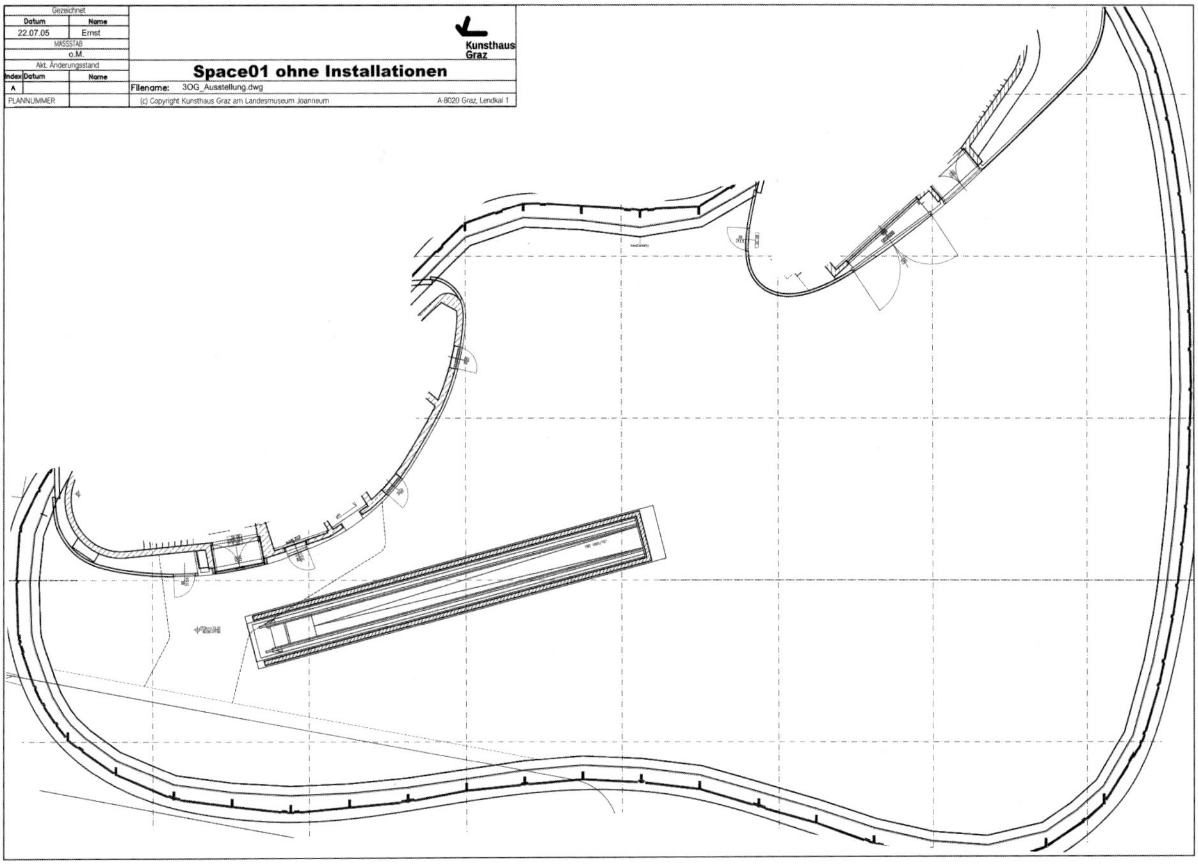
Gezeichnet
Datum
Name
22.07.05
Ernst
MASSSTAB
o.M.
Akt. Änderungsstand
Index
Datum
Name
A
PLANNUMMER
Kunsthaus Graz
Space01 ohne Installationen
Filename: 3OG_Ausstellung.dwg
(c) Copyright Kunsthaus Graz am Landesmuseum Joanneum
A-8020 Graz, Lendkai 1

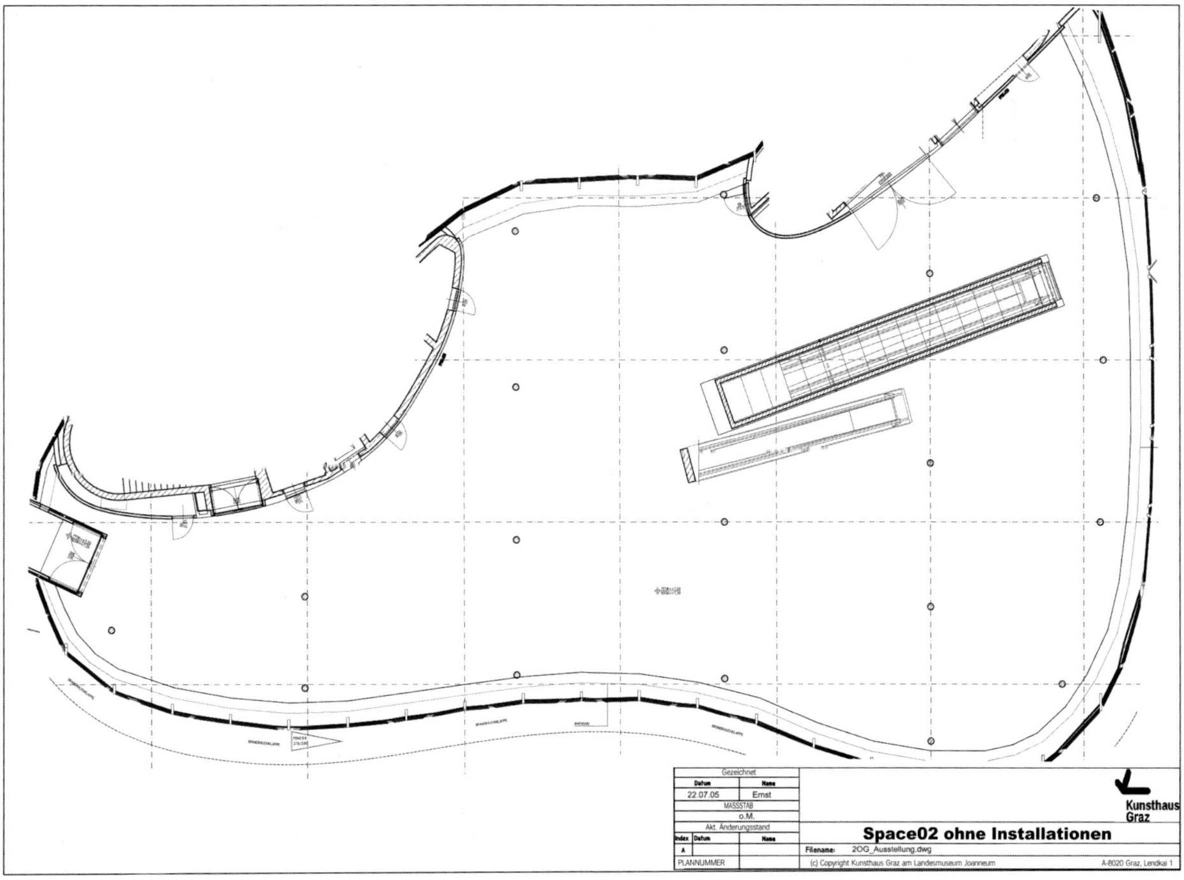
Gezeichnet
Datum
Name
22.07.05
Ernst
MASSSTAB
o.M.
Akt. Änderungsstand
Index
Datum
Name
A
PLANNUMMER
Kunsthaus Graz
Space02 ohne Installationen
Filename: 2OG_Ausstellung.dwg
(c) Copyright Kunsthaus Graz am Landesmuseum Joanneum
A-8020 Graz, Lendkai 1

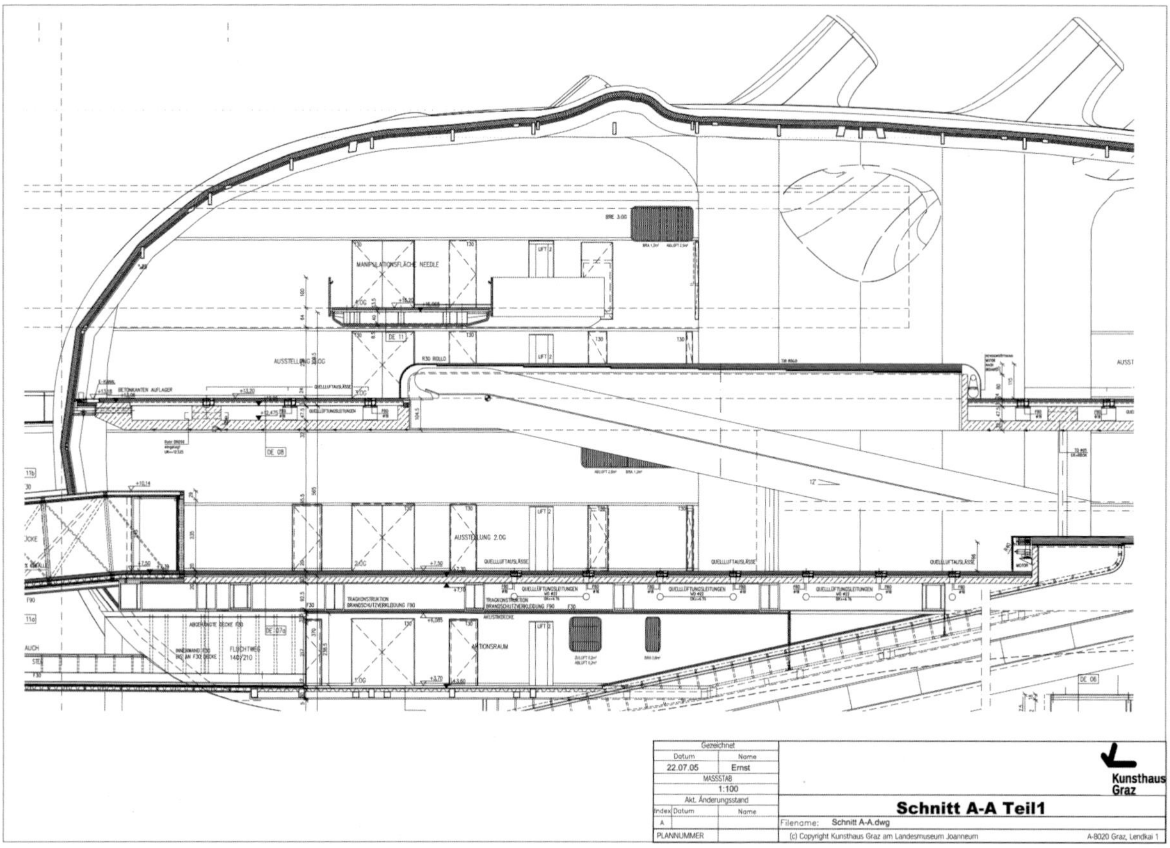
Gezeichnet
Datum
Name
22.07.05
Ernst
MASSSTAB
1:100
Akt. Änderungsstand
Index
Datum
Name
A
PLANNUMMER
Kunsthaus Graz
Schnitt A-A Teil1
Filename: Schnitt A-A.dwg
(c) Copyright Kunsthaus Graz am Landesmuseum Joanneum
A-8020 Graz, Lendkai 1

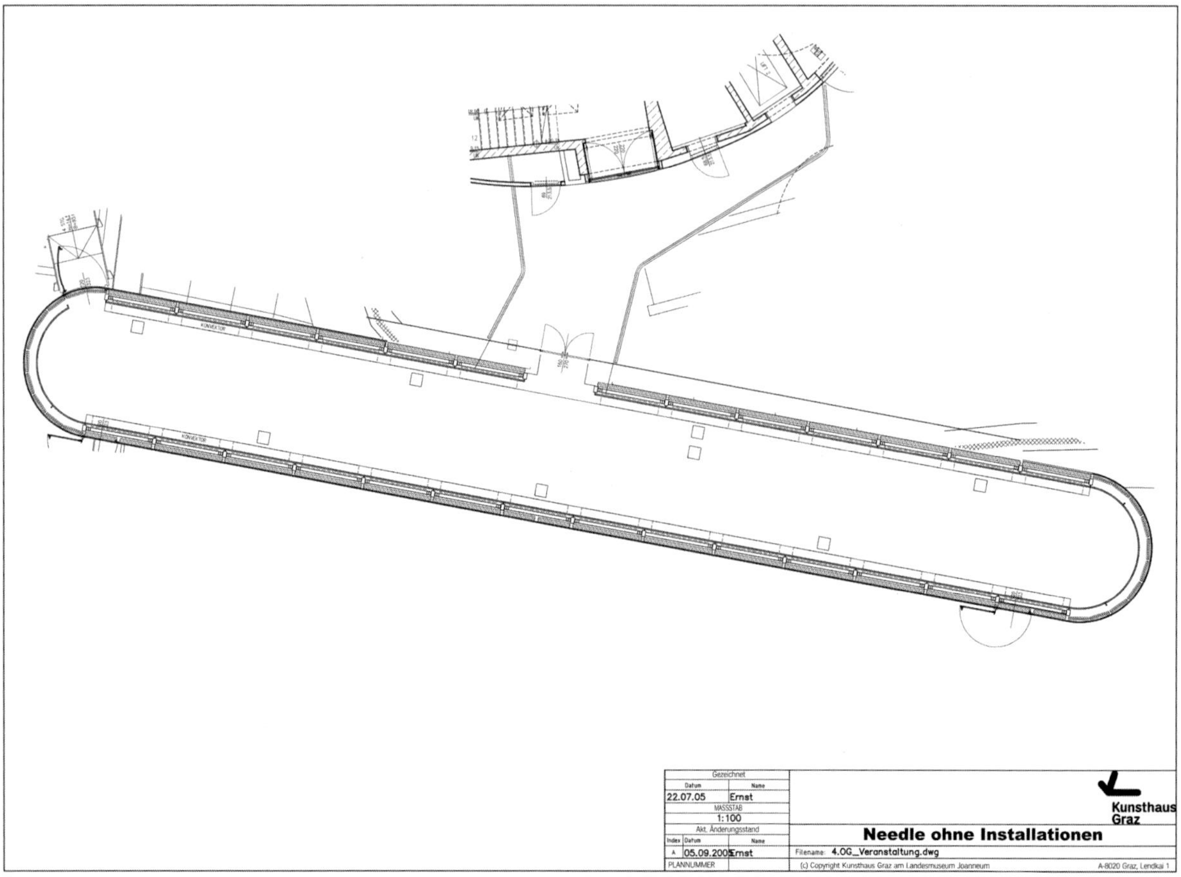
Gezeichnet
Datum
Name
22.07.05
Ernst
MASSSTAB
1:100
Akt. Änderungsstand
Index
Datum
Name
A
05.09.2005
Ernst
PLANNUMMER
Kunsthaus Graz
Needle ohne Installationen
Filename: 4.OG_Veranstaltung.dwg
(c) Copyright Kunsthaus Graz am Landesmuseum Joanneum
A-8020 Graz, Lendkai 1

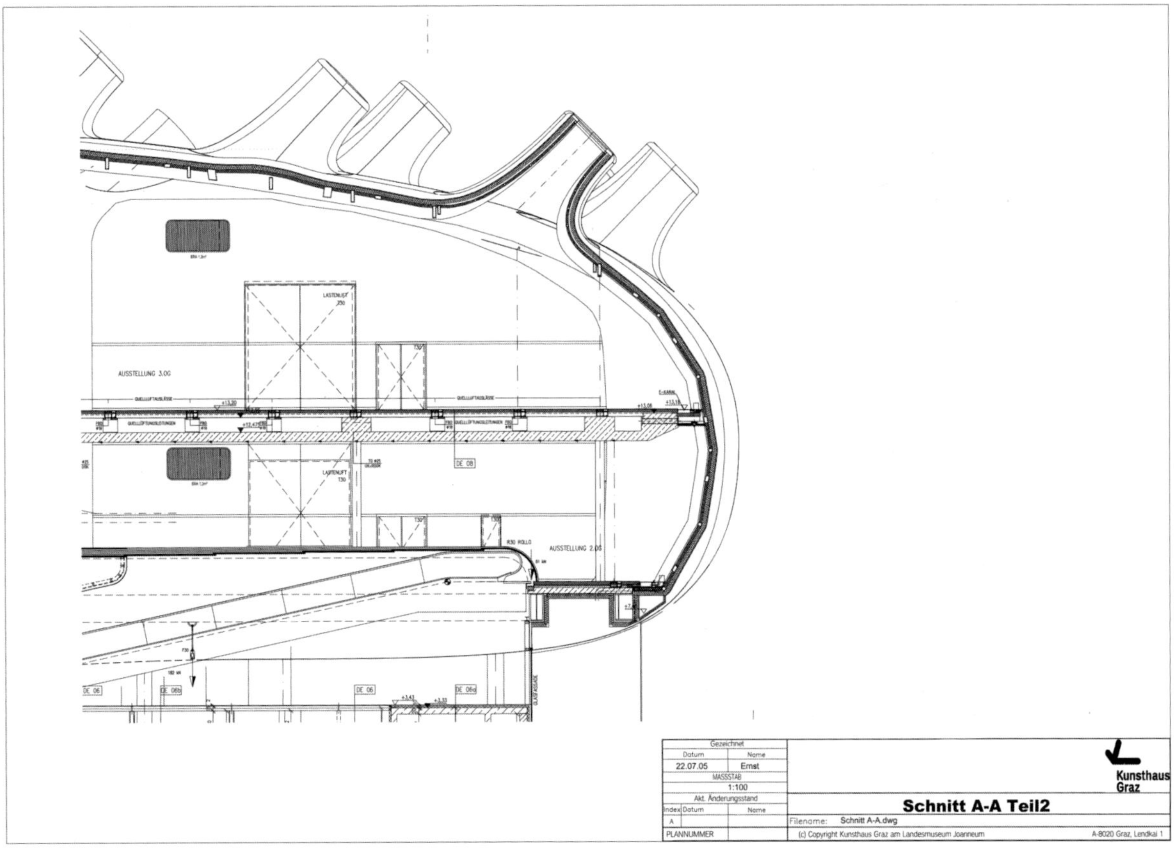
AUSSTELLUNG 3.OG
AUSSTELLUNG 2.OG
LASTENLIFT
Gezeichnet
Datum
Name
22.07.05
Ernst
MASSSTAB
1:100
Akt. Änderungsstand
Index Datum
Name
A
PLANNUMMER
Kunsthaus Graz
Schnitt A-A Teil2
Filename: Schnitt A-A.dwg
(c) Copyright Kunsthaus Graz am Landesmuseum Joanneum
A-8020 Graz, Lendkai 1

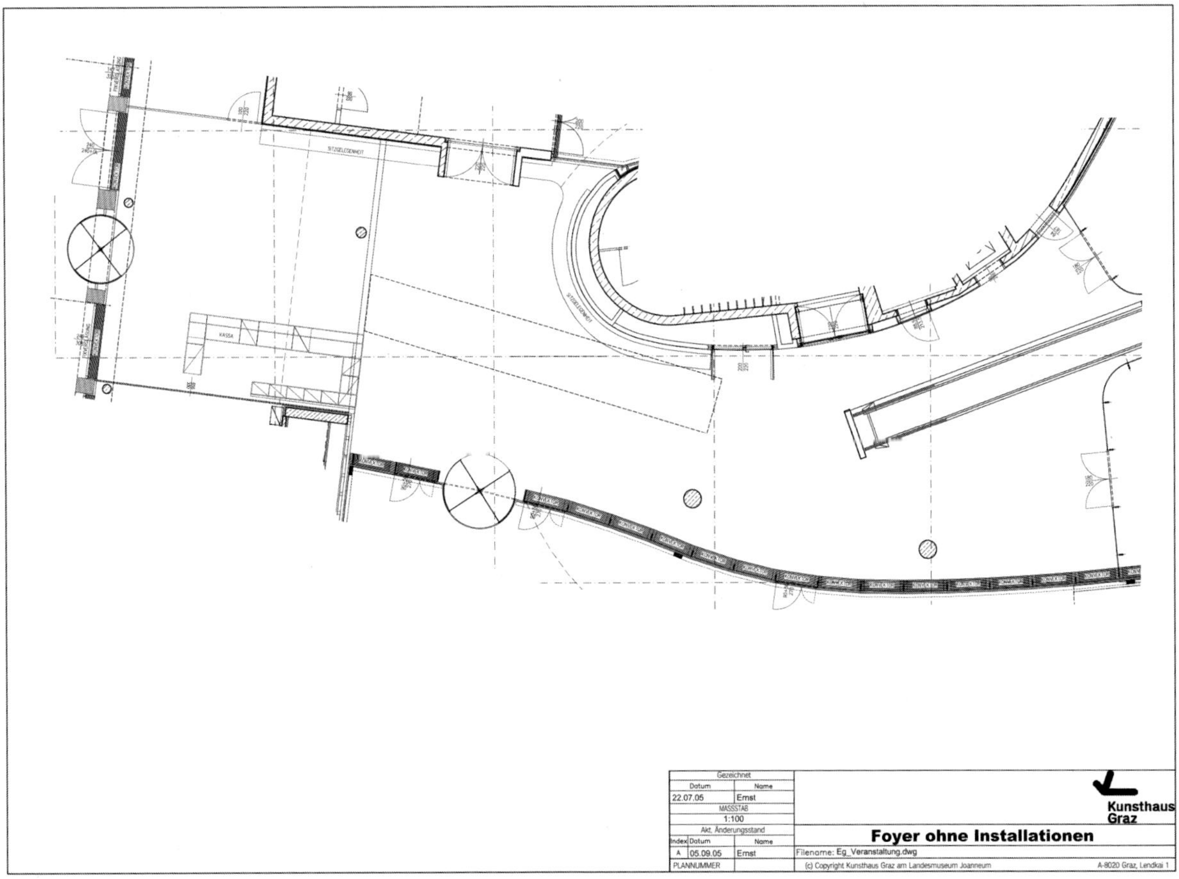
KASSA
Gezeichnet
Datum
Name
22.07.05
Ernst
MASSSTAB
1:100
Akt. Änderungsstand
Index Datum
Name
A 05.09.05 Ernst
PLANNUMMER
Kunsthaus Graz
Foyer ohne Installationen
Filename: Eg_Veranstaltung.dwg
(c) Copyright Kunsthaus Graz am Landesmuseum Joanneum
A-8020 Graz, Lendkai 1

spacelab^uk

Niederlassung Graz
Bürgergasse 8-10
8010 Graz
T: 0316 814142
F: 0316 8141424
spacelab@aon.at

Press release

KUNSTHAUS GRAZ – DESCRIPTION OF THE DESIGN

In April 2000, our competition project for the Kunsthaus Graz was selected by an international jury presided by Prof. Volker Giencke. The proposed scheme was a relatively simple but radical solution: the Kunsthaus would be made of two organically shaped gallery decks raised above ground and wrapped in a double-curved skin. This skin was to protect the Kunsthaus from the environment and to let in natural light, particularly through a series of north-facing nozzles located on the upper surface of the skin. The gallery decks were to be accessible through a long, thin travelator which we called the "pin". Hence the name of the project: " Skin and Pin".

Now, one year later, the design of the project has progressed considerably and we have reached the end of the Entwurf stage. We are pleased to say that all the key ideas that gave the scheme its quality have been maintained and have been successfully developed further by our team in terms of design quality and technical feasibility.

In particular the skin (which is the most functionally sensitive and geometrically complex part of the project, and the one that has of course attracted the most questions in the last few months), has now been developed with precision in terms of structure and materials. The outer layer will be made of transparent rectangular sheets of 15mm acryl with double curvature. Beneath this layer, there will be a steel structure made of triangulated facets. Some of these facets will be opaque, while others will be made of glass, so that approximately 20% of the surface of the skin will be translucent, allowing filtered natural light into parts of the exhibition area. There will also be some small, completely transparent areas, to allow selective views to the outside.

The general organisation of the scheme remains the same except on the ground floor, where we have had to position both access ramps to the car park within the footprint of the building, leading to a slight reduction in floor area and therefore to a few design changes: the service areas (delivery zone, kitchen, etc...) are now grouped in two islands inserted under the belly of the museum and the "longest bar in Austria" is now a free form rather than the original straight line.

The challenging dream of the competition proposal has now become, with this Entwurf, a precisely formulated functional reality which we believe enhances and sharpens its architectural quality as well as clearly demonstrating its viability.

spacelab^uk Ltd., company number 3971084

Protocol of the jury /
Kunsthaus Graz Competition 1999/2000
Project 33 /
Winning Project

Competition authors
Peter Cook
Colin Fournier
Niels Jonkhans
Mathis Osterhage
Marcos Cruz

Collaborators
Nicola Haines
Jamie Norden
Karim Hamza
David Erkan
Anja Leonhauser
Wanda Hu
Steve Pike
Charles Walker

The project is a free-form, free-standing building. It won less through its size and radicality than because of its elegance and perfection.

The main body fits in successfully with its surroundings. It yields itself to the context of the existing building material and at the same time swings right out to the boundaries of the ground plan.
The building is suspended over the site, leaving the space under it free. The main body is very similar to its surroundings. Along with its enveloping and isolating function, the outer shell also serves to give form. It consists of a two-shelled membrane that acts as a physical construction between the inside and outside. The outer membrane is coated with Teflon, non-flammable, unbreakable and translucent. Sections of transparent membrane can be inserted where necessary.
The façade gives the impression of a solid construction – although this is not really the case. New technologies and high-grade processing help in this respect. In the dark, the building throws an unobtrusive glow onto its surroundings. The three-storey inside space includes a media centre for young people on the lower floor, while the upper floors are devoted exclusively to exhibition space. All technical rooms are contained within the double-walled outer shell. Within the exhibition space, light will be introduced into the inner space via a north-facing cone of light. Light control defines the spatial atmosphere and enables a pure and expansive spatial experience ('Architecture is a game of forms in light,' Le Corbusier, 1924).
The Kunsthaus is not a conventional building, not a building which can or should be compared with existing ones. It is far removed from current architectural interpretation in its sheer verve; it is untouched by any current trend, but instead informs them. Its function as a magnet for the 'uncompromising' is evident in the playful lightness of its artistic conception.

Exhibitions 2003–2020

2003

25.10.2003–18.01.2004
**Einbildung.
The Perception in Art**
Curated by
Peter Pakesch,
Katrin Bucher
With works by
Marc Adrian, Mario Ballocco, Darren Almond, Alberto Biasi, Angela Bulloch, Anthony Caro, Chuck Close, Gianni Colombo, Jan Dibbets, Olafur Eliasson, Heinz Gappmayr, Taft Green, Robert Irwin, Elsworth Kelly, Rachel Khedoori, Liz Larner, Richard Kriesche, Sarah Morris, Ernesto Neto, Max Neuhaus, Matthew Ngui, Helga Phillip, Qiu Shihua, Markus Raetz, Bridget Riley, David Rokeby, Alfons Schilling, Henryk Stazewski, Michael Schuster, Esther Stocker, Manfred Willmann, Rémy Zaugg
(**Space01**)
(**Space02**)
→ 115)

2004

28.02.2004–02.05.2004
Sol LeWitt. Wall
Curated by
Peter Pakesch,
Katrin Bucher
(**Space01**)
→ 108)

28.02.2004–02.05.2004
**Vera Lutter.
Inside In**
Curated by Peter Pakesch, Adam Budak
(**Space02**)

15.05.2004–15.08.2004
**Living in Motion.
Design and Architecture for Flexible Dwelling**
An exhibition of the Vitra Design Museums, Weil am Rhein, curated by Mathias Schwartz-Clauss
(**Space01**)
(**Space02**)

15.05.2004–19.09.2004
Videodreams. Between the Cinematic and the Theatrical
Curated by Adam Budak, Peter Pakesch
With works by Fabienne Audéoud / John Russell, Janet Cardiff / George Bures Miller, Stan Douglas, Rodney Graham, Teresa Hubbard / Alexander Birchler, Mark Lewis, Sharon Lockhart, Aernout Mik, Tony Oursler, Judy Radul, Catherine Sullivan, Barbara Bloom, Joan Jonas, Artur Żmijewski
(**Space02**)
→ 085)

09.10.2004–16.01.2005
Moveable Parts. Forms of the Kinetic
Curated by Katrin Bucher, Peter Pakesch, Heinz Stahlhut, Peter Weibel
With works by Yakoov Agam, Thomas Baumann, Werner Bauer, Julien Berthier, Martha Boto, Pol Bury, Gianni Colombo, Siegfried Cremer, Attila Csörgö, Olafur Eliasson, Malachi Farrell, Joachim Fleischer, Hans Haacke, István Haraszty, Jeppe Hein, Rebecca Horn, Wendy Jacob, Peter Könitz, Piotr Kowalski, Julio Le Parc, Lia, Paul McCarthy, Bruce Nauman, Fernando Palma Rodriguez, Michelangelo Pistoletto, Sigmar Polke, Tim Prentice, Sabrina Raaf, Werner Reiterer, Jason Rhoades, George Rickey, Michael Sailstorfer, Nicolas Schöffer, Jeffrey Shaw, Roman Signer, Jesus-Rafaël Soto, Takis, Jean Tinguely, Günther Uecker, Gregorio Vardanega, Gerhard von Graevenitz, Stephan von Huene, Martin Walde, Tsai Wen-Ying, Krysztof Wodiczko, Christiaan Zwanikken
(**Space01**)
(**Space02**)

2005

29.01.2005–13.02.2005
Now's the time. Montage audiovisual
Curated by Sandro Droschl
With works by Doug Aitken, Thomas Baumann, D-Fuse, Christoph Draeger, Tina Frank, Alexander Györfi, Dariusz Krzeczek, Lia, Michel Majerus, m.ash, Maix Mayer, Sarah Morris, N.I.C.J.O.B., Olaf Nicolai, Pfaffenbichler / Schreiber, Daniel Pflumm, Richard Prince, Franc Purg, reMI, Gerwald Rockenschaub, Lisa Ruyter, Axel Stockburger, Johannes Wohnseifer
(**Space02**)

12.02.2005–16.05.2005
Michel Majerus. Installations 92-02
Curated by Günther Holler-Schuster, Peter Pakesch
(**Space01**)

05.03.2005–16.05.2005
John Baldessari. Life's balance. Werke 84-04
Curated by Adam Budak, Peter Pakesch
(**Space02**)

04.06.2005–11.09.2005
Chikaku. Time and Memory in Japan
Curated by Toshiharu Ito with Adam Budak (Kunsthaus Graz), Seiichi Furuya (Camera Austria), Miki Okabe (The Japan Foundation)
With works by Masaki Fujihata, Rieko Hidaka, Takashi Ito, Emiko Kasahara, Tadashi Kawamata, Yayoi Kusama, Trinh T. Minh-ha, Hiroyuki Moriwaki, Daido Moriyama, Takuma Nakahira, Tetsuya Nakamura, Motohiko Odani, Taro Okamoto, Yoko Ono, Yutaka Sone, Yoshihiro Suda, Hiroshi Sugimoto, Makoto Sei Watanabe, Masaaki Yamada, Miwa Yanagi
(**Space01**)
(**Space02**)
→ 114)

01.10.2005–08.01.2006
M City. European Cityscapes
Curated by Marco De Michelis with Katrin Bucher and Peter Pakesch
With works by Thomas Baumann / Martin Kaltner, Chris Burden, Cibic & Partners, Hans-Peter Feldmann, Sylvie Fleury, Masaki Fujihata, Carlos Garaicoa, Dan Graham, Vicente Guallart, Andreas Gursky, Duane Hanson, Richard Ingersoll, Matthieu Laurette, Deborah Ligorio, Bart Lootsma, meinGraz, Werner von Mutzenbecher, MIT SENSEable City Laboratory, Simon Neri, Julian Opie, Osservatorio Nomade, Kyong Park, Marjetica Potrč, ReD, Thomas Rentmeister, Gerhard Richter, Wilhelm Sasnal, Stiletto, Gavin Turk, Paola Viganó
(**Space01**)
(**Space02**)
→ 092)
→ 119)

2006

13.01.2006–25.01.2006
Paju Book City. Current Architecture in Korea
An exhibition by AedesBerlin, curated by Kim Young-joon
(**foyer**)
→ 045)

25.01.2006–19.02.2006
Jessica Hausner. Toast
(**Space02**)

04.02.2006–07.05.2006
Maria Lassnig, Liz Larner. Two or Three or Something
Curated by Peter Pakesch, Adam Budak
(**Space01**)
→ 124)

04.03.2006–07.05. 2006
Gods in Exile. Salvador Dalí, Albert Oehlen et al.
Curated by Peter Pakesch, Katrin Bucher
With works by Albert Oehlen, Christian Ludwig Attersee, Arnold Böcklin, Salvador Dalí, Philippe Halsman, Max Klinger, Karel Teige
(**Space02**)

10.06.2006–03.09.2006
Inventory. Works from the Herbert collection
Curated by Peter Pakesch, Katrin Bucher
With works by Carl Andre, Giovanni Anselmo, Art & Language, John Baldessari, Robert Barry, Marcel Broodthaers, Stanley Brouwn, Daniel Buren, Jean-Marc Bustamante, André Cadere, Hanne Darboven, Jan Dibbets, Luciano Fabro, Gilbert & George, Dan Graham, Douglas Huebler, Donald Judd, On Kawara, Mike Kelley, Martin Kippenberger, Joseph Kosuth, Sol LeWitt, Richard Long, Mario Merz, Reinhard Mucha, Bruce Nauman, Giulio Paolini, A.R. Penck, Michelangelo Pistoletto, Gerhard Richter, Thomas Schütte, Robert Smithson, Niele Toroni, Jan Vercruysse, Didier Vermeiren, Lawrence Weiner, Franz West, Ian Wilson, Heimo Zobernig
(**Space01**)
(**Space02**)
→ 088)

28.06.2006–02.07.2006
Intuitive Spaces. Visible memory of a friendly alien
An exhibition in cooperation with FH Joanneum, concept by Karl H. Lampret, Marion Winter, Josef Greimel, Gerd Kertz, Kira Howanietz
(**foyer**)

23.09.2006–22.10.2006
Protections.
This is not an exhibition
Co-produced by steirischer herbst, curated by Adam Budak, Christine Peters
With works by Cezary Bodzianowski, The Centre Of Attention, Katrina Daschner, Elmgreen & Dragset, Tim Etchells, Vlatka Horvat, Christian Jankowski, Marysia Lewandowska & Neil Cummings, Katarina Löfström, Daria Martin, Kris Martin, Frédéric Moser & Philippe Schwinger, Warren Neidich, Roman Ondak, Elisabeth Penker, Philippe Rahm, Markus Schinwald & Oleg Soulimenko, Dejan Spasovik, Apolonija Šušteršic, Mark Wallinger, Markus Weisbeck, Herwig Weiser
(**Space01**)
(**Space02**)
→ 089)

04.11.2006–14.01.2007
Narratives. -35/65+
Two Generations
Curated by Katrin Bucher Trantow, Katia Schurl
With works by Janez Bernik, Ákos Birkás, Nick Bötticher, Martin Bricelj, Vesna Bukovec, Lada Cerar, VALIE EXPORT, Hubert Fichte & Leonore Mau, Robert Freund, Franziska Furter, Heinz Gappmayr, Daniel Hafner, Caroline Heider, Luisa Kasalicky, Július Koller, Zenita Komad, Felicitas Kruse, Denisa Lehocka, Constantin Luser, Julian Mullan, Christian Niccoli, Drago Persic, Tobias Putrih, Miriam Raggam & Barbara Wilding, Andres Ramirez Gaviria, Bjørn Segschneider, Martina Steckholzer, Rudolf Steckholzer, Stefanie Wuschitz, Metka Zupanič
(**Space01**)
(**Space02**)
→ 080)

2007

03.02.2007–13.05.2007
Cerith Wyn Evans.
Bubble Peddler
Curated by Adam Budak
(**Needle**)
(**BIX**)
(**Space01**)
→ 212)

03.02.2007–11.02.2007
Kenneth Anger.
Eaux d'Artifice
Curated by Adam Budak
(**Space04**)

03.03.2007–13.05.2007
Werner Reiterer.
Eye sucks world
Curated by Peter Pakesch, Katia Schurl
(**Space02**)
→ 087)

07.06.2007–02.09.2007
China welcomes you ...
Desires, Struggles,
New Identities
Curated by Katrin Bucher Trantow, Peter Pakesch
(**Space01**)
(**Space02**)
(**Needle**)
→ 118)
→ 146)

15.09.2007–06.01.2008
Modell Martin
Kippenberger.
Utopia for Everyone
Curated by Peter Pakesch, Daniel Baumann
(**Space01**)

22.09.2007–13.01.2008
Volksgarten.
Politics of Belonging
Curated by Adam Budak, Katia Schurl, Peter Pakesch
(**Space02**)
(**public space**)

2008

19.01.2008–03.02.2008
Hanspeter Hofmann.
Bonheur automatique
Curated by Christoph Doswald, Katia Schurl
(**Space04**)
→ 068)

26.01.2008–16.05.2008
Manuel Knapp.
stroboscopic noise
Curated by Adam Budak
(**Space02**)

02.02.2008–18.05.2008
Pedro Cabrita Reis.
True Gardens #6
Curated by Adam Budak, Peter Pakesch
(**Space01**)
→ 131)

06.03.2008–26.10.2008
Thyssen-Bornesmisza
Art Contemporary.
Collection as Aleph
Curated by Adam Budak, Daniela Zyman
(**Space01**)
(**Space02**)
(**foyer**)

07.06.2008–31.08.2008
Joe Colombo.
Design and the Invention
of the Future
An exhibition of the Vitra Design Museums and La Triennale di Milano in cooperation with the Studio Joe Colombo, Mailand, curated by Mateo Kries, Ignazia Favata
(**Space01**)

26.06.2008–03.08.2008
Nieto Sobejano
Arquitectos, Madrid.
Arquitectura concreta
(**foyer**)

17.09.2008–26.09.2008
Surface of the World.
Retrospective
Michelangelo Antonioni
feat. Johanna Billing:
Project for a Revolution
Curated by Adam Budak
(**Space04**)

27.09.2008–11.01.2009
Life?
Biomorphic Forms in
Sculpture
Curated by Katrin Bucher Trantow, Peter Pakesch
With works by Ruth Asawa, Louise Bourgeois, Berlinde De Bruyckere, Lee Bul, Wolfgang Flad, Gabríela Friðriksdóttir, Siobhán Hapaska, Julie Hayward, Georg Herold, Agnieszka Kalinowska, Liz Larner, Ernesto Neto, Carsten Nicolai, Pino Pascali, Jill Spector, eva helene stern***, Franz West, Xiao Yu, Xu Zhen
(**Space01**)
(**Space02**)

15.11.2008–22.02.2009
Richard Kriesche.
Capital + Code
Curated by Katrin Bucher Trantow, Peter Pakesch
(**Space02**)

2009

31.01.2009–17.05.2009
Diana Thater.
gorillagorillagorilla
Curated by Adam Budak, Peter Pakesch
(**Space01**)
→ 127)

06.03.2009–26.04.2009
Dariusz Kowalski.
Interrogation Room
Curated by Katrin Bucher Trantow
(**Space02**)

08.05.2009–24.05.2009
A Secret Understanding.
Produced by Forma
(**foyer**)

06.06.2009–30.08.2009
Rock – Paper – Scissors.
Pop-Music as Subject
of Visual Art
Curated by Diedrich Diederichsen
With works by Saâdane Afif, Cory Arcangel,

Art & Language with The Red Krayola, Sam Durant, Kim Gordon & Jutta Koether, Renée Green, Stefan Hablützel, Mike Kelley, Klara Lidén, Lucy McKenzie, Dave Muller, Albert Oehlen, Katrin Plavcak, Mathias Poledna, Uwe Schinn, Nico Vascellari
(**Space01**)
(**Space02**)
→ 113)

26.09.2009–10.01.2010
Warhol Wool Newman. Painting Real
Curated by
Peter Pakesch
With works by
Barnett Newman, Andy Warhol, Christopher Wool
(**Space01**)

26.09.2009–10.01.2010
Screening Real. Conner Lockhart Warhol
Curated by
Peter Pakesch
With works by
Bruce Conner, Sharon Lockhart, Andy Warhol
(**Space02**)

2010

06.02.2010–25.04.2010
Catch me! Grasping Speed
Curated by
Katrin Bucher Trantow
With works by
Gwenaël Bélanger, Christian Eisenberger, Peter Fischli und David Weiss, Daniel Hafner, Carsten Höller, Erika Giovanna Klien, Lu Qing, Aleksandra Mir, Lisi Raskin, Ludwig Reutterer, Wilhelm Rösler, Ed Ruscha, Anri Sala, Roman Signer, Xavier Veilhan, Stella Weissenberg, Markus Wilfling et al.
(**Space01**)

06.02.2010–16.05.2010
Tatiana Trouvé. Il Grande Ritratto
Curated by
Adam Budak
(**Space02**)
→ 102)

22.05.2010–29.08.2010
Bless N°41. Retrospektives Home
Curated by
Katrin Bucher Trantow, Peter Pakesch
(**Space02**)
→ 121)

12.06.2010–12.09.2010
Human Condition. Empathy and Emancipation in Precarious Times
Curated by
Adam Budak
(**Space01**)
(**Space02**)

25.09.2010–09.01.2011
Franz West. Auto-Theatre, Cologne – Naples – Graz
Curated by
Peter Pakesch (Kunsthaus Graz), Kasper König, Katia Baudin (Museum Ludwig Köln), Mario Codognato (MADRE Neapel)
(**Space01**)

09.10.2010–09.01.2011
ATOROT. Are there other robots out there?
John Dekron in collaboration with A1 and Fachhochschule Salzburg, department Augmented Reality & Games
(**Needle**)
(**Space01**)
(**Space02**)
(**virtueller Raum**)

09.10.2010–20.02.2011
Robot Dreams
Coproduction with Museum Tinguely, Basel
Curated by
Katrin Bucher Trantow, Peter Pakesch, Andres Pardey, Roland Wetzel
(**Space01**)
(**Space02**)

11.11.2010–21.11.2010
Mieke Bal. nothing is missing
Curated by
Adam Budak
(**Space03**)
→ 179)

2011

29.01.2011–27.02.2011
Design Impulse. Bikes/Boats/Cars & Flying Machines
An exhibition of the Joanneum University of Applied Sciences (FH JOANNEUM) and Creative Industries Styria/ designforum Steiermark
(**Space04**)

05.02.2011–15.05.2011
Anti/Form. Sculptures from the MUMOK Collection
Curated by
Peter Pakesch
(**Space01**)
(**Space02**)

11.03.2011–15.05.2011
Hollerer/Marte. 'Do we need to have an accident?'
Curated by
Katrin Bucher Trantow
With works by Clemens Hollerer, Sabine Marte
(**Space02**)
→ 097)

10.06.2011–30.09.2011
Simon Starling & SUPERFLEX. e.g.
Curated by
Adam Budak
(**Space01**)
(**Space02**)
(**at different locations of the Joanneum**)

11.06.2011–04.09.2011
Measuring the World. Heterotopias and Knowledge Spaces in Art
Curated by
Peter Pakesch, Katrin Bucher Trantow
(**Space01**)
(**Space02**)

17.09.2011–05.02.2012
Ai Weiwei. Interlacing
An exhibition by Fotomuseum Winterthur, curated by
Urs Stahel, Ai Weiwei
(**Space02**)

01.10.2011–15.01.2012
Antje Majewski. The World of Gimel. How to Make Objects Talk
Curated by
Adam Budak, Antje Majewski; assistant curator: Katia Huemer
With works by
Antje Majewski, Thomas Bayrle, Helke Bayrle, Marcel Duchamp, Didier Faustino, Pawel Freisler, Delia Gonzalez, Alejandro Jodorowsky, Edward Krasinski, Leonore Mau, Markus Miessen & Ralf Pflugfelder, Dirk Peuker, Agnieszka Polska, Mathilde Rosier, Gavin Russom, Issa Samb, Juliane Solmsdorf, Simon Starling & SUPERFLEX, El Hadji Sy, Neal Tait
(**Space01**)
→ 112)

2012

03.03.2012–06.05.2012
Sofie Thorsen. Cut A-A'
Curated by
Katrin Bucher Trantow, Katia Huemer
(**Space02**)
→ 098)

03.03.2012–06.05.2012
Michael Kienzer. Logic and Self-Will
Curated by
Katrin Bucher Trantow
(**Space01**)
→ 111)

06.06.2012–02.09.2012
Liu Xiaodong. The Process of Painting
Curated by
Günther Holler-Schuster
(**Space01**)

16.06.2012–02.06.2013
media.art.collecting. Perspectives of a Collection
Curated by
Günther Holler-Schuster, Katrin Bucher Trantow, Katia Huemer
(**Space02**)

29.02.2012–20.01.2013
Cittadellarte. Sharing Transformation
Curated by Katrin Bucher Trantow (Kunsthaus Graz), Juan Estaban Sandova (Cittadellarte), co-curated by Katia Huemer (Kunsthaus Graz), Paolo Naldini (Cittadellarte)
(**Space01**)
→ 139)

2013

15.02.2013–12.05.2013
Berlinde De Bruyckere. In the Flesh
Curated by Katrin Bucher Trantow
(**Space01**)
→ 125)

01.03.2013–28.04.2013
Josef Dabernig. Panorama
Curated by Katrin Bucher Trantow
(**Needle**)

07.06.2013–01.09.2013
Heimo Zobernig
Curated by Peter Pakesch
(**Space01**)

28.06.2013–13.10.2013
Culture:City. Cultural Buildings from Bilbao to Zeche Zollverein
An exhibition of the Akademie der Künste, Berlin, curated by Matthias Sauerbruch, co-curated by Wulf Walter Biettger, Caroline Wolf
(**Space02**)

21.09.2013–12.01.2014
Romuald Hazoumè. Beninese Solidarity with Endangered Westerners
Curated by Günther Holler-Schuster
(**Space01**)
→ 136)

28.09.2013–01.12.2013
Karl Salzmann. Rotation/Notation
Curated by Katia Huemer
(**Project Space**)

08.11.2013–23.03.2014
Promotion Prize of the Province of Styria 2013
Curated by Jaroslaw Suchan
(**Space02**)

12.12.2013–09.02.2014
Ulrike Königshofer. The See-Through Machine
Curated by Katia Huemer
(**Project Space**)

2014

07.02.2014–11.05.2014
El Lissitzky – Ilya and Emilia Kabakov. Utopia and Reality
Curated by Charles Esche, Ilya Kabakov & Emilia Kabakov, co-curated by Peter Pakesch, Katrin Bucher Trantow, Willem Jan Renders
(**Space01**)

20.02.2014–21.04.2014
Michaela Grill. My Restless Heart
Curated by Katia Huemer
(**Project Space**)

07.03.2014–01.06.2014
James Benning. Decoding Fear
Curated by Peter Pakesch
(**Space02**)
→ 101)

30.04.2014–29.06.2014
Rosemarie Lukasser. Thoughts on '… I'm on the'
Curated by Katia Huemer
(**Project Space**)

06.06.2014–12.10.2014
Katharina Grosse. 'Who, I? Whom, You?'
Curated by Katrin Bucher Trantow
(**Space01**)
→ 130)

18.06.2014–19.10.2014
Karl Neubacher. Media Artist, 1926–1978
Curated by Günther Holler-Schuster
(**Space02**)
→ 100)

10.07.2014–22.07.2014
Cäcilia Brown. Eau de Vinci
Curated by Katia Huemer
(**Project Space**)

12.09.2014–16.11.2014
Dino Zrnec. ensure for size
Curated by Katia Huemer
(**Project Space**)

27.09.2014–12.10.2014
Richard Mosse. The Enclave
An exhibition by ORF musikprotokoll, Kunsthaus Graz, curated by Susanne Niedermayr
(**Space04**)

04.10.2014
The Big Draw Graz – Das große Zeichnen
An education project by Astrid Bernhard, Monika Holzer-Kernbichler
(**entire building**)

14.11.2014–15.02.2015
Damage Control. Art and Destruction Since 1950
An exhibition by the Hirshhorn Museum, Smithsonian Institution, Washington D.C.; curated by Kerry Brougher, Russell Ferguson with Katrin Bucher Trantow; assistant curator: Elisabeth Schlögl
(**Space01**)
(**Space02**)

2015

13.03.2015–26.10.2015
Landscape in Motion. Cinematic Visions of an Uncertain Tomorrow
Curated by Peter Pakesch, Katrin Bucher Trantow; assistant curator: Elisabeth Schlögl
(**Space02**)

10.04.2015–30.08.2015
HyperAmerica. Landscape – Image – Reality
Curated by Peter Pakesch, Katia Huemer
(**Space01**)

27.06.–05.07.2015
Industrial Design Show 2015. Bachelor- and Master Thesis from the 'Industrial Design' Programme of the FH Joanneum
(**Space05**)

11.07.–06.09.2015
Political Landscape. Art Resistance Salzkammergut
An exhibition by the Institut für Kunst im öffentlichen Raum Steiermark, curated by Dirck Möllmann, Elisabeth Fiedler
With works by Clegg & Guttmann, Eva Grubinger, Florian Hüttner, Angelika Loderer, Susan Philipsz, Bojan Šarčević
(**Space05**)

25.09.2015–10.01.2016
Corporate. Xu Zhen (Produced by MadeIn Company)
Curated by Katrin Bucher Trantow, Peter Pakesch
(**Space01**)
→ 135)

03.10.2015
The Big Draw Graz –
An education project by Astrid Bernhard, Monika Holzer-Kernbichler
(**entire building**)
→ 188)

20.11.2015–07.02.2016
The Paradise the Downfall. Hartmut Skerbisch – Media Works
Curated by
Günther Holler-Schuster
(**Space02**)
→ 099)

2016

12.02.–03.04.2016
Sasha Pirker | Lotte Schreiber. FILM
Curated by
Roman Grabner
(**Space05**)

26.02.–01.05.2016
Constantin Luser. Music Tames the Beast
Curated by Katrin Bucher Trantow, Katia Huemer; assistant curator: Elisabeth Schlögl
(**Space01**)
→ 126)

11.03.–21.08.2016
The Painter's Cabinet. Terry Winter's Dialogue with Nature
Curated by Peter Pakesch; assistant curator: Katia Huemer
(**Space02**)

06.04.–17.04.2016
RESANITA. Wilde Frau
Curated by
Katrin Bucher Trantow
(**Space05**)

05.05.–02.06.2016
Yaruya. The Sculptor Samson Ogiamien between African tradition and European reality
Curated by
Günther Holler-Schuster
(**Space05**)

26.05.–28.08.2016
Bittersweet Transformation. Alina Szapocznikow, Kateřina Vincourová and Camille Henrot
Curated by Katrin Bucher Trantow; assistant curator: Elisabeth Schlögl
(**Space01**)

17.06.–03.07.2016 / 22.07.–28.08.2016
Stories from the Edge 1 & 2. A Road Trip to the Identities of the Adriatic Coast
A project by Daily Rhythms Collective, curated by Nayari Castillo, Kate Howlett-Jones, Francesca Lazzarini, co-curated by Katrin Bucher Trantow
With works by
Nayari Castillo, Kate Howlett-Jones, Polonca Lovsin, Ryts Monet, Renata Poljak, Pila Rusjan, Nika Rukavina, Alessandro Sambini and Marina Sartori and other participating artists: Marta Cereda, Sabina Damiani, Paola Pasquaretta, Petra Počanić, Mirko Smerdel of the Discipula collective, Una Rebić and Helene Thümmel from the#JUHA collective, Aleksander Velišček, Andreas Vormayr
(**Space05**)

12.06.–21.08.2016
The Museum as a Gym. Fitness trail at the Kunsthaus Graz. A Project by Aldo Giannotti
Curated by Katia Huemer, Elisabeth Schlögl
(**entire building**)
→ 145)
→ 184)

06.09.–18.09.2016
Josef Schützenhöfer. 71
A project by Intro Graz Spection, in collaboration with Katrin Bucher Trantow
(**Space05**)

19.09.2016–19.02.2017
Site/Cite. Speaking in Tongues While Splitting One's Own. A Project by Birke Gorm
Curated by Katia Huemer, Elisabeth Schlögl
(**visitor staircase**)
(**west façade**)
→ 182)

30.09.–30.10.2016
The Logic of Angels. Llullophon
A production by ORF musikprotokolls at the steirischen herbst, curated by Fränk Zimmer, co-curated by Katrin Bucher Trantow
(**Space05**)

24.09.2016–19.02.2017
Kneaded Knowledge. The Language of Ceramics
Curated by
Peter Pakesch, Edmund de Waal
With works by
Ai Weiwei, Edmund de Waal, Lynda Benglis, Alison Britton, Hans Coper, Lucio Fontana, Asger Jorn, Kasimir Malewitsch, Fausto Melotti, Joan Miró, Isamu Noguchi, Pablo Picasso, Lucie Rie, Marit Tingleff, Peter Voulkos
(**Space01**)

24.09.2016–08.01.2017
Body Luggage. Migration of Gestures
Commissioned by the festival steirischer herbst, curated by Zasha Colah
With works by
Kemi Bassene, Padmini Chettur, Jimmy Chishi, Chaw Ei Thein, Caecilia Tripp, Milica Tomić, Simon Wachsmuth, Gernot Wieland, Sawangwongse Yawnghwe, Portia Zvavahera as well as works from the archives of Hilde Holger, Chandralekha, Shiavax Chavda, Htein Lin, et al.
(**Space02**)

01.10.2016
The Big Draw Graz – ARTopie – Drawing Makes Sense!
An education project by Gerald Hartwig, Monika Holzer-Kernbichler
(**entire building**)
→ 183)

2017

10.02.2017–21.05.2017
Dizziness. Navigating the Unknown
Curated by Ruth Anderwald, Katrin Bucher Trantow, Leonhard Grond; assistant curator: Elisabeth Schlögl
With works by
Bas Jan Ader, Marc Adrian, Ruth Anderwald + Leonhard Grond, Ólafur Elíasson, Robert Filliou, Oliver Hangl, Cameron Jamie, Ann Veronica Janssens, Anna Jermolaewa, Joachim Koester, Michael Landy, Henri Michaux, Bruce Nauman, Laurel Nakadate, Trevor Paglen, Philippe Parreno, Helga Philipp, Oliver Ressler & Dario Azzellini, Ariel Schlesinger und Jonathan Monk, Ben Russell, Viktor Landström and Sebastian Wahlforss, Esther Stocker, SUPERFLEX, Catherine Yass
(**Space02**)
→ 143)

24.03.2017–20.08.2017
Erwin Wurm. Football-sized lump of clay on light blue car roof
Curated by
Günther Holler-Schuster
(**Space01**)
→ 116)

21.04.–23.04.2017
Big Wirbel. Line and String
An education project by Monika Holzer-Kernbichler
(**entire building**)

23.06.2017–28.01.2018
Haegue Yang. VIP's Union Phase I
Curated by
Barbara Steiner, co-curated by
Katrin Bucher Trantow
(**foyer**)
→ 050)
→ 051)
→ 060)

23.06.2017–27.98.2017
Koki Tanaka. Provisional Studies (Working Title)
Curated by Barbara Steiner; assistant curator: Elisabeth Schlögl
(**Space02**)

23.09.2017–28.01.2018
Graz Architecture. Rationalists, Aesthetes, Gut Instinct Architects, Democrats, Mediacrats
Curated by Barbara Steiner with Katia Huemer
With works by Günther Domenig, Konrad Frey, Julia Gaisbacher, Volker Giencke, Bernhard Hafner, Oliver Hangl, Eilfried Huth, Mischa Kuball, Anna Meyer, Szyszkowitz-Kowalski, Manfred Wolff-Plottegg, Arthur Zalewski
(**Space02**)
→ 093)

23.09.2017–25.03.2018
Up into the Unknown. Peter Cook, Colin Fournier and the Kunsthaus
Curated by Barbara Steiner with Katia Huemer
With works by Archigram, Bollinger + Grohmann, Peter Cook, Colin Fournier, Jessica Hausner, Niels Jonkhans, Mischa Kuball, Vera Lutter, Anna Meyer, realities:united, Isa Rosenberger, Gernot Stangl, Arthur Zalewski
(**Space01**)
→ 037)
→ 107)

28.09.2017–29.10.2017
play! Translocal: Museum as a Toolbox
Curated and activated by Lidia Cekic, Jasmin Edegger, Katharina Grabner, Ramona Haderer, Christina Hahn, Keyvan Paydar, Sarah Resch, Valerie Taus, Alexandra Trost, Monika Holzer-Kernbichler, Katrin Bucher Trantow
With works by Oaza Collective (Maja Kolar & Maša Poljanec), Marcin Polak, Aldo Giannotti, Lasnaidee (Maria Derlōš und Jekaterina Kljutšnik), Luigi Coppola, Josef Bauer, Gerwald Rockenschaub, Candida Höfer, Giulio Paolini, Josef Dabernig, Robert Filliou and others
(**Needle**)
(**foyer**)
(**staircase**)

22.10.2017
keep drawing!
An education project as part of the UNIQA Family Day
(**entire building**)
→ 147)

2018

23.01.2018–28.01.2018
Lokal: Initiative Kunstverleih. Licht Luft Sonne, Kunst!
Curated by Andreas Heller, Isa Riedl and zweintopf
With works by Helga Chibidziura, Michael Fanta, Heribert Friedl, Max Gansberger, Christoph Grill, Michael Gumhold, Veronika Hauer, Andreas Heller, Markus Jeschaunig, Ulrike Königshofer, Renate Krammer, Marianne Lang, Martin Osterider, Erwin Polanc, Wendelin Pressl, Alfons Pressnitz, Isa Riedl, Karoline Rudolf, Maria Schnabl, Nina Schuiki, studio ASYNCHROME, Lea Titz, Roswitha Weingrill, Bernhard Wolf, zweintopf
(**Space04**)

15.02.2018–02.04.2018
Haegue Yang. VIP's Union Phase II. Surrender
Curated by Barbara Steiner, Katrin Bucher Trantow
(**Space02**)

13.04.2018–26.08.2018
Faith Love Hope. 800 Years of the Graz-Seckau Dioceze
An exhibition by Kunsthaus Graz and KULTUM, curated by Katrin Bucher Trantow, Johannes Rauchenberger, Barbara Steiner; assistant curators: Elisabeth Schlögl, Teresa Schnider
With works by Adel Abdessemed, Azra Akšamija, Iris Andraschek, Maja Bajević, Anna Baranowski and Luise Schröder, Maja Bekan, Monica Bonvicini, Louise Bourgeois, Guillaume Bruère, Günter Brus, Berlinde De Bruyckere, Willem De Rooij, Marlene Dumas, Manfred Erjautz, VALIE EXPORT, Harun Farocki, Linda Fregni Nagler, Hilde Fuchs, Dan Graham, Maria Hahnenkamp, Fritz Hartlauer, Anna Jermolaewa, Birgit Jürgenssen, Franz Kapfer, Zlatko Kopljar, Maria Kramer, Kris Martin, Anna Meyer, Inge Morath, Muntean / Rosenblum, Alois Neuhold, Hermann Nitsch, Adrian Paci, Hannes Priesch, Karol Radziszewski, Werner Reiterer, Ulrike Rosenbach, Anri Sala, Christoph Schmidberger, Santiago Sierra, Slavs and Tatars, TEER (Wolfgang Temmel, Fedo Ertl), Norbert Trummer, Luc Tuymans, Danh Vō, Franz West, Markus Wilfling, Manfred Willmann, Artur Żmijewski
(**Space01**)
(**Space02**)

22.09.2018–27.01.2019
Congo Stars
Curated by Sammy Baloji, Bambi Ceuppens, Fiston Mwanza Mujila, Günther Holler-Schuster, Barbara Steiner, co-curated by Alexandra Trost
With works by Abis, Alfi Alfa, Sammy Baloji, Gilbert Banza Nkulu, Chéri Benga, David N. Bernatchez, Bodo, Vitshois Mwilambwe Bondo, Burozi, Dominique Bwalya Mwando, Chéri Cherin, Trésor Cherin, Djilatendo, Ekunde, Sam Ilus, Jean Kamba, Lady Kambulu, Eddy Kamuanga Ilunga, Kasongo, Jean Mukendi Katambayi, Aundu Kiala, J.P. Kiangu, Bodys Isek Kingelez, Ange Kumbi, Hilaire Balu Kuyangiko, Albert et Antoinette Lubaki, Gosette Lubondo, Ernest Lungieki, George Makaya Lusavuvu, Tinda Lwimba, Michèle Magema, Maurice Mbikayi, Maman Masamba, Matanda, Mbuëcky Jumeaux, JP Mika, Mega Mingiedi Tunga, Moke, Moke-Fils, Gedeon Ndonda, Nkaz Mav, Vincent Nkulu, Vuza Ntoko, Chéri Samba, SAPINart, Monsengo Shula, Sim Simaro, Maître SYMS, Tambwe, Tshibumba Kanda Matulu, Pathy Tshindele Kapinga, Tuur Van Balen & Revital Cohen
(**Space01**)
(**Space02**)
→ 134)

07.11.–11.11.2018
Congo-Wirbel
An education project by Monika Holzer-Kernbichler
(**entire building**)

2019

15.02.2019–19.05.2019
Jun Yang. The Artist, the Work, and the Exhibition
Curated by Barbara Steiner, Jun Yang
With works by Erwin Bauer, Mike Kelley / Paul Mc Carthy, siren eun youn jung, Lee Kit, Oliver Klimpel, Michikazu Matsune, Yuuki Nishimura, Yuki Okumura, Koki Tanaka, Maja Vukoje, Jun Yang, Bruce Yonemoto

(**Space01**)
(**Space 02**)
→ 019)
→ 117)
→ 138)

13.03.2019–23.04.2019
Johann Lurf.
Earth Series with Laura Wagner and Cavalcade
Curated by
Katrin Bucher Trantow
(**Space03**)

13.03.2019–23.04.2019
Laura Wagner. Obelisks
Curated by
Katrin Bucher Trantow
(**Cat-Tree**)

21.05.2019–23.06.2019
Karin Wintscher-Zinganel.
Uniform-Multiform
Curated by
Barbara Steiner
(**Cat-Tree**)

31.05.2019–01.06.2019
'I don't think I am trying to commit suicide.'
Performance Now
Curated by Rosemarie Brucher (University of Music and Performing Arts Graz), Ann-Grit Becker, Sabine Flach (University of Graz), Anselm Wagner (Graz University of Technology), Roman Grabner (Bruseum), Katrin Bucher Trantow, Katia Huemer, Barbara Steiner (Kunsthaus Graz)
With works by Ron Athey, boychild, Klitclique, Georg Kroneis, Michikazu Matsune, Navaridas & Deutinger, Flora Neuwirth, Franz Reimer, Barbis Ruder, Milica Tomić and students of the University of Music and Performing Arts Graz
(**Needle**)
(**Space01**)
(**Space02**)
(**Space04**)
(**foyer**)
(**freight elevator**)
(**delivery zone**)
(**staircase**)
→ 073)
→ 175)

28.06.2019–20.10.2019
Connected.
Peter Kogler with Frederick Kiesler with Hedy Lamarr with Fernand Léger with museum in progress with Otto Neurath with Charlotte Perriand with Franz Pomassl with Winfried Ritsch with Franz West ...
Curated by Katrin Bucher Trantow; assistant curator: Elisabeth Schlögl
(**Space01**)
(**Space02**)
→ 091)
→ 129)
→ 207)

05.08.2019–14.10.2019
Alive inside the Crystal.
A Project by Oliver Klimpel
Curated by Oliver Klimpel
(**Cat-Tree**)
→ 049)

04.09.2019–29.09.2019
Oliver Ressler.
What Is Democracy?
Curated by
Katrin Bucher Trantow
(**Needle**)
→ 018)
→ 021)

20.10.2019
Open House –
Silkscreen and Sound
An education project by Monika Holzer-Kernbichler
(**Needle**)
(**Space03**)
(**Space04**)
(**foyer**)

23.11.–24.11.2019
Open House – Werken!
An education project by Monika Holzer-Kernbichler
(**Needle**)
(**Space03**)
(**Space04**)
(**foyer**)

15.11.2019–16.02.2020
ARTS ↔ CRAFTS
Curated by
Barbara Steiner
With works by
Azra Akšamija, Olivier Guesselé-Garai,Plamen Dejanoff, Olaf Holzapfel, Antje Majewski, Jorge Pardo, Slavs and Tatars, Haegue Yang, Johannes Schweiger
(**Space01**)
(**Space02**)
→ 094)
→ 137)

16.11.2019–02.02.2020
Barbara Edlinger.
Fields
Curated by
Katia Huemer
(**Cat-Tree**)
→ 053)

2020

07.02.–13.03.2020
Navaridas / Deutinger / Szalay: ONÍRICA / REMAINS
Curated by
Katia Huemer
(**Cat-Tree**)
(**foyer**)
(**Space04**)
→ 069)

01.07.–20.09.2020
Where Art Might Happen.
The Early Years of CalArts
Curvated by Philipp Kaiser and Christina Végh (Kestner Gesellschaft, Hannover), in cooperation with Katrin Bucher Trantow, Barbara Steiner
With works by
Michael Asher, David Askevold, John Baldessari, Ericka Beckman, Ross Bleckner, Barbara Bloom, Troy Brauntuch, Sheila Levrant de Bretteville, Klaus vom Bruch, Judy Chicago, Eric Fischl, Simone Forti, Jack Goldstein, Douglas Huebler, Stephan von Huene, Allan Kaprow, Mike Kelley, Alison Knowles, Suzanne Lacy, Daniel Joseph Martinez, John Miller, Susan Mogul, Matt Mullican, Ann Noël,Tony Oursler, Nam June Paik, Stephen Prina, Charlemagne Palestine, Anthony Ramos, Ulrike Rosenbach, David Salle, Miriam Schapiro, Mira Schor, Jim Shaw, Wolfgang Stoerchle, Mitchell Syrop, Carrie Mae Weems, James Welling, Faith Wilding, Christopher Williams, Emmett Williams with guest artists Richard Kriesche, Margot Pilz et al.
(**Space02**)
→ 095)

01.07.–04.10.2020
Bill Fontana.
Primal Energies
Curated by
Katrin Bucher Trantow
(**Space01**)
→ 028)
→ 128)

01.07.–13.09.2020
Socially distanced
Curated by Katrin Bucher Trantow, Katia Huemer
(**Cat-Tree**)

29.09.2020-04.03.2021
Community. Visible
Curated by
Katrin Bucher Trantow,
Katia Huemer
With works by
Juka Abdilwahid, Florin Asei, Adi Brunner, Manuela Hillebrand, Peter Milosavljevic, Jörg Rath, Bettina Winter
(**Cat-Tree**)
→ 054)

23.10.2020-07.03.2021
Herbert Brandl
TOMORROW
Curated by Barbara Steiner; co-curated by Katia Huemer
(**Space01**)
(**Space02**)
→ 103)
→ 122)
→ 133)

2016–2019
Kunsthaus Foyer
Curated by Barbara Steiner
(**foyer**)
→ 186)
→ 187)

(Biographies)

A
B
C

Peter Cook
(* 1936)
Sir Peter Cook is an original member of the seminal 1960s group 'Archigram'. Subsequently a designer/academic (Emeritus Professor: Royal Academy of Arts London, University College London, Staedelschule Frankfurt-Main). He is the architect of the Kunsthaus Graz with C. Fournier and also of buildings for Bond University Queensland, Vienna Law and Commerce University, with G. Robotham and two buildings for Arts University Bournemouth. Drawings in MOMA New York, Centre Pompidou, FRAC Orleans, etc. If the outside world says early PC was 'Mr Plug-in City', Mature PC was 'Mr. Kunsthaus' – a title shared with Colin – what would they call him now?

D
E
F

Colin Fournier
(* 1944)
studied architecture and town planning at the Architectural Association in London. He is now Emeritus Professor of Architecture and Urbanism at the Bartlett School of Architecture, University College London (UCL). After winning the competition with Peter Cook, he was delighted to hear people's generally positive reaction to the design. He once overheard a girl saying to a friend that she found it 'nice but very odd, you know ... all those curves!' and said, in response: 'Animals and humans have curves, including you, why does a museum have to look like a box?' She replied with a smile: 'Because the Kunsthaus is a building, and I am a woman.' Since then, he has always told students not to let anyone, in particular architecture professors and future clients, tell them what a building should look like.

Pablo von Frankenberg
(* 1984)
studied empirical cultural studies and sociology, holds a doctorate in museum architecture and has been working since 2013 as a curator and museum consultant on themes such as architecture, history, commemoration and new forms of museum presentation. Only at the Kunsthaus Graz has he seen the presentation developed by Frederick Kiesler actually put into practice, the painting turned towards the viewer on a cantilever arm, beyond the safeness and unquestionability of the wall, offering itself in an intimate way. Why is it so difficult to reinvent the museum? Because there has been so little research into the correlation between space, design and knowledge.

G

Martin Grabner
(* 1979)
studied architecture and graduated from the College for Fine-Art Photography and MultimediaArt at the Ortweinschule Graz. After teaching and research at the Faculty of Architecture in Graz, he has been a member of the curatorial team at the Kunsthaus Graz since 2019. His photography focuses on the relationship between people and architecture in the use, reception and production of space. Although he is actually a friend of 'orthogonal Swiss concrete boxes', he has felt an almost irrationally close connection to the Kunsthaus since he cycled past the building pit every day as a young architecture student – probably because of its especially unique character.

H

Anna Lena von Helldorff
(* 1977)
studied system design at the Academy of Fine Arts Leipzig and repeatedly asks herself and her surroundings: 'What do you see? What are you thinking? What do you do with it?' and so on and so forth. She is active in various forms and formats of collaboration and in the relation between text and image – in both, spaces and infrastructures. At the Kunsthaus during the reconstruction she dealt not only with the foyer but also with the meandering interfaces and shifting perspectives of information, communication and exhibition.

Katia Huemer
(* 1977)
works as part of the curatorial team at the Kunsthaus, and has spent much of her everyday life over the last 16 years inside and with this building. In the past two years she has

focused increasingly on exploring the theatrical qualities of the Kunsthaus, which can be seen at both a visual and functional level. While working on this book she noticed two things: firstly, that even after such a long involvement with the building there are still new things to discover; and secondly, that she takes any criticism of the Kunsthaus as a personal insult.

I
J
Niels Jonkhans
(* 1970)
studied art and architecture in Maastricht, Düsseldorf and London. He is a freelance architect in Vienna and since 2011 has been Professor of Architectural Design at the Faculty of Architecture at Nuremberg Institute of Technology.
After winning the competition with spacelab/uk, the joint project office with Peter Cook and Colin Fournier, he moved from London to Graz in 2000. There, during a taxi ride, he learned his first Austrian words, 'a schiache Hittn' (an ugly hut), spoken by the driver, who was describing a new museum building planned for the banks of the Mur. Unfortunately, Niels Jonkhans has forgotten which one.

K
L
M
N
O
P
Q
R
S
Elisabeth Schlögl
(*1987)
studied history of art and collection studies. She began work with the Kunsthaus curatorial team in April 2014, at a time when there was fierce debate about what the Kunsthaus stood for in the city, how it was 'used', and whether what happened inside it had anything to do with people. These questions still accompany her everywhere, especially since she has coordinated and often curated the BIX light and media façade since 2017.
In response to a statement she often hears regarding the visibility of the BIX projects – 'But you can't recognise what it is!' – she never tires of asking: 'Does seeing always have to involve recognising?'

Barbara Steiner
(* 1964)
studied history of art and political sciences at the University of Vienna. She has been director of the Kunsthaus Graz since July 2016. Previously she was director of the Museum for Contemporary Art in Leipzig, headed art associations in Ludwigsburg and Wolfsburg, and taught for several years each at the University of Art in Linz, the Royal Academy of Arts in Copenhagen, and the Academy of Fine Arts in Leipzig. Her theoretical and practical work involves the issues around exhibiting – also concerning questions of space and architecture. Since her arrival in Graz she has regularly been told that it is not possible to exhibit at the Kunsthaus, that the building is not well suited for the purpose of showing art. The exhibitions she has curated there demonstrate that it is indeed possible, if you are first willing to engage with the building.

T
U
V
W
Anselm Wagner
(* 1965)
studied history of art, philosophy and classical archaeology in Salzburg and Munich.
In 2004 he was a fellow at the Clark Art Institute Williamstown/Massachusetts, and in 2009 Fulbright Visiting Professor at the University of Minnesota in Minneapolis. Since 2010 he has held the position of Professor of Architectural Theory at Graz University of Technology. His research interests include the cultural history of Modernism, critical architectural theory and the history of architecture in Graz. During his stays in the USA he discovered that not only did no one know of Graz, but most could also not say where Austria was. Everyone he spoke to, however, did know 'that weird Kunsthaus'.

Sophia Walk
(* 1984)
studied architecture, teaches and researches at the Institute of Architectural Theory, Art History and Cultural Studies at Graz University of Technology. She is interested in the (image) transformation that can happen to buildings, and considers the back of a building to be, in fact, the most noteworthy aspect in their architecture, since she has learned to look behind their façades. During the development phase of this book, while on the tram as it approached the stop by the Kunsthaus, she overheard one passenger say to another: 'Apparently that museum has awesome pancakes!' This was not actually the first time that she had reason to ask herself what constitutes a museum, and what the perception of it is, from both the outside and inside. But one thing she is sure of: it's not pancakes.

X
Y
Z
Arthur Zalewski
(* 1971)
is an artist and lives in Leipzig. In addition to his own photographic practice, he has realised numerous artist collaborations. The photographic examination of concrete places plays a key role in his work.
The photo essay **Favoriten** is a subjective inventory of **Graz Architecture**. The photographic sequences created for the exhibition are based on observations of the everyday: 'What has become of certain ideas and the attitudes associated with them? How have social demands shifted? What remains?'

Drawing by a pupil from BG/BRG Carneri, created during the construction phase of the Kunsthaus

A–Z, (Index)

↗ p. 105
The planning architects often also lack the specialist knowledge required for this particular building task.
↗ p. 105
very different aesthetic, cultural, political and economic interests can be invested in a museum building
↗ p. 117
The renaissance of the museum
↗ p. 119
places that offer the possibility of addressing various scientific views of the world
↗ p. 121
embodiment of a historical architectural utopia
↗ p. 137
drawing a border can quickly lead to delimitation, or even exclusion
↗ p. 141
that a house is not, or should not be, so much a building but a network of services and information
↗ p. 149
why people can't come in to the exhibition with an ice cream cone, a dog or an umbrella
↗ p. 153
The building is a magnet and a mediation tool.
↗ p. 155
how the building affects the exhibition. And how the exhibition affects the building
↗ p. 159
possible definition of museum architecture – thinking in potentialities or latencies
↗ p. 169
I can think in terms of museums. Or I can think with them.
↗ p. 297
not be on a pedestal, behind a classical façade, not an institution that would appear to be a privileged space
↗ p. 303
an open platform which could be used by different curators

staircase

T

Travelator

↗ p. 43
gliding 'into the unknown'
↗ p. 149
Gliding into the building on the Travelator is like a rite de passage
↗ p. 231
In a practical and technical sense, the Travelator is a hybrid between a moving walkway, which allows you to glide forwards, and the escalator, which transports you upwards.
↗ p. 235
'the subtle pleasure we experience when licked by the family cat's sandpaper tongue'
↗ p. 297
the notion of almost insidiously moving through three-dimensional space

U

Up Into the Unknown

usage

↗ p. 57
banal but necessary functional requirements or everyday forms of utilization
↗ p. 87
The building is defined by its use.
↗ p. 93
Defining points and zones leaves a lot of room for manoeuvre, but it gives structure to the space and the possible usage of the space.
↗ p. 103
architecture [...] gains its importance not only through its reception, but above all through its use, i.e. through social interaction
↗ p. 139
to think of the museum in terms of its use
↗ p. 141
the vital question is this: how can you succeed in making a building really permeable, not only in the sense of crossing the boundaries of the building itself, but also breaking up the divisions in how it is used?
↗ p. 143
spaces with multiple codes, i.e. spaces with different uses, also create additional work when it comes to the organisation of their use.
↗ p. 145
conventions are more likely to be found in the exhibition space.
↗ p. 147
to involve people like security officers, technical services and cleaning staff
↗ p. 155
Uses also become specific to a place, and make a place specific.
↗ p. 159
Function is related to the typology of the building, whereas use is concerned with how it is actually used.
↗ p. 163
whether changeability becomes clear through use and flexibility through functions?
↗ p. 163
The designers and the planners can influence the flexibility of the functions, but the users shape the changeability of the usage.
↗ p. 169
You have to build a space that is challenging.
↗ p. 221
When it comes to the medium of the metaphor, we also fall back on what we know.
↗ p. 227
when a building is used, it begins to be emotionalised
↗ p. 229
include a use in which something special is expected
↗ p. 229
the variety of forms of use
↗ p. 229
(individual and collective) use of the Kunsthaus
↗ p. 239
We can use architecture through language, i.e. indirectly, and we can use it directly through our actions within buildings.
↗ p. 297
architecture as theatre

Kunsthaus
→ 075)

View of the **Kunsthaus** from the Schloßberg.
Installation by Oliver Ressler, What Is Democracy?

Imprint)

Kunsthaus Graz GmbH
is owned in equal parts
by the City of Graz
and the Universalmuseum
Joanneum GmbH,
which in turn is a company
owned by the Province
of Styria

Publication

Editors
Concept
Barbara Steiner
Sophia Walk
Anna Lena von Helldorff
Katia Huemer
Proofreading
Kate Howlett-Jones
Translations
Louise Bromby
(von Frankenberg,
Steiner, Walk, Wagner,
conversations),
Teresa Faudon (Huemer),
Kate Howlett-Jones
(Schlögl, biographies)
Graphic Design
Anna Lena von Helldorff
Image Editing
Michael Neubacher
Print
Medienfabrik Graz

Paper
Magno satin, 300 g
Biotop 3, 100g
Magno satin, 150g
Typeface
Stelvio (WT)
(Many thanks to
Thomas Thiemich!)

Kunsthaus Graz
Lendkai 1
8020 Graz
Österreich

+43 (0)316/8017-9200
info@kunsthausgraz.at
www.kunsthausgraz.at

Bibliographic information published
by the Deutsche Nationalbibliothek
The Deutsche Nationalbibliothek
lists this publication in the Deutsche
Nationalbibliografie; detailed
bibliographic data are available on the
Internet at http://dnb.d-nb.de.

jovis Verlag GmbH
Lützowstraße 33
10785 Berlin

www.jovis.de

jovis books are available
worldwide in select
bookstores. Please contact
your nearest bookseller
or visit www.jovis.de for
information concerning
your local distribution.

ISBN 978-3-86859-680-9

Drawing by a pupil from BG/BRG Carneri, created during the construction phase of the Kunsthaus